The Reference Shelf®

CHALLENGES FOR HEFTY SMURF

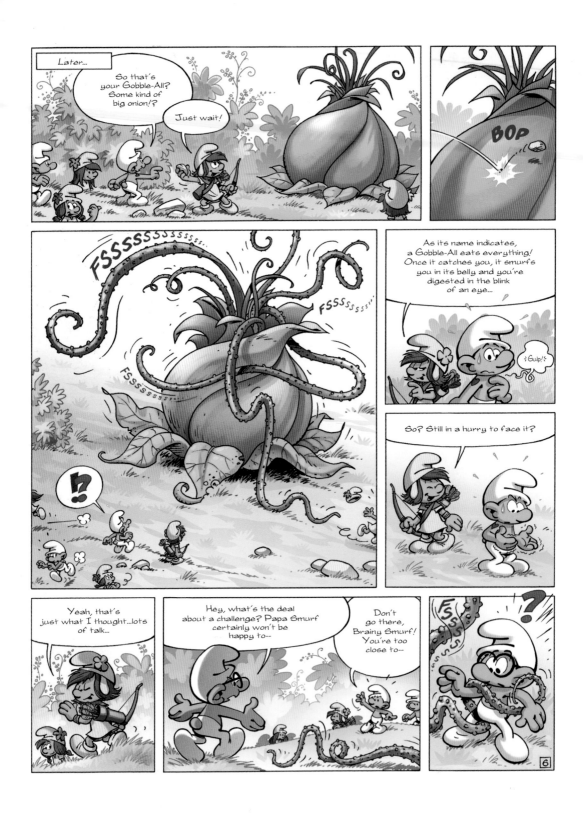

23

CLUMSY SMURF'S DRAGONFLY

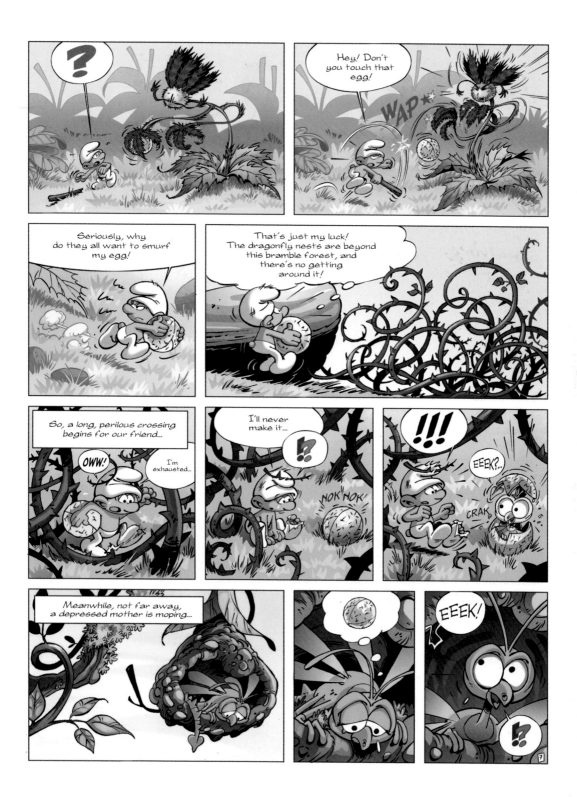

THE SQUASH SMURFS

34

35

40

A SMURFLILY STRANGE WORLD

(SMURFS VILLAGE BEHIND THE WALL 2)
THE BETRAYAL OF SMURFBLOSSOM

THE BETRAYAL OF SMURFBLOSSOM

Like every year, around this time, the girl Smurfs organize the Great SmurfTree Games in Smurfy Grove...

And, just like every year, Smurfstorm is the best of them...

But this time, she has a worthy adversary in the form of Hefty Smurf.

This is the next-to-last event, the gourd test...

They are the only two left!

If one of them misses their gourd, then it's all over! Look, Smurfstorm is going first!

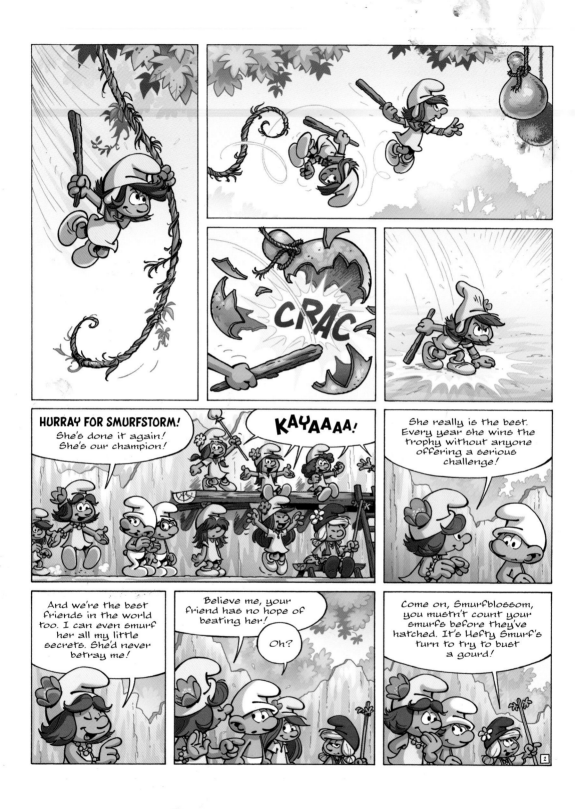

HURRAY FOR SMURFSTORM! She's done it again! She's our champion!

KAYAAAA!

She really is the best. Every year she wins the trophy without anyone offering a serious challenge!

And we're the best friends in the world too. I can even smurf her all my little secrets. She'd never betray me!

Believe me, your friend has no hope of beating her!

Oh?

Come on, Smurfblossom, you mustn't count your smurfs before they've hatched. It's Hefty Smurf's turn to try to bust a gourd!

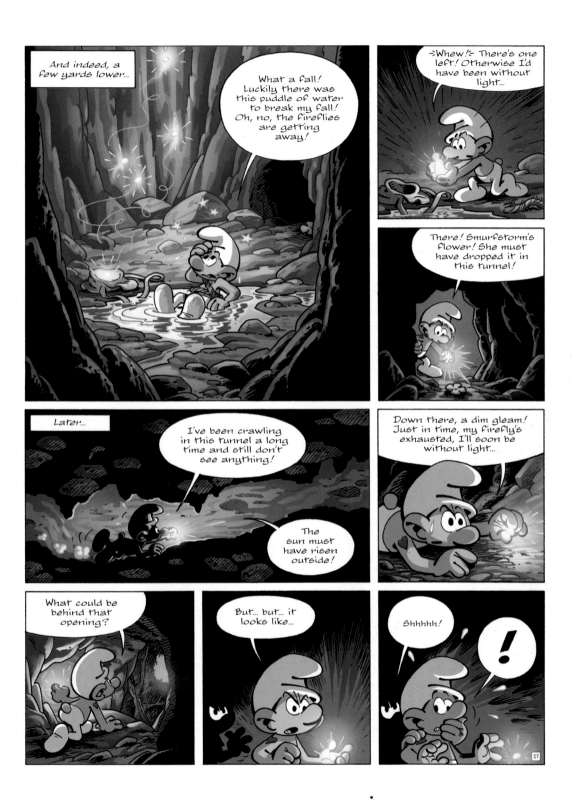

"But I couldn't stay there because I could hear the Growlers getting closer..."

"So I snuck into a little tunnel and, after crawling for a while, I saw an opening..."

"And guess what?! It opened directly onto the interior of the Growlers' nest."

"I stayed hidden there, observing them coming and going for hours..."

"And I noticed a strange detail about their behavior."

"They seem to attach a great deal of importance to a huge tree whose solidity they tested regularly ..."

31

Later... That's perfect, the wind's smurfing in the right direction. It'll push the smoke right towards the Growlers's nest! Light the fire!

And don't be stingy with the moss! There must be lots of smoke!

Our Smurf friends must have arrived by now at the tunnel entrance that-- ?

BRAINY SMURF, WHAT ARE YOU DOING HERE? AND WHERE'S SMURFSTORM? Uhhhh... Well... I... uh...

Not far away... HA! HA! HA! I'd smurf dearly to see Brainy Smurf's face right now... Hee hee!

You gotta admit you didn't leave him much choice by threatening to tell everyone he still sleeps with his binky! I'm ashamed! Heh heh...

Ah, there's the opening that let us get out of the tunnel! We just have to backtrack to the Growlers's nest!

One moment. Let's make some axes first. Or else, what will we smurf the much-talked-about trunk with?

34

In the nest, the Growlers run for their lives...

Careful, be ready, we'll have to smurf fast! Will your foot be all right?

Yes, it almost doesn't hurt anymore.

With this kerchief covering our noses, we'll be able to breathe more easily!

Taking advantage of the mayhem and the smokescreen, our two friends quickly sneak to their goal...

Come on! Let's go!

And without wasting a moment, set to work...

TCHAC
TCHAC
TCHAC

TCHAC
TCHAC
TCHAC

But outside, there is an unexpected turn of events...

36

89

91

THE CROW IN SMURFY GROVE

CAAWWW!

HA! HA! HA!

That night, strange noises were coming from Gargamel's home...

Look, Azrael! It doesn't look like much, but this insignificant bird will be the Smurfs' doom!

CAAWW! CAAWW!

?

This crow will finally let me accomplish what I've pointlessly expected from you!

HA! HA! HA! There's no point in pouting, fleabag!

It'll succeed where you've always failed because it'll always have something essential that you don't!

The power of SPEECH!

!?

99

101

114

115

123

124

125

KAYAAAA!
Down with the tyrant!
It's no use! You have no chance!
This way!
POW
There! Smurf that!
BAM
You're free now, my friends!
TCHAC
Thanks, Blossom!
Here's your bow, Stormy!
This will be fun!
LOOK OUT!
!
Hey! The prisoners are smurfing!
One down! KAYAAA!
POK
38

40

141

WATCH OUT FOR PAPERCUTZ™

Welcome to the third totally-different volume of THE SMURFS TALES by Peyo—brought to you by Papercutz, those Smurftastic smurfs dedicated to smurfing great graphic novels for all ages. I'm Jim Salicrup, Papercutz Smurf-in-Chief and winner of the Papa Smurf lookalike contest, here to talk smurf about this particular volume of THE SMURFS TALES…

If you've already picked up volumes one and two of THE SMURFS TALES you already know the story of Belgian cartoonist Pierre Culliford, who, under his pen name of Peyo, introduced a village of blue elves into a *Johan and Peewit* comic back in 1958. Those blue elves, known in America as the Smurfs, proved to be so popular they soon had a comics series of their very own, followed by movies and animated cartoon series starring them. They're currently starring in an all-new animated series on Nickelodeon, and of course, they're the stars of this graphic novel series, THE SMURFS TALES.

In our previous two volumes, we pretty much picked up where we left off with the original

Papercutz graphic novel series, THE SMURFS, which had more or less been publishing the original SMURFS graphic novels in chronological order. But for this volume we have something extra-smurfy-special for you. This volume is completely devoted to the comics adventures of the female Smurfs originally introduced in the most recent Smurfs movie, Smurfs: The Lost Village, as well as the short films, The Smurfs: A Christmas Carol and The Smurfs: The Legend of Smurfy Hollow. Collected within this volume are the two previously published graphic novels that featured the female Smurfs, The Village Behind the Wall and The Village Behind the Wall 2: The Betrayal of Smurfblossom, plus the never-before-published-by-Papercutz "The Crow in Smurfy Grove." These three SMURFS TALES are all illustrated in the same colorful style, so it made sense to us to collect them all in one volume.

But that's not all! As if there weren't more pages of Smurfs in this volume of THE SMURFS TALES than any other, we still managed to squeeze in two more Smurf stories: "The Paper Smurfs" and "Spiders Attack at Dawn." And that's still not all! We also featured good ol' *Johan and Peewit* in "The Thousand Crowns," keeping up THE SMURFS TALES tradition of also including other Peyo-created characters as part of the mix.

We could take this opportunity to tell you what's coming up in the next volume of THE SMURFS TALES, but we decided it might be more fun to leave it as a smurfy surprise. A good surprise—not like Jokey Smurf's surprise packages! In the meantime, you still have The Smurfs on Nickelodeon and a whole bunch of Smurfs graphic novels from Papercutz to quench almost any thirst for Smurfs (Gargamel excepted)!

Smurf you later,

Jim

STAY IN TOUCH!
STAY IN TOUCH!

EMAIL: salicrup@papercutz.com
WEB: papercutz.com
TWITTER: @papercutzgn
INSTAGRAM: @papercutzgn
FACEBOOK: PAPERCUTZGRAPHICNOVELS
FANMAIL: Papercutz, 160 Broadway, Suite 700, East Wing, New York, NY 10038

Go to papercutz.com and sign up for the free Papercutz e-newsletter!

THE PAPER SMURFS

Here, Baby! Smurfette smurfed some new clothes for your doll.

Arooo!

Gently, you'll--

CRAAAC

Oh! Good one! Good job!

WAAAAAAH!

Handy Smurf! Could you fix Baby's doll?

I really don't have time. I'll smurf it tomorrow.

I think I've found the spell. Now I just have to smurf my preparations.

Three drops of methylene blue...

OOPS! It's hot!

The parchment is ruined! The spell is smurfed!

148

149

153

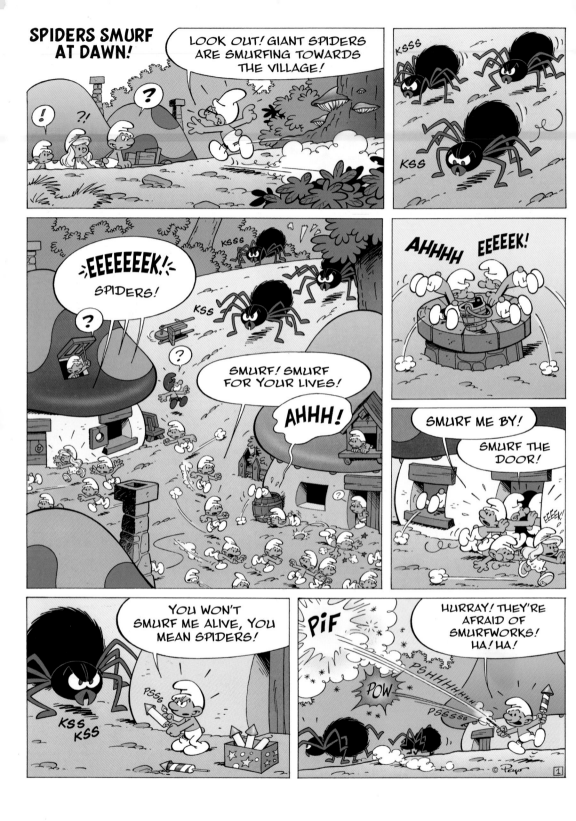

155

JOHAN AND PEEWIT in
THE THOUSAND CROWNS

TIME, IT IS A-FLEETING, NOUGHT AM I ACHIEVING...

Good Lord! He's hurting our eardrums with that box of false notes. It has got to stop!

Wait! I think I've found a way. If it works, we'll use it to play a good trick on him.

Listen closely... Tomorrow, on some sort of pretext, send Peewit to the neighboring village   and, on his path...

And the next day...

Ah! There he is!

Hello! Milord!

Do you want to do a good deed? This parchment shows where a thousand crowns are buried. Alas, I'm too old to make the trip and will give it to you for five crowns.

Agreed! Wait here a moment. I'll go get them at the castle.

Alas, I cannot wait. Couldn't you give me your instrument instead?

It's just that I'm fond of it. We have such nice evenings with it. But all the same, a thousand crowns...

Well, too bad! Here! Take it!

And here's the parchment.

159

THE END

Water Supply

Edited by Richard Joseph Stein

Editorial Advisor Paul McCaffrey

The Reference Shelf
Volume 80 • Number 2

The H.W. Wilson Company
New York • Dublin
2008

The Reference Shelf

The books in this series contain reprints of articles, excerpts from books, addresses on current issues, and studies of social trends in the United States and other countries. There are six separately bound numbers in each volume, all of which are usually published in the same calendar year. Numbers one through five are each devoted to a single subject, providing background information and discussion from various points of view and concluding with a subject index and comprehensive bibliography that lists books, pamphlets, and abstracts of additional articles on the subject. The final number of each volume is a collection of recent speeches, and it contains a cumulative speaker index. Books in the series may be purchased individually or on subscription.

Library of Congress has cataloged this serial title as follows:

Water supply / edited by Richard Joseph Stein.
     p. cm.—(The reference shelf ; v. 80, no. 2)
  Includes bibliographical references and index.
  ISBN 978-0-8242-1079-3 (alk. paper)
  1. Water-supply. 2. Water--Pollution. 3. Global warming. 4. Water rights. I. Stein, Richard Joseph.
    TD355.W385 2008
    363.6'1—dc22

                                     2008007177

Cover: Kuroyon Dam, Kurobe, Japan. Credit: © Akira Kaede/Getty Images

Visit H.W. Wilson's Web site: www.hwwilson.com

Printed in the United States of America

Contents

Preface

Water is a fundamental necessity for sustaining life on Earth. Every species on the planet depends on it for survival, from those that live in it to those that dwell in the desert. Water should be a renewable resource, continually falling from the sky and evaporating into the air. Its importance in our lives is immeasurable. We drink it, bathe in it, cook with it, grow crops with it, play in it, and, in some cases, are born in it. Indeed, 60 percent of the average adult human body is composed of water. Given its central place in human life, water is not surprisingly viewed as sacred in many cultures, both past and present.

In the industrialized world, however, this precious resource is too often taken for granted. We remain blissfully unaware of how much water is required to grow our food or make our clothes. Accustomed to water on demand, we take advantage, oftenusing more than we need. We are also not conscious of developing countries, where many people have little or no access to clean, drinkable water.

This volume of the Reference Shelf series explores the global water supply and related issues. It is divided into five chapters, the first of which provides a broad overview of conditions throughout the globe. Even though water covers 70 percent of the Earth's surface, 98 percent of it is salt water and thus unfit for human consumption. Of the two percent that is, three quarters are beyond use, frozen in ice caps and glaciers. The remaining freshwater is found in streams, lakes, ponds, rivers, groundwater, springs, and wetlands throughout the world.

Global water supply and demand is grossly unbalanced. An estimated 3.5 billion people have piped water in their homes, while 1.5 billion people have access to freshwater through springs, wells, and other means. That leaves about a billion people without access to clean water. In the United States and Canada, a person consumes an average of 150 gallons of water per day, while citizens in the United Kingdom use about 50 gallons per day. In the developing world, two-thirds of the people use less than 13 gallons per day.

Selections in the second chapter, "Water Wars," explore conflicts among nations, corporations, and ideologies over how water is distributed. That countries that share dwindling freshwater resources would come into conflict is not particularly surprising. However, as the entries in this section demonstrate, water conflicts are rarely so simple, often pitting countryman against countryman and one compelling interest against another.

Through an examination of a massive oil spill in Brooklyn, New York, and other mishaps, the articles in the third section, "Water Pollution," highlight the worldwide toll unsafe drinking water conditions has exacted.

As a growing population coninues to strain water resources worldwide, many expect climate change to further erode global water security. Increased drought, floods, desertification, and other challenges are among the likely side effects of global warming, as entries in the fourth chapter reveal.

Efficient water management is key to any successful society. Effective distrtibution and purification systems are essential in ensuring a healthy populace. The articles in the fifth chapter, "Water Management," explore various strategies for accessing and distributing water. Among the other methods analyzed are the treatment of sewer and stormwater so that they are safe for consumption.

Though this book addresses many of the issues relating to the world's water supply, it is by no means meant to be definitive. Consequently, included in the Bibliography section are lists of helpful books, Web sites, and abstracts of additional articles.

In conclusion, I would like to extend my heartfelt thanks to Paul McCaffrey and Christopher Mari for their helpful insights. I would also like to thank the many publishers and writers who kindly granted permission to republish their work.

Richard Joseph Stein
February 2008

I. THE GLOBAL WATER SUPPLY: AN OVERVIEW

Niagara Falls, as viewed from the United States.

Editor's Introduction

"Water, water, everywhere, / Nor any drop to drink," Samuel Taylor Coleridge wrote in his epic poem *The Rime of the Ancient Mariner.* Adrift on the ocean, Coleridge's forlorn and dehydrated protagonist was surrounded by water, albeit undrinkable salt water, which made his thirst all the more unbearable. Many people in the world today face a similar dilemma. Whether for reasons of climate, pollution, or poverty, they do not have regular access to potable freshwater and thus, at times, do not have "any drop to drink."

The seven articles in this chapter provide an overview of the global water supply and its often inequitable distribution. As stated in the Preface, there are an estimated one billion people without access to freshwater. Another two billion have access, but lack the resources to effectively purify and distribute it. The reality is grim, and the situation is expected to worsen. According to Eleanor J. Sterling, in "Blue Planet Blues," the first entry in this chapter, the United Nations (UN) estimates that, by 2025, 48 nations will face "freshwater stress," a term that can also mean water scarcity. Indeed, five countries—Russia, Indonesia, Canada, China, and Colombia—possess half the world's total supply of accessible freshwater. The Middle East and North Africa, on the other hand, have few water resources. While such disparities are profound, they are not without remedy: "A bounty of choices is available," Postel states, "once we decide to stop taking water for granted."

In a *UN Chronicle* report, Tushaar Shah discusses research conducted by the International Water Management Institute that illuminates the different water challenges facing nations in Africa and Asia. The developed world, Shah contends, "needs to help water-stressed developing countries devise freshwater solutions."

Though freshwater is most often associated with drinking and sanitation, it is global agriculture that puts the greatest strain on water resources. The authors of the subsequent article, "Water Scarcity: The Food Factor," anticipate that as the world's population continues to increase, more and more water will be needed to irrigate crops and care for livestock, straining water resources even further. They suggest a number of strategies to avoid such outcomes, emphasizing the need for water-efficient crops.

Katherine Mieszkowski interviews Fred Pearce in "Not a Drop to Drink." Pearce discusses *When the River Runs Dry*, his book about water depletion and consumption. Based on his extensive research, Pearce advocates a so-called "blue revolution" to make people more aware of the water they use. He also examines "virtual water," which is employed in the production of food and clothing.

3

In "Where's the Water?" Andrea Neal observes that the United States is "just starting to understand that water is a finite substance that must be protected." In order to meet the demands of a growing population, she says, we must learn to conserve. Marianne Lavelle continues the discussion of water supply problems in the United States in "Water Woes." She notes that the country's drinking and wastewater systems are aging rapidly, and upgrading them will take decades and require billions of dollars.

Finally, Wendy Priesnitz, in "Bottled Water or Tap Water?" weighs the health and environmental tradeoffs of tap and bottled water. Citing studies by scientists at the Natural Resources Defense Council (NRDC) and the University of Geneva, she notes that bottled water often contains impurities. Likewise, Priesnitz observes that similar studies of municipal water supplies indicate that these are also "far from pristine." However, an added drawback of bottled water is the damage to the environment caused by discarded bottles and shipping costs. She concludes that tap water is probably the healthier and more environmentally sound alternative.

Blue Planet Blues

By Eleanor J. Sterling
Natural History, November 2007

Water: evolving life-forms crawled out of it hundreds of millions of years ago, yet it still envelops us in our fetal state, suffuses every tissue of our body, and surrounds our drifting continents. From ancient origin myths and ritual baths, to Handel's *Water Music* and the play of ornate fountains, to water parks and water slides, we celebrate it. Water molecules move through the years and across the globe, from rivulets to rivers to oceans, rising into the atmosphere and falling back to land, connecting each of us to the rest of the world. In this global cycle, each of us is always downstream from someone else.

Despite all the water in the world, only a small fraction is available to us and other species that depend on freshwater. Salty seas account for more than 97 percent of the water on Earth. Of the remaining 3 percent or so, at least two-thirds is tied up in glaciers, ice caps, and permafrost, or else lies deep underground, of little use to those of us living on the land above.

Freshwater is not evenly distributed across the globe. The Americas have the largest amount and Oceania (Australia, New Zealand, and the Pacific islands) the smallest. Thinly inhabited Oceania, however, has the greatest per capita supply, more than 9.5 million gallons per person per year. Asia has the lowest. By country, Brazil, Canada, China, Colombia, Indonesia, and Russia together have half the world's supply of freshwater; northern Africa and the Middle East are the water-poorest. The United Nations defines water scarcity as less than 500 cubic meters (132,000 gallons) per person per year. Kuwait has a natural supply only one-fiftieth that amount, but given its huge supply of oil, it can afford to run desalination plants.

At the individual level, further inequities emerge. Although a person can manage for a few days on a gallon or two a day, an adequate supply of clean water is about thirteen gallons per person per day. Ten percent of it is needed for drinking, the rest for sanitation and hygiene (40 percent), bathing (30 percent), and cooking (20 percent). In 2006 the UN estimated that more than a billion people— one-sixth of the world's population—lack even the bare minimum gallon-plus per day of safe drinking water, and 2.6 billion lack access to basic sanitation. In contrast, those of us who live in the

United States and Canada each consume, on average, more than 150 gallons a day for domestic and municipal purposes (not including agricultural and industrial usage). In the United Kingdom people do fine with about a fifth as much.

People appropriate more than half the world's available surface freshwater. Globally, 70 percent of withdrawals from rivers and groundwater are used for agriculture, 22 percent for industry, and the remaining 8 percent for homes and municipal use. As demand increases, driven by both population growth and soaring consumption rates, water appropriation is projected to rise to 70 percent by 2025. In many ways, we are already damaging the systems that provide us with this critical natural resource.

Groundwater is one of the major systems being stressed. Overpumping, or extracting water faster than the underground systems recharge, has led to plummeting water tables, not only in the Middle East and northern Africa, but also in China, India, Iran, Mexico, and the U.S. The Ogallala aquifer, one of the world's largest, stretches under parts of eight states in the High Plains of the central U.S., from South Dakota to Texas. Water began collecting in porous sediments there some 5 million years ago; a geologically slow rate of recharge means that deep wells still bring up water from the end of the last Ice Age, more than 10,000 years ago, making it truly "fossil water." But the aquifer is being pumped out many times faster than it can be replenished. Between the early 1900s, when the Ogallala was first tapped for irrigation, and 2005, the water table dropped by more than 150 feet in some parts of Texas, Oklahoma, and Kansas. The raising of crops has become uneconomical for some Great Plains farmers, and further depletions could have substantial ripple effects on billions of people around the world who depend on American farm products.

As more land is paved over, rainwater can no longer soak into the ground or evaporate slowly to recharge the system. In coastal areas, a falling water table may open an aquifer to an influx of saltwater, impairing or even ruining it as a freshwater source.

Human activities are affecting other aquatic systems as well. Canals, dams, and levees that impede the natural flow of water can change not only the absolute quantity but the quality of water downstream: its concentration of pollutants, its sediment load, its temperature, and so on. People on both sides of the barrier are affected, whether they are growing crops or fishing for sport. Those changes can also severely alter or destroy the habitats of other species. More than half the wetlands in parts of Australia, Europe, New Zealand, and North America were destroyed during the twentieth century. When people divert water into desert regions to maintain thirsty crops, luxurious green lawns, and golf courses—instead of growing drought-adapted crops and native and ornamental plants— water resources are decimated. Even high-volume rivers such as the Colorado, the Ganges, and the Nile have been reduced, in some places, to polluted trickles.

In water-rich regions, people may wonder how their actions could have any effect on how people use water in water-deprived areas. But consumer choices obviously help drive what agriculture and industry produce and how they produce it. If agriculture and industry account for more than 90 percent of water usage, our closets, cupboards, desks, and refrigerators are filled with what has been termed "virtual water": products that require water for their growth, manufacture, and packaging. Those products now come from all over the world, including from places with limited water resources.

More than 700 gallons of water are needed to grow enough cotton to make a T-shirt. Your choice to buy the shirt could lead farmers in and Central Asia to divert water to irrigate a cotton crop. Although poor farmers may welcome the cash, such diversions have led, for instance, to a 75 percent loss of volume in the Aral Sea. Once the fourth-largest inland body of water by area, the Aral has now shrunk so much that its former lakebed is littered with rusty ships, rimmed with abandoned fishing villages miles from the water's edge, and scoured by storms of toxic dust.

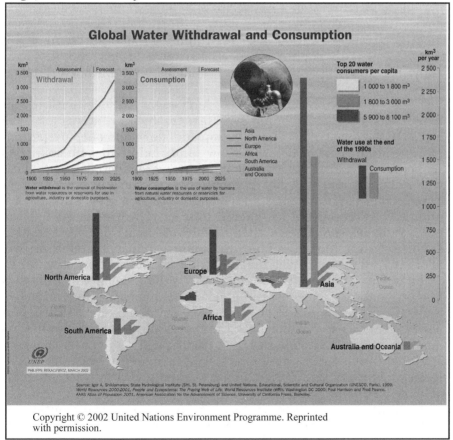

Conserving water helps not only to preserve irreplaceable natural resources such as the Aral, but also to reduce the strain on urban wastewater management systems. Wastewater is costly to treat, and requires continuous investment to ensure that the water we return to our waterways is as clean as possible. During storms, rainwater runs off the pavement, collecting pollutants as it goes. Where storm sewers and sanitary sewers are connected, the influx of storm water can overwhelm sewage treatment facilities, leading to the release of untreated sewage and polluted storm water directly into local waterways. Forty billion gallons of such a toxic cocktail flow into the Hudson River and its estuary each year. Several towns and cities around the world are installing innovative solutions to such problems that also benefit surrounding ecosystems. Rainwater overflow, for instance, can be channeled into wetland systems instead of into storm sewers.

Human activities affect water quality in other ways as well. Particularly in large cities, once water has disappeared down the drain or into a storm sewer, it is rarely thought of again. But what becomes of the household chemicals poured daily into the water supply—cleansers, antibacterial soaps, medicines? Ecologists are just now learning about their downstream effects. One that is well documented is the disruption of growth and reproduction in frogs and fish. Cities with sophisticated treatment systems can filter out many chemicals, but antibiotics, hormones, and antibacterial compounds remain hard to handle.

The UN estimates that by 2025, forty-eight nations, with a combined population of 2.8 billion, will face freshwater "stress" or "scarcity." Water shortages already impede development, perpetuate poverty, and damage health in low- and middle-income countries. As populations grow and the demand for water increases, problems will intensify and will not be contained within national borders. Population displacements and conflict over shared surface and groundwater resources are bound to exacerbate international turmoil. It is no coincidence that the word "rival" derives from the Latin word for "one living on an opposite bank of a stream from another."

The world also faces the uncertain effects of global warming. The loss of mountain ice caps and glaciers, for instance, may alter the quantity and reliability of water for drinking, agriculture, and power generation. California's Central Valley, which produces a quarter of the food sold in the U.S., depends on timely seasonal snowmelt from surrounding mountains; farmers could face failing or lower-yielding crops as the climate warms and less water is available in the growing season.

Water policy makers have focused on technological solutions to increase water supplies—diverting surface water, pumping up groundwater, extracting the salt from seawater. Such solutions often have high costs, both monetary and environmental. And so the focus has shifted to reducing demand. Hydrologists estimate that as much as 60 percent of the water extracted from aquatic systems for human use is simply wasted—lost to leakage, evaporation, inefficient appliances, and human carelessness. Changes in various technologies and in everyday behavior could slash that number in half. Saving water in the home calls for installing water-efficient appliances and fixtures, fixing leaks, refilling water bottles from the tap, landscaping with native plants, and generally being more conscious about water use. Municipalities could construct wetlands or, better yet, refrain from destroying existing ones. Towns and businesses could pave with a permeable material that enables water to seep back into aquifers. Industries and municipalities can reuse water that has been treated but does not reach drinking-water standards. A bounty of choices is available, once we decide to stop taking water for granted.

PopulationWatch

"More Crop per Drop"

BY TUSHAAR SHAH
UN CHRONICLE ONLINE, MARCH/MAY 2003

Intensification of water scarcity is an unpleasant reality in many emerging economies of the world. However, the causes of water scarcity sometimes differ. Research at the International Water Management Institute (IWMI) suggests that tackling water scarcity implies quite different challenges in Africa where it is predominantly "economic" and in Asia where it is "physical". In Africa, it is a question of promoting judicious creation of new hydraulic capital, but in Asia water scarcity is about an unsustainably large number of rural poor living off a limited base of natural resources, particularly fresh water. In the UN Millennium Summit in September 2000, UN Secretary-General Kofi Annan echoed a decade of IWMI research when he said that "we need a 'Blue Revolution' in agriculture that focuses on increasing productivity per unit of water— 'more crop per drop'."

New IWMI research suggests we also need more "cash per drop" and "more jobs per drop".

Over decades of economic progress, the industrialized world has evolved approaches that are now helping them manage their freshwater well. These approaches have held a powerful sway over global water thinking in recent years and yielded stylized approaches, whose common refrain is integrated management of water and land resources in a river basin framework. Policy prescriptions implied are: transform fragmented territorial water institutions into integrated river basin organizations; price water to reflect its scarcity; institute tradable property rights; and establish appropriate legal and regulatory mechanisms for effective demand management.

Adopting these policies, however, creates new difficulties and tensions because they fail to factor in three aspects of the freshwater challenge facing water-scarce countries: what drives their irrigation economies; how best to influence their water users; and how will their fresh water situation respond to their overall economic evolution.

Irrigation is at the heart of the water scarcity in water-stressed regions. But for irrigation, India's freshwater challenge would be much easier to meet. And the first world has never dealt with irrigation on the scale we find in water stressed countries. Seventy per cent of the world's irrigated areas are in Asia, and much future irrigation development will occur in Africa. These countries need irrigation because of three reasons—extreme climate, high population pressure, and low levels of economic development, occurring all at once.

South Asian and North China plains would find it easier to preserve their freshwater if they had lower population density as in Australia or Israel, better water endowments as in Canada, a more favourable rainfall pattern and climate as in Europe, a well-developed industrial and service economy as in the Asian tigers, or a strategic resource like oil as in Iraq, Iran or Saudi Arabia. Since they have none of these, their only hope is in squeezing more crops, cash and livelihoods from every drop of water, until they can substantially ease population pressure on agriculture. Growing food for their large populations is formidable enough a challenge for South Asia and China; but even more formidable is the challenge of providing secure livelihoods for large segments of rural population dependent on farming.

In the industrialized world today, notions of how water should be managed are conditioned by the way the water sector is organized. After centuries of economic growth, populations have concentrated in urban agglomerations near the estuaries. Municipal and industrial uses of water have rapidly increased, while agricultural use of "managed" water has shrunk. Most water users are served by service-providing agencies that are amenable to regulation and economic management.

Water has become an "industry"; and like in any industry, pricing has become an effective tool for water demand management, as well as for funds generation for maintaining and improving hydraulic infrastructure. The key freshwater management challenge is allocating water between alternative uses, and the stage is set for river basin management.

Developing countries in Asia and Africa are decades away from evolving their water sectors to this stage of maturity. Here, the water sector is largely informal; the majority of users get their water requirements directly from nature, from small decentralized storages or from groundwater, untrammeled by laws and regulatory frameworks and unmediated by service providers. Management of water demand is critical but nearly impossible, because of the challenge of regulating a vast number of tiny users.

Just take the case of groundwater regulation. South Asia and North China's virtually unmanaged groundwater aquifers are being depleted by a colossal, informal groundwater economy whose growth has responded more to population density than to the availability of the resource (*Debroy and Shah*). This is as much a challenge in the western United States and Mexico. Yet, the problem is far more complex in Asia. The United States uses 100 km^3 of groundwater every year, but the bulk of this is pumped by around

200,000 large pumps and benefits 2 per cent of the American people. In contrast, India's 150 km^3 of annual groundwater use is extracted by 20 million small pump owners and supports over half of India's population. And yet, the United States and Mexico have not been particularly more effective in regulating groundwater depletion and degradation than India and China (*Shah 2003a*).

Ironically, economic growth may well be the best healer for the ailing freshwater ecologies of the water-stressed world. As long as smallholder agriculture in Asia and Africa continues to act as the parking lot for the rural poor, their Governments will find it difficult to resist irrigation development. As economic progress generates off-farm livelihood opportunities, freshwater use in agriculture declines or becomes easier to regulate. During three decades of rapid growth in some parts of east Asia, for example, irrigated areas fell by 40 per cent; and a similar trend is emerging in Mexico.

> Ironically, economic growth may well be the best healer for the ailing freshwater ecologies of the water-stressed world.

The IWMI analysis, with the help of the new Water Poverty Index developed by scientists at Keel and Wallingford, suggests that the access to water depends not so much on physical water resources of a country but on its GNP/capita.

It shows that the quality of freshwater too seems to follow the inverted Kuznets' curve: declining in early stages of economic growth but rising as countries improve their standard of living, regardless of physical endowments of water resources (*Shah 2003b*). The challenge before the water-stressed world is to chalk out what Peter Gleick has called the "soft water path" to economic growth, which is more mindful of the value of preserving freshwater in the strategic choices it makes for growing its economy.

NGO efforts to popularize low-cost micro-irrigation technologies in South Asia, people's movement to use rainwater harvesting and recharge aquifers in western India and upland areas of China, the enthusiasm in southern India, the United Republic of Tanzania and Ghana to reinvent the social uses of age-old tanks and ponds in local water supply and irrigation systems—all these exemplify unique responses of water-stressed regions to their unique freshwater challenges.

These deserve more and empathetic international attention and support than they get now. In part, this is because of the dominant belief that today's developing world will solve its freshwater problems in much the same way as the first world did decades ago.

It is doubtful if this will be the case entirely. The world needs to help water-stressed developing countries devise freshwater management strategies appropriate to their socio-ecological context and the genius of their people.

The most important role the United Nations can play is that of creating a larger common ground between the water wisdom developed in the industrialized world and a textured understanding of the freshwater challenges facing the water-stressed regions and of unique innovations being tried out in parts of Asia and Africa.

References

Shah, Tushaar, Ian Makin, R. Sakthivadivel and M. Samad (2002) "Limits to Leapfrogging: Issues in Transposing Successful River Basin Management Institutions in the Developing World". Charles L. Abernethy, Ed.

Intersectoral Management of River Basins. Colombo: International Water Management Institute.

Debroy, Aditi and Tushaar Shah (2003) "Groundwater Socio-ecology of South Asia".

Custodio, E. and R. Llamas, Eds. *Intensive Use of Groundwater: Challenges and Opportunities*. Amsterdam: Swets & Zeillinger.

Shah, Tushaar (2003a) "Governing the Groundwater Economy: Comparative Analysis of National Institutions and Policies In South Asia, China and Mexico". Paper presented at SINEX Conference, Valencia, Spain, 7–10 December 2002.

Shah, Tushaar (2003b) "Water Poverty of Nations: Its Causes and Remedies". Internal paper. Anand: International Water Management Institute.

Water Scarcity

The Food Factor

BY DAVID MOLDEN, CHARLOTTE DE FRAITURE, AND FRANK RIJSBERMAN
ISSUES IN SCIENCE & TECHNOLOGY, SUMMER 2007

With ever more water needed to raise crops to feed the burgeoning global population, efforts to produce more food with less water are critical to averting a crisis. With so much talk about a global water crisis, about water scarcity, and about increasing competition and conflicts over water, it would be easy to get the impression that Earth is running dry. You could be forgiven for wondering whether, in the not-too-distant future, there will be sufficient water to produce enough to eat and drink.

But the truth is that the world is far from running out of water. There is land and human resources and water enough to grow food and provide drinking water for everyone. That doesn't mean, however, that the global water crisis is imaginary. Around the world there are already severe water problems.

The problem is the quantity of water required for food production. People will need more and more water for more and more agriculture. Yet the way people use water in agriculture is the most significant contributor to ecosystem degradation and to water scarcity. Added together, these problems amount to an emergency requiring immediate attention from government institutions that make policy, from water managers, from agricultural producers—and from the rest of us, because we are all consumers of food and water.

The crisis is even more complex than it first appears to be because many policies that on the surface appear to have nothing to do with water and food make a bigger difference to water resources and food production than even agricultural and water management practices. But people who make these decisions often do not consider water to be part of them. Water professionals need to communicate these concerns better, and policymakers need to be more water-aware.

In early 2007, the Comprehensive Assessment of Water Management in Agriculture, which explored ways to cope with this crisis, was released. The assessment gathered research and opinions from more than 700 researchers and practitioners from around the world. They addressed these questions: How can water be developed and managed in agriculture to help end poverty and hunger, promote environmentally sustainable practices, and find a balance between food and environmental security? The Comprehensive Assessment provides a picture of how people used water for agriculture in the past, the water challenges that people are facing today, and policy-relevant recommendations charting the way forward. Food and environmental communities joined efforts to produce the assessment, which was jointly sponsored by the United Nations Food and Agricultural Organization, the Convention on Biological Diversity, the Consultative Group on Agricultural Research, and the Ramsar Convention on Wetlands.

> If there's plenty of water for drinking and growing food, then what's the crisis all about?

Crisis, What Crisis?

If there's plenty of water for drinking and growing food, then what's the crisis all about? Many in the developed world are complacent about the supply of water and food. Global food production has outpaced population growth during the past 30 years. The world's farmers produce enough for everyone, and food is cheap. Water resources development, which has played a critical role in fueling agricultural growth, can be seen as one of humankind's great achievements. Why isn't the type of water resource development that served us well in the past sustainable?

For one thing, agriculture must feed another 2 to 3 billion people in the next 50 years, putting additional pressure on water resources. More than 70% of the world's 850 million undernourished people live in rural areas, and most depend directly or indirectly on water for their livelihoods. Yet for millions of rural people, accessing enough food, enough water, or both is a daily struggle. Rain may be plentiful for some farmers, but in many places it falls when it is not needed and vanishes during drought. The Indian rural development worker Kalpanatai Salunkhe put it succinctly: "Water is the divide between poverty and prosperity."

In addition, policies seemingly unrelated to water drive increased water use. For example, using biofuels may be a way to reduce greenhouse gases, but growing the crops to produce them demands additional water. Increased reliance on biofuels could create scarcity by pushing up agricultural water use. In India, increased biofuel production to meet 10% of its transportation fuel demand by 2030 will require an estimated 22 cubic kilometers more irrigation water, about 5% of what is currently used in Indian food production, pushing the country further into water scarcity. India can ill afford these additional water resources.

Trade has the potential to markedly reduce water use. Yet trade policies rarely if ever take water into account. As a first step, trade officials could consider the water implications of trade. Subsidies and economic incentives lead to better soil and water management. Countries set subsidy policies as an economic incentive. If farmers have access to cheaper fertilizer or water, or the prospect of higher prices for their crops, they will invest in better practices. But agricultural subsidies consider a country's political interests (such as rural employment) rather than water. Subsidies in countries such as the United States allow cheaper food to be exported and drive down the prices of commodities such as corn and wheat. Farmers in Africa and poor countries elsewhere then have trouble competing with these artificially low prices. Local, national, and international policymakers should carefully consider the water implications of their actions along with local politics.

How Much Water Do We Eat?

The water-food-environment dilemma starts with everybody because everybody eats. The water people need for drinking is essential, but it is only about 0.01% of the water people require to produce their food.

Why does food production need so much water? It is largely because of the physiologic process of plant transpiration. Huge amounts of water are evaporated constantly from pores on the surface of a plant's leaves. This evaporation is part of the process of photosynthesis, in which a plant manufactures its own energy from sunlight. Evaporation also helps cool the plant and carries nutrients to all its parts. In addition to transpiration, some liquid water is turned to vapor through evaporation from wet soils or leaves.

Crop yield is roughly proportional to transpiration; more yield requires more transpiration. It takes between 500 and 4,000 liters of evapotranspiration (ET, the combined process of evaporation and transpiration) to produce just one kilogram of grain. When that grain is fed to animals, producing a kilogram of meat takes much more water—between 5,000 and 15,000 liters. Thus, vegetarian diets require less water (2,000 liters of ET daily) than do high-calorie diets that include grain-fed meat (5,000 liters of ET daily.)

The bottom line is that although people individually need just 2 to 5 liters of drinking water and 20 to 400 liters of water for household use every day, in reality they use far more: between 2,000 and 5,000 liters of water per person per day, depending largely on how productive their agriculture is and what kind of food they eat. An estimated 7,100 cubic kilometers of water are vaporized to produce food for today's 6.6 billion people. On average, each of us requires about 1,000 cubic meters of water each year for food, or about 3 cubic meters (3 tons, or 3,000 liters!) of water per day. For country-level food security, about 2,800 to 3,000 calories must reach the market in order for each of us to consume about 2,000 calories. Thus, about one liter of water is required per calorie of food supply.

Water for crops comes either directly from rain or indirectly from irrigation. Growing food with rainwater has much different water and land-use implications than does intensive irrigation. Meat produced on rangeland uses much less water than industrial meat production in feed-based systems. In addition, although both grazing and industrial livestock systems need water, the soil moisture in grazing land cannot be piped into a city and therefore does not reduce the domestic water supply, although it does reduce the amount of water available to the natural ecosystem that is being grazed.

The importance of meat to water consumption and livelihoods is quite different in developed and developing countries. Animal products are extremely important in the nutrition of families who otherwise consume little protein. They are also precious to African herders and farmers who use livestock for transport, for plowing, for living food storage, and often for a walking bank account as well. In the developed world, by contrast, most livestock production is for meat and comes from industrial feed-based processes.

Reaching the Limits

Every year, the rain falling on Earth's surface amounts to about 110,000 cubic kilometers. About 40,000 cubic kilometers contributes to rivers and groundwater. The remainder evaporates directly from soil. People withdraw 3,700 cubic kilometers from rivers and aquifers for cities, industries, and agriculture. Agricultural irrigation takes most of that: 2,600 cubic kilometers or 70% of total withdrawals. Agriculture also consumes 7,100 cubic kilometers per year through ET, about 80% of which comes directly from rain and 20% from irrigation. Rainfall supplies plenty of water for food production. But often it fails to rain in the right place or at the right time.

Limits have already been reached or breached in several river basins. These basins are "closed" because people have used all the water, leaving just an inadequate trickle for the ecosystem. The list of closed basins includes important breadbaskets around the Colorado River in the United States, the Indus River in southern Asia, the Yellow River in China, the Jordan River in the Middle East, and the Murray Darling River in Australia.

Many agricultural and city users prefer groundwater, the underground water in aquifers and streams beneath Earth's surface that supplies springs and wells. The present boom in groundwater use for irrigation that began in the 1970s is occurring because this water is easy to tap with cheap pumps and the supply is reliable. But for millions of people, the groundwater boom has turned to bust as groundwater levels plummet, often at rates of 1 to 2 meters per year. Groundwater is declining in key agricultural areas in Mexico, the North China plains, the Ogallala aquifer in the U.S. high plains, and in northwest India.

Patterns of water use are also changing in response to changes in the amount of grazing land and the productivity of fisheries. Further expansion of grazing is unlikely to be available to support expanded meat and milk production, so more livestock will have to come from industrial feed-based systems. That will require more water, especially for feed production. Ocean and freshwater fisheries have in many cases surpassed their limits, yet consumption of fish and fish products is booming. So in the future, more fish products will come from aquaculture, which requires yet more fresh water.

Water scarcity resulting from physical, economic, or institutional constraints is already a problem for one-third of the world's population. About 1.2 billion people live in areas plagued by physical water scarcity, meaning they lack enough water to satisfy demand, including enough water to sustain ecosystems. These are Earth's deserts and other arid regions. Physical water scarcity also occurs in areas with plenty of water, but where supply is strained by the overdevelopment of hydraulic infrastructure. Another 500 million people live where the limit to water resources is fast approaching. All of these people are beginning to experience the symptoms of physical water scarcity: severe environmental degradation, pollution, declining groundwater supplies, and water allocations in which some groups win at the expense of others.

> About 1.2 billion people live in areas plagued by physical water scarcity, meaning they lack enough water to satisfy demand.

Economically water-scarce basins are home to more than 1.5 billion people. In these places, human capacity or financial resources are likely to be insufficient to develop local water, even though the supply might be adequate if it could be exploited. Much of this scarcity is due to the way in which institutions function, favoring one group while not hearing the voices of others, especially women. Symptoms of economic water scarcity include scant infrastructure development, meaning that there are few pipes or canals to get water to the people. Even where infrastructure exists, the distribution of water may be inequitable. Sub-Saharan Africa is characterized by economic water scarcity. Water development could do much to reduce poverty there.

Both economic and physical water scarcity pose special problems that can be particularly difficult to deal with. But, as we have said, water problems also occur in areas with adequate water. Institutions—laws, rules, and a supportive organizational framework—are key to mitigating water problems. Where there is inequitable water distribution or ecosystem degradation, water problems can be traced back to ill-adapted or poorly functioning institutions. Rarely is there an overriding technological constraint.

As economies develop and people's incomes rise, their diets tend to change. In developed areas, more grain is grown for feeding animals than for feeding people. The reverse is true in sub-Saharan Africa, where grains are a major part of the human diet. With economic development, the trend is toward much more meat in the diet, as in East Asia. There, average annual meat consumption is expected to double, from 40 to 80 kg per person, by 2050.

With growing incomes and changes in diet worldwide, food and feed demand could double by the year 2050. If there is no increase in water productivity—the amount of water it takes to produce a unit of food—water consumed by agriculture must double as well. The environmental impact of that massive human demand for water would be stunning. Therefore, the amount of food per unit of water, which has tended to grow in the past, needs to grow much faster.

Water for More Food

There are five main options for getting water for more food:

- Expand irrigated areas by diverting more from rivers, lakes, and aquifers

- Expand rain-fed areas by turning more natural area into arable land

- Get "more crop per drop" through increases in water productivity

- Trade food from areas of high to low water productivity

- Look beyond water and crops by managing demand through dietary changes or reduced food wasting

Irrigation has been the key water resources development strategy in Asia and the Western industrialized countries: Build dams, divert water to irrigate crops, and intensify production. Irrigation has succeeded in combating famine and poverty and has helped stimulate economic growth in early stages of development; for example, in India and China. Particularly in Asia, this achievement is often referred to as the Green Revolution, which combined improved crop varieties with increased chemical fertilizer use and irrigation. In Asia there were few other options, because the population density in many countries precluded converting land to agriculture.

In Africa, on the other hand, the key strategy has been the opposite: to expand the area under cultivation with very little irrigation or agricultural intensification. Latin America has adopted a mixed strategy.

A downside of irrigation expansion is its several effects on aquatic ecosystems. Dams fragment rivers. Increased ET causes river flows to diminish and groundwater levels to drop. Intensive irrigation has led to closed basins where all water is allocated to specific uses, including water for the environment. In fact, irrigation has been the single most important reason for closing river basins and creating physical water scarcity.

Nevertheless, the continued expansion of irrigated land remains an important strategy. Storing water behind dams or in groundwater is arguably an important way of coping with climate change because it helps reduce uncertainties of supply. Scenario analysis shows that irrigation could contribute 55% of the total value of food supply by 2050, up from 45% today. But that expansion would require 40% more water to be withdrawn for agriculture, surely a threat to many aquatic ecosystems and fisheries. Fisheries would compete with irrigated crops for water. Highly nutritious fish products, important for some of the poorest of the poor, are threatened when water is diverted to crops.

Sub-Saharan Africa is a special case because there is now so little irrigation there. Irrigation expansion seems warranted. Doubling the irrigated land in sub-Saharan Africa would increase irrigation's contribution to the food supply from only 5% today to, optimistically, 11% by 2050.

Typical water productivity figures for the staple cereal crops rice and wheat are 0.5 kilogram per cubic meter in low-performing irrigation systems, 0.2 kilogram per cubic meter in rain-fed sub-Saharan Africa, and up to 2 kilogram per cubic meter in both Asian state-of-the-art irrigation systems and rain-fed systems in Europe and North America. Today, 55% of the gross value of our food is produced by rainfall on nearly 72% of the world's cropland.

Rain-fed agriculture could be upgraded to meet food and livelihood needs through better management, not just of water but also of soil and land. These tactics can increase water productivity, adding a component of irrigation water through smaller-scale interventions such as rainwater harvesting: capturing rain before it gets to rivers by building small earthen dams across streams or diverting water from roads or rooftops into storage.

At the global level, the potential for rain-fed agriculture is large enough to meet present and future food demand through increased productivity alone. An optimistic scenario, in which farmers reach 80% of the maximum practically obtainable yield, assumes significant progress in upgrading rain-fed systems while relying on minimal increases in irrigation. This leads to annual growth of 1%, increasing an average rain-fed yield of 2.7 metric tons per hectare in 2000 to 4.5 tons in 2050. From 1961 to 2000, the clearing of land expanded the cropped area by 24%, at the expense of terrestrial ecosystems. But with productivity gains, expansion can be limited to 7% from now until 2050, in spite of the rising demand for agricultural commodities. The Millennium Ecosystem Assessment identified agricultural land expansion as the most important driver of ecosystem change, so limiting this expansion would have important ecological payoffs.

But it has been extremely difficult to improve yields from rainfall alone. If adoption rates of improved technologies are low and yield improvements do not materialize, the rain-fed cropped area required to meet rising food demand by 2050 would need to expand by 53% instead of 7%. Globally, the land for this is available. But additional natural ecosystems would have to be converted to agriculture, which would encroach on marginally suitable lands and add to environmental degradation.

There are reasons to be optimistic about water productivity gains. There is still ample scope for higher physical water productivity in low-yielding rain-fed areas and in poorly performing irrigation systems, where poverty and food insecurity prevail. Good agricultural practices—managing soil fertility and reducing land degradation—are important for increasing crop per drop. The Comprehensive Assessment reveals scope for improvements in livestock and fisheries as well, which is important because of the growing demand for meat and fish. Farmers and water managers can do these things with the right incentives.

But caution and care must be mixed with this optimism. There are misperceptions about the scope for increasing physical water productivity. Much of the potential gain in physical water productivity has already been met in high-productivity regions. There is less water wasted in irrigation than commonly thought. Irrigation water is often reused locally or downstream; farmers thirsty for water do not carelessly let it flow down the drain. A water productivity gain by one user may be a loss to another. Upstream gain may be offset by a loss in fisheries, or the gain may put more agrochemicals into the environment.

But increases in yield almost always require that more water be transformed to water vapor through ET. Most gains in water productivity can be made by increasing yields in areas of the world where yield is extremely low, roughly 1 to 2 tons per hectare. Doubling crop yield by improved soil and water management can actually triple water productivity in these areas, because plants stressed by thirst perform so poorly and because there is excess evaporation from soils.

Today's low-yielding areas can generate the biggest increases in water productivity. These are the rain-fed areas of sub-Saharan African and South Asia, where improved soil fertility combined with better water management can make big differences. Adding supplemental irrigation will be a key. A second payoff is that these are areas with a lot of rural poverty and few jobs outside agriculture. Increases in agricultural productivity can boost incomes and economic growth.

Where yields are already fairly high, say 6 tons per hectare, increasing yield by one-third typically takes about one-third more water. Still, even at these higher yields water productivity can be bettered, although improvements are more difficult to obtain.

Major gains and breakthroughs, such as those in the past from breeding and biotechnology programs, are much less likely to take place in the future. In fact, the Comprehensive Assessment concluded that although breeding had played the most significant role in water productivity gains in the past, today it is improved management that is most likely to generate more increases. Drought- and disease-resistant varieties are crucial for reducing the risks of farming, but higher yields from these crops tend to consume more water. Perhaps a breakthrough will come by breeding traits of water-efficient crops (such as maize and sugarcane) and low-transpiration crops (such as cactus and pineapple) into the more common but thirstier crops (such as wheat and barley).

Many view water pricing as the way to improve water productivity by reducing water waste in irrigation. But this has proven extremely difficult to implement because of political realities and lack of water rights. Gains are also hard to realize because of the complex web of hydrological flows. But well-crafted incentives that align society's interest in using water better with farmers' interest in profitable crops still hold promise. One such incentive: Urban users could compensate farmers for moving water originally intended for irrigation (and stored behind dams) from agriculture to cities facing rising demand.

There is more reason to be optimistic about increasing economic water productivity. Switching to crops with higher value or reducing crop production costs both lead to higher economic water productivity. Integrated approaches—agriculture/aquaculture systems, better integrating livestock into irrigated and rain-fed systems, using irrigation water for households and small industries—all are important for increasing value and jobs per drop.

Increases in physical and economic water productivity reduce poverty in two ways. First, targeted interventions enable poor people or marginal producers to gain access to water or to use it more productively for nutrition and income generation. Second, the multiplier effects on food security, employment, and income can benefit the poor. But programs must ensure that the gains reach the poor, especially poor rural women, and are not captured by wealthier or more powerful users. Inclusive negotiations increase the chance that all voices will be heard.

Can Trade Avert Water Stress?

By importing agricultural commodities, a country "saves" the amount of water it would have required to produce those commodities domestically. Many contend that this trade in virtual water—the equivalent water it takes to grow food—could solve problems of water scarcity. Egypt, a highly water-stressed country, imported 8 million metric tons of grain from the United States in 2000. To produce this amount of grain Egypt would have needed about 8.5 cubic kilometers of irrigation water, a substantial proportion of Egypt's annual supply from Lake Nasser of 55.6 cubic kilometers.

The cereal trade has a moderating impact on the demand for irrigation water because the major grain exporters—the United States, Canada, France, Australia, and Argentina—produce grain with highly productive rainfall. A contrasting example is found in Japan, a land-scarce country and the world's biggest grain importer. Japan would require an additional 30 billion cubic meters of crop water to grow the food it imports. A strategic increase in international food trade, and thus trade in virtual water, could mitigate water scarcity and reduce environmental degradation. Instead of striving for food self-sufficiency, water-short countries would import food from water-abundant countries. But there are forces working against this trade.

Poor countries depend, to a large extent, on their national agriculture sector, and they often lack funds to buy food from the world market. At present, for example, Uganda and Ethiopia simply cannot afford to buy their food from other countries, and even if they could, getting it to people through the local marketing system would be a daunting task. Struggling with food security, these countries remain wary of depending on imports to satisfy basic needs. Even countries such as India and China that could afford to import more food instead of expanding irrigation may instead embrace a politically appealing degree of national food self-sufficiency. Australia, on the other hand, is a major exporter of food and virtual water in spite of scarce water and the environmental problems arising from it.

At present, countries trade for economic or political reasons, not for water. So it is unlikely that food trade will solve water scarcity problems in the near term. But water, food, and their environmental implications should enter more firmly into discussions of trade.

> Poor countries depend . . . on their national agriculture sector, and they often lack funds to buy food from the world market.

Looking for More Water

Where else can water gains be found? Water resources rarely enter the discussions of livestock scientists and managers, and if they do, the talk usually concerns livestock drinking water. But water needed to generate food for livestock far surpasses what animals need for drinking. Yet these are areas where significant increases could be found. Colleagues at the International Livestock Research Institute have shown that the water productivity of livestock could easily be doubled or tripled by, for example, changing the type of food fed to animals or enhancing the production of milk, meat, and eggs. Better grazing practices could help reduce the environmental impact. There are large gains to be had in aquaculture systems too, but these are rarely quantified.

In addition, policies that focus on diets could have a profound impact on water resource use. Although for many people undernourishment is a key concern and better diets an issue, the opposite is also true. Households in the developed world waste as much as 20% to 30% of their food, and therefore the water it took to produce it. In developing countries much food is wasted too, particularly in moving it from farm to market. And although overeating may not waste food, it still wastes water.

The ultimate cause of our water problems is inadequate institutions. Behind water scarcity, unequal distribution of benefits from water development, and failure to take advantage of known technologies lie policies, laws, and organizations that influence how water is managed. With rapidly growing cities, expanding agriculture, and changing societal demands, the water situation is changing rapidly in most places in the world. Yet institutions rarely adapt rapidly enough to keep pace. Reform is needed.

A prime example is the slow adoption of productivity-enhancing measures. Technologies that boost water productivity are known or could be readily developed, but the institutional environment does not support it. Risk-averse farmers are unlikely to invest in water technologies or improved management practices if there might be a dry spell that will ruin crops. In much of sub-Saharan Africa, crops could be grown, but there is no market or else no roads to take the goods to market. Farmers are asked to employ water-saving technologies that benefit cities, but rarely are there sufficient incentives and compensation for farmers to do so.

Compounding this are the hydrologic complexities brought about by the increasingly intertwined nature of water users. The development of upstream water for crops may take water away from downstream fisheries, but there is no mechanism to bring both types of agricultural producers to the table to discuss the issue. Institutions need to become much better at integrating policies across sectors and at using science to see opportunities and pitfalls when making changes.

Donor agencies and international institutions have advocated a host of panaceas—water pricing, water markets, farmer management of irrigation systems, drip irrigation—using blueprint solutions, donor funds, and leverage to hasten reforms. It is frustrating when these ideas are ignored. A major reason is that reforms are simply not right for local conditions. For example, new river basin organizations may be promoted, but they ignore or replace informal arrangements that already exist.

What is needed is a reform of this reform process, one in which solutions can be better crafted to meet local needs in the specific political and institutional context. This will require building coalitions among the partners. Civil society and the private sector are key actors. Government institutions are key, too, but often the slowest to take up reform.

Actions are required now. Here are some possibilities:

- All of us should think about the water implications of the food we eat—and waste.

- Consumers and the private sector should be prepared to pay the environmental costs of food production.

- Politicians and trade negotiators should consider the water implications of trade and energy use and pay the water costs.

- Governments should fund the development of water for food.

- City dwellers should compensate farming communities for water that is taken away from them.

- Governments should set up mechanisms for negotiating water disputes.

- Governments, civil society, and the private sector should spend time and money to empower poorer water users to compete equally with wealthier ones.

We tend to defer these choices to the next generation, which will feel the consequences of scarcer groundwater or ecosystem degradation. But we can learn from the mistakes of the past. We can provide incentives to produce more food with less water. All of us and our governments should recognize that there are limits to water, and that more and more water is not always a solution.

Not a Drop to Drink

By Katharine Mieszkowski
Salon, April 25, 2006

Leave the tap running while brushing your teeth, and you're dumping four and a half gallons of water down the drain, according to the U.S. Environmental Protection Agency.

That's the kind of shiny stat trotted out to inspire profligate water-wasters to conserve. Just shut off the tap, save water. It's easy! Huzzah! Yet, as British science journalist Fred Pearce makes crystal clear in "When the Rivers Run Dry," the water we consume—and waste—in everyday life is hardly limited to what comes out of our own faucets.

Pearce, a longtime editor for *New Scientist*, who is now an environmental consultant for the magazine, calculates that it takes 40 gallons of water to grow the ingredients for the bread in a single sandwich, not to mention 265 gallons to produce a glass of milk and 800 gallons for a hamburger. And that's just what's for lunch. Don't get him started on what you wear to this water-rich feast. Even a simple cotton T-shirt bearing some hopeful green slogan like "Save the Bay" is a huge water user. Pearce figures it takes 25 bathtubs-full of water to grow the scant 9 ounces of cotton for such a shirt.

Water is the ultimate renewable resource, literally falling from the sky back to earth after it evaporates. And since it's so heavy and cumbersome to move great distances, it's also a local resource. Yet, start quantifying the water embedded in foods and goods, the "virtual water" as economists call it, and water is fast becoming a global commodity like oil. There's Brazilian water in the coffee beans grown for an American latte; there's Pakistani water in the cotton in that T-shirt.

In "When the Rivers Run Dry," Pearce finds a growing strain on many local water resources around the globe, as the world's population grows. As he visits dozens of countries, he sees rivers that have been so diverted, depleted and dried out, such as the Rio Grande, that they no longer conform to their original map locations. Pearce reports that the fallout from the competition for water resources is enormous, exacerbating tensions between Palestinians and Israelis in the West Bank and even accidentally poisoning villagers by the millions in India and Bangladesh.

The article first appeared in Salon.com, at http//www.Salon.com. An online version remains in the Salon archives. Reprinted with permission

Yet, Pearce also finds hope in the way some communities around the world are harvesting and using water. Salon spoke with the writer by phone from England about why he thinks we need a "blue revolution."

If there are 650 gallons of water in a pound of cheddar cheese, is it futile to make small gestures like turning off the water when you brush your teeth in the name of saving it?

It helps with water bills, so it makes sense in that way. And it may make sense with local water resources, which may be constrained, just within a small town, or even a community.

At the global scale, no, it doesn't make much difference. Most of the water that each one of us uses comes from the water used to irrigate the crops that we consume. That's principally food, but not only. Cotton for our clothing is a major user of water around the world.

We don't really know as we pick up the food from the store whether our purchases are responsible for making some local crisis elsewhere worse, but it is often the case. Many countries are facing serious water shortages; often their rivers are running dry, or their water tables falling very fast, and in many cases much of that water is being exported by those countries in the form of goods. Yet, when we pay market price for those goods, that price doesn't usually include any estimate of the cost to the water resources. We still think of water as an unlimited resource rather like the air we breathe.

Now some countries are entirely dependent on water from elsewhere to feed their people, on this "virtual water."

Many countries have run out of water for growing their own crops and are now importing water in the form of food. Egypt really, for instance, lost the ability to feed itself perhaps 30 years ago. It now imports a large amount of water in the form of food. That is the only way it can do it. Water is pretty heavy stuff to move, but the trade in products produced with water is huge, and in many ways can be seen as a trade in water.

What are some of the rivers around the world that have run dry, or are most in danger of it?

There are two rivers in a bad way in the U.S., one of which is the Colorado. There's a U.S. treaty with Mexico to deliver water over the border, and the U.S. has considerable difficulty in providing any water over the border to meet its minimum treaty requirement, because all the water is used up essentially by farmers and increasingly by cities along the Colorado.

The water goes off to Southern California, Phoenix, Tucson [Ariz.]. By the time the river crosses the border into Mexico, which is close to its delta, it is really very dry. There's not a lot of water left.

The Rio Grande is another interesting example. It essentially dries up about a thousand kilometers from the sea near El Paso [Texas]. The riverbed is virtually dry for 300 kilometers before some more water comes back in from tributaries coming in from Mexico.

So, whatever it looks like on the map, really the Rio Grande is two rivers. There's a river that gives out at El Paso, and there's the tributary that comes in and replenishes the last run to the Gulf of Mexico. There are very serious economic repercussions from the drying up of the Rio Grande. I met farmers who simply no longer have water to irrigate their crops, and that's on both sides of the border, on the Mexican side and on the Texas side.

If you look around the world, virtually no water flows from the Nile into the Mediterranean; very little water flows from the Indus through Pakistan into the Arabian Sea; the Yellow River in Northern China, one of the world's longest rivers, is essentially dry for much of the year. A little flow goes down to the sea, but very little. So, this is close to becoming a global phenomenon, some of the world's largest rivers, and longest rivers, simply not reaching the sea.

One response to rivers running dry is to move water enormous distances, at the cost of hundreds of billions of dollars. What do you make of such grand projects?

There are plans now for huge transfers of water across some of the world's biggest, most densely populated countries in order to provide water for the new mega-cities, and for farming. China's got one of the largest, and that's going to take a large amount of water out of the River Yangtze, which runs through the south of the country, and deliver it into the northern plains, to the Yellow River, which has essentially run dry for much of its course.

Essentially, the Yangtze is going to replenish the waters of the north of China. This project is already underway. Two of the three branches that are planned are already under construction. China hopes to be delivering water from the Yangtze to Beijing in time for the Olympics in 2008. This project will probably cost something like $60 billion. It's a major enterprise in order to keep northern China from running dry. India has talked about something even larger.

Yet, in these vast projects to move water around, aren't incredible amounts of the water lost through evaporation or seepage from canals?

Many large engineering projects suffer from a huge range of inefficiencies, which is why—in general—I'm not in favor of them. It's much better to do things locally, because you can control the water more. One thing that surprised me greatly was discovering that with Lake Nasser behind the Aswan High Dam in Egypt—one of the world's kind of totemic dams—that the evaporation from the reservoir behind that dam annually amounts to, in metric, 15 cubic kilometers of water [3.6 cubic miles], if you can imagine a vast amount like that.

That is roughly the amount of water that is used by the whole of the United Kingdom in a year. In other words, you could fill every tap, meet every water demand in the U.K., a country of more than 50 million people, simply by the water that evaporates from the surface behind the Aswan Dam.

Now, that's an amazing statistic, but there are other reservoirs that lose similar amounts of water, especially in the hot tropical regions. That can't make much sense, if you have a country which is desperately short of water, and desperately trying to collect it up to deliver it to farmers. There are also huge evaporation rates from some of the distribution canals. Also, seepage from beneath distribution canals can be a major loss of water.

What's the solution?

With seepage, often, farmers, being rather practical people, simply sink some drilling rigs into the ground, and stick a pump in and pump that water up again. So, they tend to recycle it. But evaporation is a real loss. I'm not quite sure what you do about it other than manage water more locally. One of the most heartening trends I've seen traveling around the world—and I've seen it in China and India and in other places—is the effort by farmers and villagers to harvest the rain as it falls. They don't let the water go into the rivers and run away to perhaps a large dam, or run away to the sea. They simply capture it locally, and even pour it back down their wells, creating a storage system so that they can pump it up later in the year. So, particularly in India where most of the rain falls in 100 hours over 100 days, you simply have to capture that and store it locally in ponds, or even underground in wells. That's a rather efficient way for a local community to manage its water supply. It's being very effectively applied in thousands of villages across India.

Are you optimistic that there will be a kind of "blue revolution" of innovative ways to conserve and capture water?

I'm an optimist, not a pessimist. I'm a pessimist in the sense that we use water so inefficiently and so carelessly now that it makes you despair, but I'm an optimist also because there is so much potential for doing things better. When you find that irrigation systems waste 60 or 70 percent of their water it does make you despair, but you realize that there is a huge potential to do things better. I find that given the chance farmers and local communities, and even towns and countries, will and can do a lot of things better.

Still, conserving water in one location can mean just donating it to someone else to squander.

Unlike many of the resources that we rely on, water does move—down rivers and between countries—in ways that we can't do much about. When water gets short, the conflicts that arise over water do get very complicated.

On the West Bank, for instance, the Israelis and the Palestinians are almost as much in conflict over water as they are over land. The Palestinians are very angry that they are not allowed to sink more wells and drill more boreholes on the West Bank region, because the Israelis say that the water is already fully used, when most of that water is in fact used by Israelis not only in their settlements, but also in Israel proper.

While we often see water as a kind of free resource, provided by nature, once it gets in short supply the powerful do have an ability to grab hold and keep water—whether behind dams, or by sticking pumps into the ground. We haven't quite reached the situation where water wars are breaking out, but we're getting quite close in some parts of the world.

Where do you see potential for future water wars?

The River Nile is one, which is often talked about. The Egyptian government has said in the past that if a war is likely to be fought in their region, in North East Africa, it is almost certainly going to be about the River Nile. Egypt is absolutely and totally dependent on the Nile water to survive. The Nile flows through 10 countries before it reaches Egypt, which is very concerned that a country upstream, like Ethiopia, might start to build large dams, which would interrupt the flow of water down the Nile to Egypt.

People have also rattled their sabers over the Tigris and the Euphrates, both of which flow out of Turkey through Iraq on their way to the sea. In fact, during the first Gulf War, Turkey threatened to stop the flow of water down into Iraq as an act of war, using the dams it was building. It never did it, but it threatened to, and that caused a great deal of unease in that region.

India and Pakistan have a treaty over the River Indus, which flows through India. In fact, it collects most of its water in India, and then flows on into Pakistan, which is heavily dependent on that river for its survival. There is an agreement about who can have what water from that river, but if that treaty would break down then that again could be the basis for a very nasty water war. Of course, now you're talking about two countries that are both nuclear powers.

Is the American lifestyle more consumptive of water than other countries, as it is of energy resources, like oil and natural gas? And do you think the U.S. might end up importing water from Canada in the future?

It's an issue that keeps coming up. Canada has a great deal of water, particularly in the West, and America has quite a lot of demand for water, particularly in the West. So, you can imagine circumstances under which the U.S. would like to get its hands on Canadian water. Canadians are adamantly opposed to this, and I think that you'd have a great deal of difficulty getting any water out of them. They are prepared to use their rivers to generate hydroelectricity to sell electricity to the U.S., but they're not prepared to sell their water.

Domestically, American users are among the highest water users in the world, but you [Americans] stabilized your water consumption in recent years, principally by having more efficient toilets that use much less water in the flush. Canadians have not changed their toilets in the same way. They are probably now the No. 1 domestic users of water in individual homes. But neither the U.S. nor Canada reaches anything like the per capita water consumption of Uzbekistan and Turkmenistan.

Both of those use absolutely vast amounts of water to irrigate their cotton crops. It's a system set up by the Soviet Union, which has been carried on through today. They produce huge amounts of cotton grown using water taken out of the rivers in what is in many ways an arid region. The main consequence of that huge use of water is that they've dried up the Aral Sea, which was once the fourth biggest inland sea. It's sitting in Central Asia not far from the Caspian Sea, which is even bigger. They dried up the rivers that fed that sea, virtually no water reaches the sea anymore, and the sea has retreated fantastically.

I have been to see it, and you stand on the shoreline or what was the shoreline of the Aral Sea, and look out towards what once were waters where fishing boats got good catches, and all there is is desert. The water is over the horizon 60 miles away. It's one of the most extraordinary sights you'll see in the world—how the Aral Sea has disappeared. People call it one of the great ecological catastrophes in the world, and I really think that's true. It has happened entirely as a result of misuse of water to pour the contents of what were large rivers onto fields to grow cotton, and it destroyed a sea in the process.

[Editor's note: A recent report in the *New York Times* found that the Aral Sea is being brought back in some places.]

Aside from rivers and seas, how is water disappearing that we can't so readily see, underground water?

As rivers are running dry, in many countries of the world, and I've seen this especially in India, farmers are beginning to rely more and more on pumping out underground water reserves. There is usually a lot of water underground one way or another, some of it recent from rainfall, some of it essentially fossil water that's been there for thousands of years. Farmers are pumping this water out, which is lowering the water table.

That is causing an emerging water crisis in a number of Asian countries, but India is probably the worst example. They call it a creeping anarchy because nobody has any control over what the farmers do. They simply get a private drilling rig. They drill down, and they stick a pump into the ground, and start pumping the water up.

In some parts of India where they're relying more and more on underground water, they're bringing up unexpected poisons, perfectly natural poisons, but ones which have lain in the rock beneath them undisturbed for hundreds of thousands of years. The two big examples are fluoride and arsenic. Both of these turn out to be absorbed by underground water. Because there is no great tradition of using underground water, until recent years, nobody really knew. But as farmers and people start pumping this water up, they're finding that there are huge rates of poisoning—especially in Bangladesh and in West Bengal in India.

What are some of the effects of those poisons?

Well, they kill ultimately. They're slow-acting poisons, so you can drink the water for a number of years and then you slowly start having effects. Scientists from the World Health Organization have said that they believe this is one of the world's worst poisoning epidemics ever seen, because it involves tens of millions of people in both Bangladesh and parts of eastern India.

What impact will climate change likely have on water supplies around the world?

Nobody knows exactly what is going to happen to rainfall under global warming. We're fairly certain that climate change will make most of the world warmer. There are uncertainties about how weather systems are going to change, but the bottom line probably is that the wet places will get wetter, and the places that are dry will get still drier.

Where's the Water?

By Andrea Neal
The Saturday Evening Post, November/December 2006

It's a familiar drill to people living in drought-plagued parts of the country. Folks who live at an even-numbered address water the lawn on Mondays, Wednesdays and Fridays between 4 p.m. and 10 a.m. Odd-numbered addresses sprinkle on Tuesdays, Thursdays and Saturdays.

When things get really dry—as seems to be happening more often—there's no watering at all. Violators will be charged anywhere from $100 to $1,000 a day.

If water use restrictions like these bring to mind visions of the parched Great Plains or the arid Southwest, the headlines tell another story. In the summer of 2006, communities in two Great Lakes states—Minnesota and Wisconsin—issued total watering bans during dry periods. Ditto for areas in and around normally lush Atlanta, Georgia. From New England to California, municipal planners are dealing with serious concerns about future water resources.

The proverb says, "When the well is dry, we know the worth of water." In the United States, we are just starting to understand that water is a finite substance that must be protected. *National Geographic* warned us in October 1993, "All the water that will ever be is, right now." No matter how technologically advanced our water processing becomes, we can't do a thing to increase nature's fresh water. To meet the growing demand for water caused by population growth, food production and economic development, we must conserve, be creative and use what we have more efficiently.

Water, Water Everywhere

Water is humanity's most plentiful resource, covering almost 70 percent of the Earth's surface. But 97 percent of it is ocean water, too salty for drinking or for watering crops.

Of the 3 percent that is fresh water, most is locked in the ice caps of Antarctica and Greenland or in underground rock layers too deep to mine. A tiny fraction is found in bodies of water or beneath the soil in aquifers that can be tapped for wells.

As countries go, the United States is generously endowed with this precious resource. Annual precipitation here equals 4.2 trillion gallons. That's enough to cover the entire country with 30 inches of standing water. It's not all available as drinking water or for energy production, of course. Two thirds evaporates and transpires back to the atmosphere in what is called the hydrologic cycle. The remainder seeps into the ground or goes into the nation's lakes, rivers, reservoirs, and eventually oceans. It's a lot of water, 15 times what Americans currently consume. So how could there possibly be a supply problem?

The answer is twofold: demand and distribution.

Water doesn't always go where it's needed most. A downpour in Nevada doesn't help an Illinois farmer in the middle of a drought. A full reservoir in Texas is of no use to a depleted one in New York. As a general rule, droughts create local and regional shortages that are as unpredictable as local and regional weather. To date, no one has proposed pumping water cross-country in order to share the wealth.

Making matters worse, droughts are becoming more severe and widespread, according to the World Water Council. Expected climate change in coming years will make rainy seasons shorter and more intense in some regions, and droughts longer and more severe in others, the council warns.

> In the Southwest, the effects of irrigation are especially pronounced.

Demand is rising, too, although less so in the United States than in newer industrialized nations. Blame irrigation, the great giver of life, which is responsible for virtually all of the growth in U.S. water demand in recent years. Farms need a lot of water. It takes eight gallons to grow a single, juicy tomato. Notably, industrial use of water has actually dropped since 1980.

Irrigation accounts for almost 40 percent of water use, the single largest use of fresh water in the United States. Irrigated acreage more than doubled in size from 1950 to 1980, then leveled off before increasing 7 percent from 1995 to 2000. The number of acres irrigated with sprinkler and micro-irrigation systems has increased, too; lawn and garden and small commercial systems account for almost half the total irrigated acreage.

In the Southwest, the effects of irrigation are especially pronounced. According to a report by the Rocky Mountain Institute, 88 percent of the nation's irrigation water goes to 17 western states where groundwater is being pulled out faster than it is being recharged. "The states along the Colorado River, including five of the 10 fastest-growing states in the United States, have already allocated on paper more water than is actually in the river, and in many years the river never reaches the sea."

Preserving Natural Resources

Few would suggest that we save water at the expense of agriculture or any other sector of the economy. The link between water consumption and prosperity is too compelling.

"Development always takes place where water is," notes former City-County Council President Beurt SerVaas of Indianapolis, who championed the city's 2002 purchase of the local water company for

$540 million. The privately held NiSource had placed the water utility for sale, and SerVaas, among other city leaders, didn't want to take a chance such a valuable commodity could fall into the wrong hands.

More recently, SerVaas proposed building a pipeline to transport water to the state capital from the Monroe Reservoir an hour south of Indianapolis. The reservoir, operated by the Army Corps of Engineers, currently provides the city of Bloomington with 14 million to 24 million gallons of water per day. SerVaas envisions pumping another 60 million to Indianapolis and surrounding counties.

"We are progressing here but without water we can easily retrogress," said SerVaas, who worries about projections that Indianapolis surface water use will exceed supply around the year 2017.

"We just don't have enough water here, period," SerVaas says. "You can go down to Dallas and you can buy power and you can ship it up here on the grid. And you can go down to Dallas and you can buy natural gas and ship it up here on a pipeline. But you can't go down to Dallas and buy water and ship it up here on anything. You have to get it locally."

SerVaas's proposal drew criticism from the mayor of Bloomington, worried about the impact on his own city's water needs. People will fight over water, as Mikhail Gorbachev once warned. The Indianapolis Department of Waterworks is preparing a feasibility study of the idea.

Innovation and Conservation

The idea behind Monroe Reservoir—along with 80,000 other dams and reservoirs in the United States—was to ensure water supply while controlling floods, the great technological challenge of 20th century water planning. While reservoirs continue to provide water for drinking, energy production and commercial use, planners of the 21st century have turned to emerging technologies to increase efficiency and productivity of water generation. The days of reservoir construction are over.

Creativity is the name of the game. Automatic leak-monitoring systems combined with advanced meter reading systems are on the market now for residential and commercial use. Wastewater is being reclaimed for nonpotable uses at much lower cost than treatment of water for drinking. Salt Lake City and St. Petersburg, Florida, have dual distribution systems that reuse brackish water for tasks such as flushing toilets.

Private industry has invested aggressively in projects to decrease water reliance in the industrial process. The Pacific Coca-Cola Bottling Company reduced a can line's need for rinse water by using air instead of water to clean the insides of cans before filling. The Smorgon Steel Group plant in Kansas City relies mostly on recycled water from its own processes, and purifies the water in settling ponds between uses.

Forty states have a water conservation program, the U.S. Environmental Protection Agency says. Nationwide, surveys indicate more than 80 percent of water utility customers support some form of conservation measure.

Consumer-based programs cover the gamut, from voluntary promotions—"Don't keep the water running while you brush your teeth"—to equipment upgrade offers to mandatory conservation ordinances. One such ordinance in Waukesha, Wisconsin, saw immediate results: a 10 percent drop in water usage during the first seven months of 2006 over the previous year.

"The fact is, in the next 20 years, conservation is being looked at as a source of supply in southern California," says Bob Muir, spokesman for the Metropolitan Water District (MWD) of Southern California. "We can no longer turn to another river, a stream or a lake. We're going to have to meet that demand by what we do in our own backyards."

That philosophy prompted the creation of an MWD side project called Bewaterwise, which works with residential consumers to cut water use and with homebuilders to incorporate water-saving features into new construction. The efforts have been so successful that southern California hasn't had to impose lawn-watering restrictions like many cities of the East Coast and Midwest have done in recent years.

From 2003 to 2005, southern Californians reduced the amount of time spent watering yards from 64 minutes a week to 34 minutes, notes Lynn Lipinski of Bewaterwise. One reason is that homeowners have been encouraged to use less grass and more native plants and shrubs that consume less water in their landscapes. Another reason is that residents have been taught exactly how much water is needed to maintain grass and plant health: a lot less than most households were applying.

Among other water saving tips encouraged by Lipinski's organization:

• Replace your old washing machine with a new, high-efficiency model. Saves 20 to 30 gallons per load.

• Run only full loads in the washing machine and dishwasher. Saves 300 to 800 gallons a month.

• Use a broom instead of a hose to clean driveways and sidewalks. Saves 150 gallons or more each time.

• Shorten your showers. Even a one- or two-minute reduction can save up to 700 gallons per month.

• Don't water the sidewalks, driveway or gutter. Adjust your sprinklers so that water lands on your lawn or garden where it belongs—and only there. Saves 500 gallons a month.

Recovering rainwater and gray water is another strategy becoming commonplace in parts of the South and Southwest. Gray water refers to the normally discarded water discharged from showers, sinks, tubs and washing machines (not toilets, whose discharge is referred to as black water). In California, gray water may be used for subsurface irrigation; it cannot be applied on food crops.

In Menard, Texas, homeowner Billy Kniffen and his wife rely entirely on harvested rainwater to supply their consumption needs. Kniffen's system of gutters—connecting pipes, filters and tanks— allows him to capture 2,900 gallons of water per inch of rain. The Kniffens have opted for a water conservation lifestyle as well, using low flow showerheads, on-demand hot-water-recirculating systems, and taking quickie military-style showers (i.e. soap down when the water's not running).

The system is so impressive that others in his community, including a school, are starting to harvest rainwater. In three years since Kniffen built his cabin-style home, he's never run out. "No shortage and we're in a drought right now," he reports. At peak usage times, the Kniffens consume 36 gallons of water a day, compared to average U.S. consumption of 84 gallons.

Looking to the Future

Mikhail Gorbachev, the former Soviet leader who now works for global resource preservation, says that water is like religion and ideology because of its power over people. "Since the very birth of human civilization, people have moved to settle close to it. People move when there is too little of it. People move when there is too much of it. People journey down it. People write, sing and dance about it. People fight over it. And all people, everywhere and every day, need it."

Because we need water to survive, American ingenuity will be pushed to develop even more creative ways of using water more efficiently, of recycling it more cheaply, of tapping it at deeper levels in aquifers once considered unreachable.

And if worst comes to worst, there is always the sea. Although the cost and efficiency of purifying saltwater is exorbitant now, it may not be so forever. The Massachusetts Institute of Technology recently reported on a water desalination system using carbon nanotube-based membranes that could significantly reduce the cost of purifying saltwater. Such advances could provide a long-term solution to water shortages in the United States and worldwide. But that's the future, and droughts are occurring now. It benefits all of us to turn off the faucet while brushing, to sprinkle our lawns less often, and to catch a little rain. Water is just too precious to waste.

Water Woes

By Marianne Lavelle
U.S. News & World Report, May 27, 2007

The nation's hidden water problem rushed into the basement apartments of 51st Street in West New York, N.J., last February 9, shortly after 4 a.m. That's when a 2-foot-wide pipe ruptured under Bergenline Avenue, New Jersey's longest commercial thoroughfare. Water burst through the asphalt with the force of a geyser, then cascaded downhill. "It came down the street like rapids," says Anthony Avillo, the deputy fire chief on the scene. Families were awakened by water cresting over the sides of their beds or by neighbors screaming.

In the 18-degree cold, North Hudson Regional Fire and Rescue crew members lowered themselves chest-deep into the drink and deployed life rafts to help people escape. "We had one woman holding a baby and offering it up from the water like Moses," Avillo recalls.

Miraculously, no one was seriously hurt in the deluge, but 31 people, including 14 children, were forced from their homes—some for almost a month. And as is often the case with a major water-main break, the impact rippled far beyond the uprooted families. Water service abruptly stopped for 200,000 people in five of the nation's most densely populated towns, directly across the Hudson River from Manhattan.

Even when taps began to flow again, residents were warned to boil water because a main break can be a gateway for harmful bacteria. "It was really a nightmare, and it was dangerous," says Christopher Irizarry, chief executive of the North Hudson Community Action Corp., which assisted the stranded residents. The worst fear was that a fire would break out, because hydrants were dry. Water tankers were called in from miles away to stand by.

For the North Jersey communities, the crisis was over in 60 hours, when the break was repaired and the water deemed safe. But those who've examined the state of water around the nation and the globe say the crisis is only beginning. Mismanagement and climate change are shrinking clean water supplies worldwide.

The brunt of the problem is borne by the poor on every continent; those who have the resources, like denizens of that flashy desert capital of conspicuous wealth, Las Vegas, grab all the water they can find. In less arid regions, Americans take tap water for granted, but that's only because of hundreds of thousands of miles of underground pipe laid generations ago, much of it now decaying.

Studies by government and utilities agree that cities and towns will need to spend $250 billion to $500 billion more over the next 20 years to maintain the drinking water and waste-water systems we equate with modern living. The only debate is how to pay for it, in a country accustomed to paying about $2.50 per 1,000 gallons—the lowest price for tap water in the developed world.

"There's a very widespread perception that water is a free good," says Steve Maxwell, a Boulder, Colo., consultant specializing in water and environmental issues. "It falls out of the sky—why should we pay for it? What's lost is the fact that we have to treat it, move it around, store it, and distribute it to homes in a process that costs a heck of a lot of money."

Omen. Maxwell is among those who believe it will take a catastrophic infrastructure failure causing widespread illness or death to spur action. Fortunately, that did not occur in West New York, but the break was a warning sign. The pipes most vulnerable to frigid temperatures are those that are deteriorating because they are nearing the end of their useful lives. Rich Henning, spokesman for system operator United Water New Jersey, says some pipes in that area are 70 to 80 years old, and although many are in good working order, "this happened to be one where it was its time to go."

The American Water Works Association, the trade group for the nation's drinking water utilities, estimates that there are 250,000 to 300,000 main breaks per year, and the numbers are increasing as the infrastructure ages. United Water—one of a handful of private companies running U.S. water systems—is a good example; although it is now a subsidiary of the French utility company Suez, serving 7 million people in 20 states, it still operates some of the same network that it laid when the company was founded in North Jersey in 1869.

A major problem, at least in the view of the Bush administration, is that utilities haven't been charging their citizens the true cost of providing water but instead subsidize the service with other revenues. The Environmental Protection Agency promotes the idea of what it calls "full-cost pricing" as one of its "four pillars" of sustainable water systems, along with conservation, better management, and cooperation among communities in the same watershed.

Says Benjamin Grumbles, EPA assistant administrator for water, "The more people understand the true value of water as the lifeblood of the community, and the value of infrastructure as the organs and bones that help support the system, the more they'll realize prices need to reflect that."

Pillow Talk. Ken Kirk, executive director of the National Association of Clean Water Agencies, representing sewer systems, wryly refers to the administration's idea as "the four pillows," because "they're kind of soft," he says. Although all make sense, he says, they wouldn't close the funding gap. In fact, in the topsy-turvy world of water, efficiency worsens the fiscal picture. The more water consumers save, the less revenue for utilities, which charge by the gallon.

> Atlanta [Georgia], over the past five years, tackled a water system in crisis with a $3.9 billion improvement program.

Kirk's group is one of several pushing the concept of a federal trust fund for water, much like the one that finances the highway system through the federal gas tax. Advocates have put forth funding ideas like a surcharge on bottled water, fees on toilet paper and other "flushables," or some other broad revenue source, but it all sounds like a tax to those on Capitol Hill and is a hard sell. Federal funding for drinking water and waste-water treatment, in fact, has declined 24 percent since 2001.

Since federal largess cannot be counted on, the problem is squarely in the lap of local water systems. Some have had success. Atlanta, over the past five years, tackled a water system in crisis with a $3.9 billion improvement program. The city doubled water rates, and voters approved a 1 percent sales tax to help turn around a system in which raw sewage spilled into waterways, and dangerous street sinkholes and advisories to boil water were a regular occurrence due to water-main breaks.

Aqua America, the largest U.S.-based publicly traded water company, has obtained approval in some states for regular limited rate increases to address infrastructure. Chief Executive Nicholas DeBenedictis says his company is at full-cost pricing, and consumers have seen rate hikes of no more than 2.5 percent every two years. That has enabled Aqua America to ramp up its pipe-replacement program, which was so behind in the early 1990s that it would have taken 900 years to deal with aging infrastructure.

Now, the company, which serves 2.8 million customers in 13 states, boasts it is able to replace 1 percent of its pipes annually. It's still a daunting job, however, since full replacement would take 100 years. And Aqua America continues to suffer its share of main breaks; in fact, the cost of the ruptures held the company's profit increase below 2 percent in the last quarter even as revenues soared 16 percent.

Risk Averse. The economics have discouraged some would-be water saviors. German utility giant RWE wants to spin off its American water business just four years after entering the market here with great fanfare. Minutes of RWE corporate board meetings show that its executives concluded they had underestimated the business risk posed by decaying infrastructure and neglect.

Still, plenty of potential investors look at the same landscape—especially the prospect of monopoly ownership—and see an opportunity. Private-equity funds have moved onto the scene, scooping up two relatively small U.S. water systems last year at high premiums. But Jack Hoffbuhr, executive director of the American Water Works Association, isn't ready to identify it as a trend. "Water utilities are three to four times more capital intensive than any other utility," he says. "Once private-equity firms look at when they'd begin to see a return on their funds, they might not be quite as interested in investment."

Meanwhile, back in New Jersey, United Water still copes with water-main breaks even though it says it has spent $240 million in the past decade on capital improvements, including new pipelines. Now, it is trying to recoup some of those costs.

Just two weeks after the West New York main break, but unrelated to the incident, United Water announced it would ask its customers to pay 28 percent more for water, its first rate hike in a dozen years. Although that would add only $95 a year to the average bill, it will be a blow to the many poor residents in its service area.

In other words, it may make sense to pay more for water, but it still feels unfair to those who must buy this essential service, whatever the price. Water consultant Maxwell says the challenge is being faced worldwide. "How do we treat water more and more as an economic commodity—just like copper or oil or aluminum—and make rational economic decisions about it on the one hand," he says, "and on the other hand, accept that it's a fundamental human right and everybody has to have it to exist?"

Ask Natural Life

Bottled Water or Tap Water?

BY WENDY PRIESNITZ
NATURAL LIFE MAGAZINE, MARCH/APRIL 2007

Q: We've all heard about the necessity of drinking eight glasses of water a day. Which is better—from both health and environment perspectives—tap water or bottled water?

A: In a word: tap water.

First the health perspective. A study conducted in 2001 for The World Wide Fund for Nature (WWF) confirmed the widespread belief that consumers associate bottled water with social status and healthy living. However, that association is largely a result of good marketing by the bottled water companies (which include Nestlé, Coca-Cola, Pepsi and others). The global consumption of bottled water reached 154 billion liters (41 billion gallons) in 2004, up 57 percent from the 98 billion liters consumed five years earlier. But there is little evidence that—except in cases of disasters that create tainted water emergencies—bottled water is safer or healthier than tap water.

In fact, consumer groups have long warned about a range of micro-organisms and chemicals that have been found in bottled water. In a four-year scientific study, the Natural Resources Defense Council (NRDC) tested more than 1,000 bottles of 103 brands of bottled water. In a 1999 report "Bottled Water, Pure Drink or Pure Hype?" the group concluded, "Although most bottled water tested was of good quality, some brands' quality was spotty." The report also notes that "while much tap water is indeed risky, having compared available data, we conclude that there is no assurance that bottled water is any safer than tap water." In fact, a third of the tested brands were found to contain contaminants such as arsenic and carcinogenic compounds in at least some samples at levels exceeding state or industry standards.

Scientists at the University of Geneva arrived at the same conclusion when they tested bottled and top water for the 2001 WWF study. They found that, in 50 percent of the cases they studied, the only difference between tap and bottled water was that the latter contained added minerals and salts, "which do not actually mean the water is healthier." In 1997, the United Nations Food and Agriculture Organization concluded that bottled water does not have greater nutritional value than tap water.

The regulations in North America governing bottled water tend to be as spotty as the water's quality, although activists are pushing politicians to tighten up the rules, which they say are not as stringent as those for municipal water supplies.

In Canada, Health Canada determines the classifications of bottled water under its Food and Drugs Act. If bottled water is labeled as spring or mineral water, it must come from an underground source rather than a public water supply. And mineral water is the same as spring water except that it contains a larger amount of dissolved mineral salts. Under the regulations, chemicals cannot be used to change the composition of mineral and spring waters. However, carbon dioxide and ozone may be added to protect the freshness. In addition, the source of the spring or mineral water must be identified. If bottled water is not labeled as spring or mineral water, it can come from any source, including a well or a municipal water supply, and be treated to make it fit for human consumption.

Bottled water that is not from a spring may be altered before it is presented for sale in Canada. It can be treated in different ways including carbonation, ozonation, ultraviolet radiation or filtration to remove harmful bacteria. It may be distilled or deionized to remove the minerals. The regulations require that these treatments be identified as such on the label.

The Canadian Food Inspection Agency periodically samples and analyzes imported and domestic bottled waters, focusing primarily on testing for bacterial contamination.

In the U.S., the Food and Drug Administration (FDA) is responsible for bottled water safety, but its rules completely exempt waters that are packaged and sold within the same state, which account for between 60 and 70 percent of all bottled water sold in the country. The FDA also exempts carbonated water and seltzer, and fewer than half of the states require carbonated waters to meet their own bottled water standards. FDA rules allow bottlers to call their product "spring water" even though it may be brought to the surface using a pumped well, and it may be treated with chemicals. But the actual source of water is not always made clear—some bottled water marketing is misleading, implying the water comes from pristine sources when it does not.

According to the NRDC study, "Even when bottled waters are covered by FDA's specific bottled water standards, those rules are weaker in many ways than EPA rules that apply to big city tap water." For instance, city tap water can have no confirmed E.coli or fecal coliform bacteria, but FDA bottled water rules include no such prohibition.

City tap water must also meet standards for certain important toxic or cancer-causing chemicals, such as phthalate, a chemical that can leach from plastic, including some water bottles.

In spite of all the testing, municipal water supplies are far from pristine, as the NRDC has found. It analyzed data compiled by the U.S. Environmental Protection Agency on arsenic in drinking water in 25 states. And its most conservative estimates indicated that more than 34 million Americans drink tap water supplied by systems containing average levels of arsenic that pose unacceptable cancer risks. Arsenic is a byproduct of industrial processes like copper smelting, mining and coal burning, and is used in agriculture. Some arsenic contamination results from leaching from old waste dumps, mines or tailings, or from past use of arsenic-containing pesticides.

But switching to bottled water is no way to avoid arsenic—NRDC's study found arsenic there too. Other toxic chemicals that appear in water are added by municipal water treatment facilities. They include fluoride and chlorine, both of which are controversial. Fluoride is linked with arthritis, hip fractures, cancer and other diseases, and even premature skin wrinkling. It has been banned or discontinued in many European countries. Chlorinated water has been linked to increased risks of cancer, birth defects, miscarriages and stillbirths. It mixes readily with organic matter in water to form hundreds of chemical byproducts, many of which have never been studied.

Some municipalities are using newer technologies, such as membrane filtration, ultraviolet irradiation and ozone disinfection in an attempt to improve their water supplies.

Since much of the bottled water for sale comes from municipal taps (40 percent in the U.S., according to the NRDC), consumers can presume that it at least meets those standards . . . which begs the question: Why buy water that you could get from your kitchen faucet?

That also brings us to the environmental perspective.

The Earth Policy Institute has estimated that bottled water is 10,000 times more environmentally damaging than tap water. First of all, there is the pollution created by the manufacture of the plastic bottles. According to the WWF's 2001 report "Bottled Water: Understanding a Social Phenomenon," roughly 1.5 million tons of plastic are expended in the bottling of 89 billion liters of water each year. Most of the bottles are made of the oil-derived polyethylene terephthalate, which is known as PET. While PET is less toxic than many plastics, the Berkeley Ecology Center says that manufacturing PET generates more than 100 times the toxic emissions—in the form of nickel, ethylbenzene, ethylene oxide and benzene—compared to making the same amount of glass.

In addition, the energy required to manufacture and transport the bottles to market severely depletes our supplies of fossil fuels and adds to greenhouse gas emissions. Tap water, on the other hand, is delivered by a mostly pre-existing infrastructure of underground pipes and plumbing.

The post-market waste produced by discarded water bottles exacerbates the environmental problem. Even though they are accepted by most recycling programs, many plastic water bottles end up in landfills. A 2003 study by the California Department of Conservation found that more than one billion of them are tossed into the trash in California each year. A biodegradable corn-based water bottle is on sale in the UK and some of the large bottlers claim to be testing their own versions. But they are no substitute for not buying the packaging in the first place.

As if this weren't enough, there's another environmental issue. A variety of groups

> Be sure your water source is a deep, drilled well, rather than a shallow, dug one.

are fighting the expanding bottled water industry on the basis of threats to local wells, streams and wetlands. Bottling companies can pump up to 500 gallons per minute, or even more, out of each well, and many wells run 24 hours a day, 365 days a year. There is a growing concern that taking too much water can reduce or deplete groundwater reserves and reduce the flow of streams and lakes, causing stress on ecosystems. Although groundwater systems can be recharged, it's not clear how much water can be taken without causing water tables to drop and streams and rivers to dry up.

"Our attitudes towards tap water are being shaped by the pollution choking the rivers and streams which should be veins of life," says Richard Holland, Director of WWF's Living Waters Campaign. "We must clean up and properly protect these waters at source, and not just at the treatment works, so that we can all rest easy in drinking from the tap."

Meanwhile, how do we get those eight glasses of water a day, some of it while we're on the go?

Bottling your own seems to be the answer. Point-of-use water treatment, with a quality in-home water filtration system, seems to be the most economical and environmentally sensible way to get the healthiest water.

The best solution is a reverse osmosis water filter, which will eliminate or substantially reduce a wide variety of contaminants, including much of the fluoride and chlorine. It is also the system used by many of the companies that bottle tap water.

If you have a water softener, be sure to divert the softened water away from the kitchen tap connected to the reverse osmosis system.

Avoid drinking distilled water as it has the wrong ionization, pH, polarization and oxidation. It will also drain your body of minerals.

If you live in the country and get your tap water from a well, you have a whole set of other concerns, including farm chemicals and other dangerous materials such as contaminated sludge that could be applied to fields, from antibiotics given to animals that can contaminate farm runoff, from your own septic system, and so on. Be sure your water source is a deep, drilled well, rather than a shallow, dug one. Have the water tested regularly and filter it before use.

However you improve the quality of water from your tap, you'll be improving the quality of the environment by avoiding all those plastic bottles.

II. WATER WARS

Editor's Introduction

"**I**f the wars of this century were fought over oil, the wars of the next century will be fought over water," Ismail Seraheldin, a former World Bank vice president, stated in 1995. Since that time, Seraheldin's remark has proven prescient. Indeed, as the population has increased and the industrial revolution taken hold over the last few centuries, humanity's water needs have expanded dramatically and taxed what is ultimately a finite resource. As the competition for water has increased, so too has conflict, particularly in recent years. Indeed, many believe that the troubles in the Darfur region of Sudan, where militias backed by the national government have been engaged in a campaign of ethnic cleansing, and even the Arab-Israeli conflict are in part the result of competition for water. Consequently, the term "water wars" has emerged as a global catchphrase. However, as entries in this chapter reveal, these conflicts are not always wars in the traditional sense. They do not always involve guns and tanks, and often the fault lines do not run along ethnic or national lines.

The Middle East and North Africa are among the driest regions in the world. Complicating this dilemma, many of these nations share the same water systems—such as the Tigris-Euphrates, Nile, and Jordan Rivers—creating the potential for conflict. Meanwhile, in South America, water privatization in Bolivia resulted in violent protests. Water sharing disputes are also rampant in Asia, as rising temperatures melt the snow of the Himalayas—the source for most of Asia's rivers.

In "The Rise of Big Water," the first article in this chapter, Charles Mann describes how some cities in the developing world have privatized their municipal water systems. Nearly 10 percent of the Earth's population is served by private water firms, according to *Pinsent Masons Water Yearbook*, an industry textbook. The rational for privatization rests on the belief that the utilities, once exposed to market forces, would be forced to function more efficiently, presumably cutting waste and lowering costs to the consumer. However, privatization has engendered widespread opposition as many don't believe such an essential service should be run for profit. Jon Luoma further examines the privatization of water in "Water for Profit." Luoma states that "the argument behind privatization is that only corporate efficiency can rescue the nation's aging waterworks." But, citing lapses in service, corruption and high costs, he asserts that the private sector's "record is less than encouraging."

Water conflict is not limited to developing nations, however. The United States has had its share, both past and present. Perhaps the most famous such dispute, which inspired the 1974 film *Chinatown*, was between the city of Los Angeles and the outlying Owens Valley. In recent years the state governments of North and South Dakota have been feuding with that of Missouri over the flow of the Missouri River, Bill Lambrecht reports in "The New Water Wars." The conflict pits a burgeoning recreation industry against the river's aging barge industry.

In "Water War", the author reports on the condition of Georgia's Lake Lanier, a vital source of water for the state as well as Alabama and Florida. Unfortunately, a drought of historic proportions has made the lake a battleground, pitting the three states against one another.

In "Sharing the River Out of Eden," Sandra Postel examines the significance of the Jordan River, which provides water to Israel, Jordan, Lebanon, Syria and the Palestinian Territories. Sharing a river among five distinct political entities that are often at odds with one another has proven a difficult challenge and emerged as one of the central disputes in the Arab-Israeli conflict. Not surprisingly, no consensus has emerged on a viable distribution plan. Global warming and its associated droughts and higher evaporation rates may intensify current water shortages and further increase the potential for conflict. But, there is hope. As Postel states, "Cooperative efforts between scientists and citizen groups, advancements in water-management technology, and agreements reached during peace talks in the early 1990s have already laid a foundation upon which such water-sharing arrangements could be based."

The Rise of Big Water

By Charles C. Mann
Vanity Fair, May 2007

Qin Huairen went back to Changzhou, the city of his birth, in 1977. He was 42 years old and had spent his entire adulthood working as an iron-ore prospector in southern China. He had arrived there in 1957, just before Mao Zedong's delusional Great Leap Forward, when peasants were supposed to drive China to industrial supremacy by smelting steel in their villages. Gangs of them denuded entire mountainsides—Qin saw ancient forests vanish in a day—to fuel backyard mills that couldn't make steel but could and did poison the fields. Ten years later the Cultural Revolution, Mao's attempt to drive China into permanent revolutionary ecstasy, led to deprivation so intense that villagers stripped the remaining forests for fuel and ate most of the nation's birds. Qin went back to Changzhou with a clear vision of the environmental damage that China was doing to itself. Soon after his return, the country instituted its free-market economic reforms, setting off three decades of frenzied growth. Neither Qin nor anyone else could have anticipated that the ecological devastation of the Great Leap Forward was nothing compared with what China's real leap forward would bring.

Changzhou, where Qin grew up, is a city of 3.4 million people, about 100 miles up the Yangtze River, China's most important waterway, from Shanghai. The Grand Canal, built more than two millennia ago to link northern and southern China, loops around the city center, eventually crossing the Yangtze. From the Grand Canal extend dozens of smaller canals, a spiderweb network once jammed with men in fishing boats and women doing laundry. Along the banks there used to be rice paddies irrigated by canal water— Changzhou is located in one of China's most prominent rice belts.

Changzhou had been a traditional silk center. As the market reforms took hold, new textile factories sprang up along the canals and on the city's periphery. Dark, brutally shabby, operating around the clock, the factories today spin the fabrics used in America's shirts and sneakers and S.U.V.'s. In the process they flush vast quantities of waste—dyes, inks, bleaches, detergents—into Changzhou's canals. The canals channel the waste into the Yangtze, where it joins sewage from the hastily erected apartment complexes that house the factory workers. First the fish died, Qin remembers. Then the water turned dark. Walk across the ancient bridges today, he says, and the smell will "make you choke."

Originally published in *Vanity Fair*, May 2007. Reprinted with permission.

Qin became a teacher at a middle school and was determined to make himself a force for good. Slight and energetic, with a ready smile that fills a gaunt face, he spent the years between 1985 and 1995 helping his students draw water from the canals, perform simple tests on the samples, and send the water and the test results to the city government. Every year the results got worse.

Fearful of the water in the canals and the river, the people of Changzhou frantically began digging wells. Today, visitors to the city see advertisements spray-painted by the thousands on the walls of buildings: the Chinese characters for "well digging," followed by a cell-phone number. So many wells have been dug in Changzhou that its groundwater has been over-exploited, and the local ground level has sunk by two feet. The city has officially banned new wells and mandated the installation of pollution controls, but China's endemic corruption ensures that neither measure has much meaning. Meanwhile, farmers have stopped irrigating their paddies with canal water, because the rice is absorbing heavy metals. Cancer rates in the city are climbing, Qin says.

To the idealistic Qin, the way ahead was obvious. If Changzhou's people could only be educated about the environment, they would demand a massive cleanup—and they would get one. Qin created the grandly titled Changzhou Environmental Education Research Society, headquartered in an unheated room in his middle school. He delivered spirited eco-homilies to local citizens, and distributed copies of his laboriously printed reports documenting the degradation of the city's water supply. He came up with ideas for environmental projects that children could pursue, and circulated them to the city's classrooms. Qin is the sort of man who keeps a steady eye on the future—"Teach the children," he says, "and they will teach their families"—and somehow maintains his faith in the power of reasonableness and goodwill. "The government," he told me without a trace of irony, "will take care of us."

In September 2005, the Changzhou city government finally took a dramatic step—but it was not a step that Qin would ever have imagined. Rather than forcing local factories to clean up after themselves, Changzhou decided to outsource the job of managing its water supply to a French company named Veolia—one of a handful of corporate giants now scrambling to take over city water systems around the planet, especially in the often polluted and water-short developing world. These water companies might be thought of collectively as Big Water. Today about 10 percent of the Earth's population is served by private water companies, according to *Pinsent Masons Water Yearbook*, an industry bible. The figure is far higher in urban areas and the proportion is growing fast.

Big Water makes an argument straight out of Economics 101. The best way to deliver water to people's homes efficiently, the water barons argue, is to put the process in the hands of the market. If water is scarce, then raise the price—let the law of supply and demand take over! If people want water that is not only plentiful but actually clean, then raise the price again. The market will find the point of balance between what consumers want and what they can afford. And if the water company does not make good on its promises, it can be ejected in favor of another firm. The threat of competition will force utilities to be accountable.

Cash-strapped cities in nations from Argentina to Albania have begun to turn over their municipal water systems to Big Water, often under lease arrangements that can continue in force for decades. Some of the poorest places in the world have been suddenly exposed to the discipline of the market. All too often, the results do not resemble the cheerful predictions of Economics 101. In the messy real world of unstable governments, corrupt bureaucrats, and volatile currencies, Big Water has often been unable—and sometimes unwilling—to deliver what it has promised. Rather than supinely allowing the market to work its magic, fearful customers have reacted to abrupt price hikes by filling the streets. Public fury has led to the cancellation of water contracts on three continents—only to have new managers discover that the former public utilities cannot easily be reconstituted, because the state no longer has the necessary engineers and administrators.

> Cash-strapped cities in nations from Argentina to Albania have begun to turn over their municipal water systems to Big Water.

The battle over water is also being fought on U.S. soil. More than a century ago, the majority of U.S. water systems were private, according to Peter Gleick, the president of the Pacific Institute, an environmental think tank in Oakland. "Because the private systems were not serving the poor in the cities," he says, American municipalities "moved to a public water system"—they bought out most private companies and placed them under public ownership. Public water systems have supplied drinking water to 85 percent of Americans since the Second World War. But rising populations, aging infrastructure, and laws mandating increasingly pure water are pushing cities across the country to consider returning to the past. Cities that have gone private with drinking water or wastewater treatment include Atlanta, Indianapolis, Milwaukee, and Lexington, Kentucky. Some have met with fierce resistance—angry town meetings, newspaper op-eds, and, this being America, costly downpours of litigation.

At bottom, the fights are all about the same thing, says Oliver Hoedeman of Corporate Europe Observatory, an anti-big-business group in Amsterdam. "Nobody ever looked at their water bill and said, 'Oh, this is too costly—I guess I won't drink anything this month.'" Putting the control of water into private hands, Hoedeman says, "is asking for abuse."

The stakes—environmental and political—could hardly be higher. According to a report prepared by the International Water Management Institute (I.W.M.I.), a respected international research group, one person out of every three on the planet today lacks reliable access to freshwater, whether because the water is unsafe, unaffordable, or unavailable. Some 2.6 billion people, the World Health Organization estimates, have inadequate sanitation—they do not even have proper latrines that prevent wastes from spreading into the environment. "Every day more children die from dirty water than H.I.V./AIDS, malaria, war, and accidents all put together," says Maude Barlow, national chair of the Council of Canadians, a citizens' advocacy group, and the co-author of *Blue Gold: The Battle Against Corporate Theft of the World's Water*. The water crisis, she says, is not something that besets only the megalopolises of the Third World. France instituted water rationing last summer; Thames Water applied for a drought order in London; Los Angeles is in its driest rainy season in more than a hundred years. According to a 2003 survey by the European Environment Agency, nitrates, toxins, heavy metals, or harmful micro-organisms contaminate groundwater in nearly every European country and former Soviet republic. That same year, the U.S. General Accounting Office reported that "water managers in 36 states anticipate water shortages locally, regionally, or statewide within the next 10 years." By 2025, according to the I.W.M.I., all of Africa and the Middle East, and almost all of South and Central America and Asia, will either be running out of water or unable to afford its cost.

Water, Barlow says, "is the most important environmental and human-rights issue of them all." Global warming is a present reality, but the worst consequences of pumping carbon dioxide into the atmosphere will be felt decades from now. Meanwhile, she says, "the world is running out of fresh water today."

China is in particular trouble. The country's State Environmental Protection Administration grades water on a scale from one to five, with three being minimally acceptable and five a direct health hazard. According to SEPA, for much of their length, five of China's seven main river basins are rated at four or five—poisoned by rampant industrialization. Almost half of China's municipalities—and most of its rural areas—have no systems in place for treating waste at all. Between a quarter and a third of China's population still do not have piped water. So desperately short of water is northern China, home to about 500 million people, that the country is undertaking the largest water project in human history—three enormous, 700-mile channels that will send about 12 trillion gallons of water a year from the South. In order to build just one of those channels, the government will force up to 400,000 people from their homes. Prime Minister Wen Jiabao has stated flatly that China's water shortages and water pollution threaten "the survival of the Chinese nation."

To deal with their water crisis the Chinese have—astonishingly for a country with a long history of suspicion toward foreigners—opened their doors to Big Water. Scores of Chinese cities have outsourced part or all of their water treatment and distribution to private companies; at least 40 ventures are with the French alone.

Veolia, probably the fastest-growing foreign operator in China, now manages water systems in 17 Chinese cities, including Changzhou and Shanghai.

The bitter global struggle over water remains almost unknown in the United States, where older toilets send more clean water down the drain in a single flush than many Africans use in an entire day. Americans can perhaps be forgiven for thinking that they live in a golden age of water. Competing brands of bottled water glisten in refrigerated displays, vying with one another in proclamations of health and purity. Meanwhile, much of the rest of the world worries about where to get the next drop, how much it will cost, and whether it will be lethal.

Bad for Humanity, Good for Business

Veolia Environnement, the $38 billion company that administers Changzhou's water supply, operates out of a neoclassical building in Paris, just a few blocks from the Arc de Triomphe. The company's water division, Veolia Water, serves 108 million people in 57 countries, has 70,000 employees, and is the world's biggest water-services provider. Connoisseurs of ironic juxtaposition would savor the contrast between Veolia's Paris headquarters and the manic, gritty clamor of Changzhou. The quiet lobby atrium is sleek and glassy, with flat-screen monitors depicting a multicultural parade of smiling, satisfied customers. Electronic gates give admittance to the offices only after the presentation of a special badge, its bulbous nubbin crammed with circuitry.

Antoine Frérot, the chief executive officer of Veolia Water, works in a large, upper-floor office. Frérot, 48, was trained as a civil engineer, and he retains an engineer's technocratic confidence. By way of background he gives me a short lecture on the power of human ingenuity. Thirty years ago, when he began his career, he explains, the Seine was a very dirty river. "We had to stop our water-treatment plants one day out of every two because they were overwhelmed by the pollution," he recalls. Eventually the company realized that the solution was to treat the tide of pollutants not as a cost but as a potential profit center. Instead of simply absorbing the expense of cleaning the water, he says, Veolia used the techniques it had learned to create "a new industry of liquid-hazardous-waste treatment" and marketed it to the polluting factories. Now, he says, the Seine is vastly cleaner. "This is what we do," he concludes. "Water is God's gift, we always say, but He forgot to lay the pipes."

Veolia's assonant, content-free corporate name conceals a long history. The company was founded in 1853 by Napoleon III, France's last emperor, and was financed by Baron de Rothschild and Charles Lafitte, with figures from France's nobility among its founding members. The Compagnie Générale des Eaux, as it was then called, became an essential part of the emperor's plan to modernize his country. Signing decades-long contracts to expand, modernize, and operate the water systems in France's biggest cities, C.G.E. became integral to the national infrastructure—a private enterprise holding a public commission, and entrusted with the water supply even of the glorious capital.

In the 1980s the company suddenly woke up to the possibilities of modern financial markets, and realized that it could use the huge revenues generated by its millions of water customers to buy other companies. It eventually changed its name to Vivendi and purchased, among other foreign companies, Seagram, the liquor-and-entertainment giant, for $34 billion, and the publisher Houghton Mifflin. Vivendi's C.E.O., Jean-Marie Messier, an investment banker, celebrated his string of acquisitions by moving his family to a $17.5 million duplex apartment on Park Avenue.

At its peak the former water company had more than 2,000 subsidiaries and made no sense at all. Capping it off, Messier invested heavily in dot-coms. Vivendi's fate may have been sealed in 1999 when James K. Glassman, the co-author of the somewhat premature *Dow 36,000*, gave Vivendi his official blessing as "a great company." The inevitable, debt-fueled implosion occurred three years later. To raise desperately needed cash, the company spun off Vivendi Environnement—the original water company. In 2003, to avoid unpleasant associations with the past, it changed its name to Veolia.

Under its new chairman and C.E.O., Henri Proglio, Veolia was as ambitious as the old Vivendi had ever been, but much less noisy. Scoffing at the glittery confluence of the media and Wall Street that had so entranced Messier, Proglio avoids puffery to the extent of refusing to allow *Who's Who* to print an entry about him. (Veolia declined to let him speak with *Vanity Fair*.) He has proudly claimed that he has never owned a tuxedo. Corporations, he says, must act as positive environmental forces. Proglio is caustically dismissive of "the Messier era" of investment in the dot-com bubble. "Water, like oil, is getting scarcer," he told the French newsweekly *Le Point* in an interview in 2005. "We're living on Earth in 2005 with the same amount of water that was available in 1900, while in the meantime the global population quadrupled." What's bad for humanity can be good for business; Veolia's revenues increased 12 percent in 2006.

Veolia needed to grow quickly, because it was saddled with debt—$19.4 billion at the beginning of this year—much of it a legacy from Vivendi. Happily for the company, the European Union wanted to promote European businesses overseas, especially businesses that were already leaders in their fields. The world's top three water companies are European. In addition to Veolia, the others are:

- Suez. A descendant of the enterprise that built the Suez Canal in the 1860s, Suez became an energy holding company that is now 90th on *Forbes*'s list of the world's 2,000 largest public firms.

After expanding its water operations at a dizzying rate, it acquired Lyonnaise des Eaux, one of France's biggest utilities, in 1997; it now operates in 31 countries and had 2006 revenues of $58.6 billion. Last year Enel, the Italian energy giant, publicly mulled a takeover. In an eyebrow-raising move, the French government scuppered the deal by approving a merger between Suez and state-controlled Gaz de France. The final decision on the merger will not occur before July.

- Thames Water. Called "Britain's most hated utility" last August by the left-leaning *Independent* newspaper, Thames provides water for most of London. It was created in its present form in 1989 as the Thatcher government privatized many of Britain's public functions. After Thames expanded internationally, in the 1990s, RWE, a German energy combine, acquired it in 2001. Last October RWE sold Thames for $14.9 billion to a consortium headed by Macquarie, Australia's biggest investment bank.

Compared to these European giants, American water ventures are small—even those from the Bechtel Group, which was awarded the contract to rebuild Iraq's bombed-out urban water and sewage systems. (The company says it completed most of the projects, but many were soon sabotaged.) Indeed, the No. 1 U.S. firm, American Water, doesn't quite exist—it is an RWE subsidiary that is in the process of being spun off. Understanding its advantage, the E.U. has leaned hard on other countries in trade talks to let European companies take over the management of their water supplies, and the intensive lobbying has worked.

Because urban populations are growing rapidly, city water systems everywhere are under pressure. Most of the world's hardest-pressed cities simply can't pay for the investment themselves, and thus have to borrow the money. Among the main potential sources are global bodies such as the World Bank, the International Monetary Fund, and the Asian Development Bank. These institutions are staffed by economists who deeply respect the power of free markets. They are predisposed to look favorably on governments that agree to outsource as many of their activities to the private sector as possible.

The intellectual argument in favor of the free market is straightforward. I heard a version of it from John Briscoe, who was for 10 years the senior adviser on water at the World Bank (he now is its director in Brazil). Briscoe keeps a doggerel poem by the late economist Kenneth Boulding on his wall that reads, in part:

> Water is politics, water's religion,
> Water is just about anyone's pigeon
> Water is tragical, water is comical,
> Water is far from the pure economical.

Many of the world's water problems arise, he contends, because the sacred aura around water induces government to treat it "as common property—it's free to use, no matter what you do with it and how much you use." In consequence, huge quantities are wasted. Farmers over-irrigate their fields. Landlords don't fix leaky pipes. Factory owners feel free to pollute. Governments don't extend and improve water networks, because they can't pay for it. All over the world, Briscoe says, "you have these hugely under-funded, very inefficient services producing very bad service. There's a hydraulic law of subsidies: they go to where the power is. They don't have enough to operate the system properly, so the existing system rations water, and of course it's the elite that gets to the front of the queue."

That was the situation in the United States 40 years ago, Briscoe says. "What happened is that we raised the effective price of water." Regulations forced farmers, landlords, factory owners, and ordinary Americans to pay for more-efficient water equipment—drip-irrigation systems, low-capacity toilets, water-treatment facilities, and so on. Per-capita water use in the United States fell by more than a quarter. But in the developing world, Briscoe believes, the situation is too dire for public utilities to fix themselves. In Africa, for example, "there is not one case of a utility that was horrible that has reformed itself and become well functioning. It has never happened."

The World Bank, he says, made five loans in a row to improve Manila's public water system. At the beginning, "something like 60 percent of the water was not accounted for. Half of this was leaks and half of this was stolen and diverted and not paid for." After five loans, the figure was . . . 70 percent. "Then you come to loan No. 6 and you say, what are we going to do?" The obvious answer, he says, is a private company with a clear contract that forces accountability. "If we didn't do that, we should be executed for not doing it."

Briscoe adds: "My grandmother would understand it. It's arithmetic—it's the most basic human incentive."

As one might expect, this argument seems equally clear at Veolia, which has its own success stories to tout. "When we took over Bucharest six years ago, the average [per capita water] consumption was 400 liters a day," Frérot says. "Today it is around 200 liters." Some of the conservation came from charging more, he says. "But much of it came from simply fixing leaks" in the distribution system. Incredibly, it is not uncommon for cities to lose half of their water to leaks. (Until an aggressive repair program in the 1990s, leaks cost Mexico City as much as 40 percent of its water supply; the city drained its aquifer so fast in the last century that the ground level sank 30 feet.) Combined with pressure from the European Union and the international banks, arguments like Briscoe's have led countries around the world to embrace Big Water. By 2000, according to United Nations statistics, governments in 93 nations had begun to privatize their drinking-water and wastewater services.

Buenos Aires was one of the first big cities to go private. Unable to keep up with the city's rampant growth, the Argentinean government in 1993 turned over its municipal water utility to a consortium formed by Suez, along with Vivendi, Aguas de Barcelona, and several local firms. (The choice of the politically powerful Suez was apparently aided by pressure from the Élysée Palace.) An Enron subsidiary took over the water system in the adjacent province of Buenos Aires. With the new private company operating the water supply for perhaps 10 million people, the World Bank issued excited press releases celebrating the rapid expansion into outlying neighborhoods. Hopeful governments signed similar deals in Australia, Indonesia, the Philippines, and South Africa.

> Reeling from the protests, the water multi-nationals lowered their profile.

But the Buenos Aires experience turned out to be nothing to celebrate. The consortium hired friends of the Argentinean president at high salaries even as it demanded rate increases for water supplied to millions of poor and working-class people. Some recently connected neighborhoods also discovered that the company had not installed proper drainage systems. The new water, having no place to go, flooded basements and streets. Demonstrators took to the plazas, chanting slogans and waving banners. When Argentina went into an economic tailspin at the end of 1998, many people could no longer pay their bills. Suez and Aguas de Barcelona pulled out of the consortium in 2005.

To its dismay, the Argentinian government, which took over the system, then discovered that the public water utility could not readily be brought back to life—the federal government took a year to approve the enabling legislation, and the city had to re-create the system almost from scratch. "This is one of the hidden costs of privatization," says André Abreu, a water activist at France Libertés, a nonprofit organization run by Danielle Mitterrand, the widow of the French president. "It's very hard to reverse. If a poor city makes a mistake, it is worse off than when it started."

Similar protest campaigns occurred in Uruguay, Ghana, India, Indonesia, Malaysia, the Philippines, and South Africa. In Cochabamba, Bolivia's third-largest city, the new private water utility, controlled by a subsidiary of Bechtel, increased water bills "up to 200 percent and sometimes higher," according to Jim Schultz, executive director of the Democracy Center in Cochabamba. (A Bechtel spokesperson has said that rates were raised by an average of 35 percent.) Demonstrators fought the police in club-swinging melees that left dozens wounded. Activists barricaded most of the major highways, and the president declared a "state of siege." Meetings of more than four people were banned. Further violence induced Bechtel executives to flee the city, and the government rescinded the contract. Later, Bolivia's president resigned.

Reeling from the protests, the water multi-nationals lowered their profile. Big Water largely withdrew from Latin America; after piously announcing that it would not go where it was not welcome, RWE began selling off most of its water holdings. Meanwhile, smaller, regional companies grabbed market share. But Big Water was far from beaten. The European giants were in fact turning their eyes toward the biggest target of all: China.

"As Black as Soy Sauce"

It would be safe to say that Long Cun (Dragon Village) lies off the beaten path. A small cluster of ramshackle farmhouses, it is just down the Liu River from Liuzhou, population 1.3 million, the furiously modernizing commercial center of the southwestern province of Guangxi. To reach the village from Liuzhou, visitors must negotiate a one-lane dirt road that winds around Guangxi's famous karst hills—the rounded, fairy-tale peaks familiar from Chinese landscape painting. The drive takes almost an hour, though the distance is scarcely 10 miles. In Liuzhou, the streets are full of chattering people on cell phones. In Long Cun, the streets are full of wagons drawn by bulls. As the geographer David Harvey once observed, modernity isn't a time. It's a place.

Like most Chinese cities these days, Liuzhou is ringed by walled-off industrial zones jammed with factories (more than 1,000 in Liuzhou) making automobile engines, processed foods, LCD screens, steel for ships, and the paper and plastic goods that fill American kitchens and living rooms. One such industrial zone lies on the river between Long Cun and Liuzhou. The centerpiece, its smokestacks easily visible from the village, is the sprawling Liu River Paper Mill. The tributary into which it dumps its wastes is, as local residents bitterly observe, "as black as soy sauce."

Before the coming of the mill, Long Cun drew its water for drinking and cleaning directly from the Liu River. After the mill, the villagers had to boil their water, a recourse that kills bacteria but does not eliminate pollutants. Then a new hydroelectric dam was built downriver. It slowed the Liu's current, concentrating the toxins powerfully. Villagers sued the factory, but got nowhere. The authorities "came and looked at the mess, but they didn't fix it," says Huang Fengju, a Long Cun farmer and mother of two. The factory owners must have known the right people in the city government, Huang assumed. There's a way things get done in China, and that's just the way it is.

Last November the city of Liuzhou handed down its solution. Rather than forcing the mill to clean up, it forced the village of Long Cun to connect to a city-run well—part of a far-flung system whose central network is operated by Veolia. A one-inch plastic pipe with a gray spigot soon appeared in front of Huang's house. The other villagers got plastic pipes, too. Although the water still needs to be boiled, it is better than what Huang had before. But it costs twice as much. When Long Cun got its water from the river, the village council charged two renminbi—about 25 cents—a month per person, no matter how much anyone used. The Huang household paid a total of about two dollars a month. Now the rate is higher, and it also fluctuates according to how much water is consumed. Today, that same Huang household pays about four dollars a month. The price by middle-class Chinese standards is extremely low. But most Chinese are not middle-class, and the villagers of Long Cun are flat-out poor. A typical village household earns $20 to $30 a month.

To economists with their spreadsheets in faraway places, the new pricing system in Long Cun represents progress. A flat fee encourages waste—there's no penalty for carelessly letting the tap dribble all day. And indeed Huang, prodded by higher prices, behaves the way those models of Homo economics say she should. She carefully monitors how much water she uses. Multiply her behavior by 1.3 billion, this view suggests, and China may solve its water problems—Economics 101 to the rescue. Meanwhile, the foreign companies providing the water to those hundreds of millions of people stand to make an enormous amount of money.

Implicit in the free-market scenario, however, is the assumption that families can actually pay the higher prices—and are willing to accept them. This leads to a curious ambiguity, if not an outright clash of interests. On the one hand, Beijing has repeatedly proclaimed that it needs Western know-how, and that Western water companies must be allowed to operate freely. On the other hand, Beijing doesn't want its own Cochabamba riots. Qiu Baoxing, China's vice minister of construction, said last September that the government would limit customer water fees to at most 20 percent of the cost of supply. If Western firms such as Veolia can't charge more than 20 percent of their costs, how can they possibly turn a profit? "I wanted to find out how they can make money with low, underpriced water tariffs," says Seungho Lee, a University of Nottingham researcher who recounts the recent history of Shanghai's water supply in a new book, *Water and Development in China*. Lee says he repeatedly pressed this issue with Veolia managers in Paris and Shanghai. "In a French way, I never got a direct answer," he says. When I put the same question to Rémi Paul, a vice president of Veolia's China division, he too replied in a French way. He would say only, "We have, I believe, a very good understanding with the government."

The conflict between private profit and public need will be played out in dozens of Chinese cities. The larger dynamic, though, is uncompromising. As Liuzhou and other cities surround themselves with more and more factories, poisoning the environment in the process, the cities will have to connect the polluted regions around them to city water systems. In addition, they will have to build sewage-treatment plants. But most Chinese cities can't afford to do either of these things. To help with its sewage, Liuzhou two years ago borrowed $100 million from the World Bank. Then it signed a

30-year contract with Veolia. Naturally, the company will need to recoup its investment. Local residents learned that the city planned to raise the cost of water.

The city fathers have not gone out of their way to explain to the citizenry that water prices are going up in order to pay back a company headquartered a few blocks from the Arc de Triomphe. As an experiment, I asked my translator to post a short description of the Veolia contract on one of Liuzhou's Internet bulletin boards. The reaction was immediate—surprise and apprehension. "Our water supply controlled by foreigners? Are you kidding?" wrote one person. "Who's ready to start digging wells and assembling rain collectors?" asked another, imagining a movement to evade the foreign water-bill collectors. "What do we do if the foreigners poison our water?" wondered a third. "Oh my God . . . "

The historic center of Liuzhou occupies a promontory in a big oxbow of the Liu River. Toward the northern tip is a beaten-up public square near an area that city maps label Maojin Chang—Towel Factory. The name comes from a factory nearby that went out of business before the current wave of modernization. Most of the neighborhood's inhabitants still live in the shuttered factory's dormitories. Many are pensioners; some are farmers who were thrown off their land to make way for the factories outside town, and who now live as boarders. Because ever more factories crowd the banks of the Liu, the cost of water treatment is rising to match. In just a few hours of wandering around the kiosks, benches, and doorways of Towel Factory square I found half a dozen men and women who were paying a quarter or more of their income just for water.

Economics 101 does not readily apply to neighborhoods like this one. A few blocks away, in Baisha Cun, lives an elderly man named Wei Wenfang. Until 1975, he explains, water was free: you simply dipped a bucket into the Liu. You could literally see the bottom of the river back then, he says. He proclaims this fact a second time, more loudly, for emphasis. But now Wei pays almost $10 a month—more than a quarter of his pension—for water that is nowhere near as good. He is afraid of what will happen when the price rises further. When I ask if he could save money by conserving water, Wei barks with laughter. Each water meter in Baisha Cun, he says, covers 60 to 70 apartments, many of which are sublet to more than one family. The total bill is divided equally among the residents. "There's no way to save," he says. "Your efforts are just lost in the mass. That's the way it is all over the city."

Evidently a local character, Wei has drawn a small crowd as he theatrically offers his thoughts. Now he looks about pugnaciously. But there is no disagreement.

The Judgment of Wu

Urban planning is easier in a dictatorship than in a democracy. Since its founding, in the 13th century, Shanghai has occupied the west bank of the Huangpu River. The east bank had always sustained the farms and gardens that provided food for the big city. Seventeen years ago the Chinese government decided that this arrangement was unsatisfactory. It bulldozed the villages and in a hot-brained hurry effectively threw up a brand-new city, called Pudong ("East of the Pu"). Pudong now has the world's fifth-tallest tower (an even taller one is under construction nearby), and about three million inhabitants, most of them mid-

> China, in short, built a city the size of Chicago in less time than it took Boston to complete the Big Dig.

dle-class, housed in faux-Mediterranean villettes as deracinated as so many Orange County strip malls. China, in short, built a city the size of Chicago in less time than it took Boston to complete the Big Dig.

In 2010, Shanghai will host a world's fair. Like the 2008 Olympics, in Beijing, it is intended to be a showcase for the New China. Three-quarters of the fairgrounds are in Pudong. Seventy million visitors, it is expected, will attend, and everything they see must be orderly, modern, and clean. To make this happen, Shanghai is kicking out some of the factories that used to line—and pollute—the Huangpu River. It also sold a 50-year, 50 percent stake in Pudong's water utility to Veolia, for $243 million.

Water services entail four basic functions: purifying the water that goes into the system, delivering it to households and businesses, cleaning up the water that leaves those homes and businesses, and extending and repairing the network of pipes, pumps, and plants. Simple to describe, these tasks are hair-pullingly complex on the ground; the technical challenge of building and operating a water system that can supply the daily onslaught of morning flushes and showers while not overwhelming users at light times is the sort of thing that keeps engineers in heavy demand.

In Pudong, Veolia has done it all. Since 2002, when the contract was signed, Veolia has laid almost 900 miles of large-diameter pipe, hooked up 300,000 new structures to the growing water system, built sewage and water-treatment plants, and hired 7,000 local workers, training them so well that Veolia now has only four non-Chinese employees in Pudong. On the ninth floor of its new office tower Veolia created a customer-service call-in center—a novelty in China—staffed round the clock by young women in powder-blue Veolia uniforms. Down the hall is a war room dominated by a 12-foot-wide LCD monitor that displays the real-time status of every water connection in Pudong.

Smooth operation is a testament to the power of private enterprise. It takes formidable organization to deliver water to so much new construction—though even here, incredible to Americans, the water must still be boiled. (Habituated to bad water, the Chinese people don't expect to be able to drink it straight from the tap.) To let Veolia recoup its costs, Shanghai is gradually raising water prices—not enough to make Pudong's nouveau riche blink, but enough to ensure that they will not leave the taps on all day. "This model is a unique combination of private efficiency within overall public ownership," argues Rémi Paul, who "hopes and believes" it can be extended throughout China. He has a hard time understanding why there have been protests against private water companies. So does his boss, Antoine Frérot, who chalks up the worldwide resistance to "a small minority of global activists," mostly from the "hard left parties," who are using water as an excuse to "contest globalization, capitalism, and all private companies." Indeed, as both men point out, public water systems have often been disasters, especially in the Third World. "Private companies can better manufacture cars" than governments, Frérot says, and water "is exactly the same."

Such views try the patience of Au Loong Yu, a Hong Kong labor and environmental activist. Water, he says, is simply not an ordinary consumer good, like lamps or shirts or smoothies. People can't put off buying water until they have a little more money in the bank. In democratic countries the citizenry has some recourse if prices on vital goods and services rise too high—they can get the government to intervene, or vote it out of power. But China isn't that kind of place. "I don't have anything against private enterprise," Au says. "But in countries with no democratic input—either because the state is too weak or, as in China, too strong—these companies can become dictators themselves." Hong Kong owns and operates its own water supply, Au notes. Because the city enjoys a measure of democratic self-rule, there is some chance that citizens can change policies they don't like. "They have to listen to us," Au says of the local authorities. "I don't want someone in charge of my water who only has to listen to the shareholders."

The rise of Big Water is due in part to politicians from wealthy nations twisting wrists in poor nations on behalf of influential corporations. More important, though, is the catastrophic failure by governments around the planet to provide services so basic to modern life that some activists regard them as human rights: affordable, potable water and safe sanitation. To make an end run around intractably venal public sectors, institutions like the World Bank and the International Monetary Fund push forward the private sector: Big Water and its regional competitors. But business cannot provide openness and accountability if the governments to which it answers are closed and unaccountable. Indeed, in such circumstances private enterprise can simply become an unwitting instrument of oppression—as in China, where provincial authorities use it to paper over the environmental havoc of unrestrained industrialization.

In Barlow's view, the solution to bad government is not the market, but good government. Yet both the activists and their nemeses in the World Bank and the I.M.F., distracted by the decade-long ideological battle over Big Water, have barely begun to use their diverse sorts of leverage to push governments to safeguard their natural resources and operate utilities in ways that actually serve the public. The prospect of these bitter opponents working together in any way seems unlikely. But the crisis over water is so unprecedented in scale that anything may happen.

A few months ago in Changzhou's northern edge I came across two women trying to wash laundry in a filthy inlet of the Yangtze. One gave her name as Wu—no first name. She was desperate, she said. The government had turned over the family farm to a chemical factory, giving her husband a job in it. But her husband soon lost the job and was out of work. Meanwhile the factory had polluted the family's well water, forcing the Wus to shift to a newly installed water line from the city. Now no money was coming in, and they couldn't pay their water bill. Mrs. Wu knew that a foreign company was running the utility. She knew that prices were rising and that this was supposed to curb waste. "I've had all that explained to me," she said. "It must sound good if you're rich."

Water for Profit

By Jon R. Luoma
Mother Jones, November/December 2002

Even before the water turned brown, Gordon Certain had plenty to worry about. With his north Atlanta neighborhood in the middle of a growth boom, the president of the North Buckhead Civic Association had been busy fielding complaints about traffic, a sewer tunnel being built near a nature preserve, and developers razing tidy postwar ranch homes to make room for mansions. But nothing compared to the volume of calls and emails that flooded Certain's home office in May, when Georgia's environmental protection agency issued an alert to North Buckhead residents: Their tap water, the agency warned, wasn't safe to drink unless they boiled it first. Some neighbors, Certain recalls, had just fed formula to their baby when they heard the alert.

"I had parents calling me in tears," he says. "The things that have happened to the water here have sure scared the hell out of a lot of people." A month later, another "boil water" alert came; this time, when Certain turned on his own tap, the liquid that gushed out was the color of rust, with bits of debris floating in it.

Atlanta's water service had never been without its critics; there had always been complaints about slow repairs and erroneous water bills. But the problems intensified three years ago, says Certain, after one of the world's largest private water companies took over the municipal system and promised to turn it into an "international showcase" for public-private partnerships. Instead of ushering in a new era of trouble-free drinking water, Atlanta's experiment with privatization has brought a host of new problems. This year there have been five boil-water alerts, indicating unsafe contaminants might be present. Fire hydrants have been useless for months. Leaking water mains have gone unrepaired for weeks. Despite all of this, the city's contractor—United Water, a subsidiary of French-based multinational Suez—has lobbied the City Council to add millions more to its $21-million-a-year contract.

Atlanta's experience has become Exhibit A in a heated controversy over the push by a rapidly growing global water industry to take over public water systems. At the heart of the debate are two questions: Should water, a basic necessity for human survival, be controlled by for-profit interests? And can multinational companies actually deliver on what they promise—better service and safe, affordable water?

Already, the two largest players in the industry, French-based conglomerates Suez and Vivendi Universal, manage water for 230 million people, mostly in Europe and the developing world. Now they are seeking access to a vast and relatively untapped market: the United States, where 85 percent of people still get their water from public utilities. Private water providers have positioned themselves as the solution to the developing world's water problems, notes Hugh Jackson, a policy analyst at the advocacy group Public Citizen. "But it's a lot harder for them to make the case when here, in the world's center of capitalism, cities are delivering tremendous amounts of high-quality, clean, inexpensive water to people."

Yet over the past decade, hundreds of U.S. cities and counties, including Indianapolis and Milwaukee, have hired private companies to manage their waterworks. Currently New Orleans; Stockton, California; and Laredo, Texas, are in the process of going private, although opposition has sprung up in all three cities. Water companies have been conducting annual "fly ins" to Washington, D.C., to press their legislative agenda, lobbying for laws that would protect companies from lawsuits over contaminated water and block municipalities from taking back troubled privatized systems. Most recently, a bipartisan group in Congress has been pushing a federal waterworks funding bill, advocated by the National Association of Water Companies, which would require cities to "consider" privatization before they can tap federal funds for upgrading or expanding public utilities and would also subsidize such privatization deals.

> The argument behind privatization is that only corporate efficiency can rescue the nation's aging waterworks.

At the municipal level the lobbying pressure is equally intense, with water companies actively courting local officials (the U.S. Conference of Mayors' Website features a large ad from Vivendi subsidiary U.S. Filter) and spending hundreds of thousands of dollars supporting privatization in local referendums. "It's hard for local guys to turn these companies away," Massachusetts' former water commissioner Douglas MacDonald has said. "They're everywhere, with arms like an octopus."

The argument behind privatization is that only corporate efficiency can rescue the nation's aging waterworks. But if success is measured in terms of delivering an essential commodity to everyone who needs it, then the industry's record is less than encouraging. Around the world, cities with private water-management companies have been plagued by lapses in service, soaring costs, and corruption. In Manila—where the water system is controlled by Suez, San Francisco-based Bechtel, and the prominent Ayala family—water is only reliably available for two hours a day and rates have increased so dramatically that the poorest families must choose each month between either paying for water or two days' worth of food. In the Bolivian city of Cochabamba, rate increases that followed privatization sparked rioting in 2000 that left six people dead. And in Atlanta, city officials are considering canceling United Water's contract as early as this winter.

"Atlanta was going to be the industry's shining example of how great privatization is," says Public Citizen's Jackson. "And now it's turned into our shining example about how it maybe isn't so great an idea after all."

On a cloudy August day that brought a welcome bit of drizzle to drought-parched Atlanta, Mayor Shirley Franklin lugged a seven-pound bound volume off a shelf and heaved it onto a table in her office. The report, prepared by a committee she appointed shortly after taking office last January, contained the city's case against United Water. It detailed violations of federal drinking-water standards, including one instance in which levels of chlorine rose to six times the level the company agreed to in its contract. The report also listed a string of maintenance problems ranging from broken security cameras and gates to open manholes and water-main leaks that went unrepaired for weeks. Some residents had to wait months for basic repairs, even though the company's contract specifies that some repairs must be made within 15 days. In fact, United failed to complete more than half of all required repairs in 2001, and it allowed rust and debris to build up, so that when the boil-water alerts forced the company to flush the system, brown water flowed from the taps.

Finally, the report noted, instead of improving collections of unpaid water bills as promised, United actually allowed collection rates to drop from 98 to 94 percent, costing the city millions of dollars.

United has succeeded at one thing, according to the city: cutting its own operating costs, chiefly by reducing the water-works staff by 25 percent even as demand for water in burgeoning Atlanta keeps rising. Staff reductions were partly responsible for the company's service troubles, the report indicated, as were higher-than-expected repair expenses: Last year United demanded that the city provide an additional $80 million for unanticipated maintenance costs. The increase was blocked when a lone City Council member refused to sign the revised contract.

In mid-August, Mayor Franklin announced that "United Water has not lived up to its responsibility" and formally notified the company that it had 90 days to fix the problems or the city would terminate its contract. "They keep telling me they are part of a world-class corporation that can bring us world-class service," she says, offering a small smile. "So I'm giving them a chance to prove it." United has offered to spend $1 million on outside inspectors to reassure city officials that it isn't, as Franklin puts it, "cutting any corners."

It wasn't supposed to turn out this way. In 1998, when Atlanta's City Council voted to contract out its water filtration and delivery system, city officials insisted that corporate management would stave off a budget crisis and drastic rate increases, and would lower costs by more than 40 percent while improving service. (Franklin herself, then a management consultant, lobbied for one of the companies bidding on the contract.) It was the largest water-privatization program ever attempted in the United States and was expected to prompt a wave of similar contracts around the country.

Water privatization has been gaining steam since the early 1990s, when market advocates began touting it as the next logical step after deregulating electricity. Many city waterworks that were built or expanded in the 1970s are now decaying, and the cost of needed repairs is staggering. The U.S. Environmental Protection Agency estimates that U.S. cities will have to spend nearly $151 billion to upgrade or replace pipes, filters, storage tanks, and other infrastructure over the next two decades. Cities will have to spend an additional $460 billion on sewage systems—another area where the corporate water giants are making inroads.

The prospect of skyrocketing infrastructure costs prompted U.S. officials to look overseas, where privatization is already a booming business. Multinational companies now run water systems for 7 percent of the world's population, and analysts say that figure could more than double, to 17 percent, by 2015. Private water management is estimated to be a $200 billion business, and the World Bank—which has encouraged governments to sell off their utilities to reduce public debt—projects it could reach $1 trillion by 2021. Fortune has called water "one of the world's great business opportunities," noting that it "promises to be to the 21st century what oil was to the 20th."

The biggest contenders for this emerging market are Suez, a corporate descendant of the company that built the Suez Canal, and the media conglomerate Vivendi Universal, which owns the USA network and Universal Studios. Together, the two companies now control about 70 percent of the world's private water-delivery systems and take in a combined $60 billion in revenues. Both have spent billions in recent years expanding in the United States: In 1999, Suez bought United Water for $1 billion, and Vivendi acquired the then-largest American company, U.S. Filter, for more than $6 billion. RWE/Thames Water, a German/British conglomerate, is currently completing its merger with the biggest remaining domestic company, American Water Works.

The water companies have been expanding even more dramatically in the developing world, where antiquated, often colonial-era, water systems are no match for rapidly increasing populations. More than 1 billion people lack access to clean drinking water, notes Peter Gleick, president of the Pacific Institute for Studies in Development, Environment and Security; a recent report he co-authored points out that "half the world's people fail to receive the level of water services available in many of the cities of ancient Greece and Rome."

Yet corporate water's record in fixing those problems—or even maintaining the industrialized world's systems—has been mixed at best. In 1989 Prime Minister Margaret Thatcher pushed through a program to privatize the United Kingdom's water supply; costs to consumers soared over the following decade, despite billions in government subsidies to the water companies. In some cities, water bills rose by as much as 141 percent in the '90s, while thousands of public-sector jobs were lost. Even the conservative *Daily Mail* declared that "Britain's top ten water companies have been able to use their position as monopoly suppliers to pull off the greatest act of licensed robbery in our history."

Last year the Ghanaian government agreed to privatize local water systems as a condition for an International Monetary Fund loan. To attract investors, the government doubled water rates, setting off protests in a country where the average annual income is less than $400 a year and the water bill—for those fortunate enough to have running water—can run upwards of $110.

> Companies scrambling for lucrative municipal water contracts have also been caught up in corruption scandals.

In Bolivia's third-largest city, Cochabamba, water rates shot up 35 percent after a consortium led by Bechtel took over the city's water system in 1999; some residents found themselves paying 20 percent of their income for water. Street protests led to riots in which six people were killed; eventually, the Bolivian government voided Bechtel's contract and told company officials it could not guarantee their safety if they stayed in town.

Privatization has also spawned protests and, in some cases, dominated elections in several other countries, including Paraguay—where police last summer turned water cannons on anti-privatization protesters—Panama, Brazil, Peru, Colombia, India, Pakistan, Hungary, and South Africa. Here in the United States, some municipalities that initially jumped on the privatization bandwagon are now having second thoughts. In Milwaukee, which turned its sewage system over to United Water in 1998, an audit released in July found that a sewer tunnel was dumping raw sewage into local waterways, including Lake Michigan. Vivendi managed Puerto Rico's water and waste-water treatment for seven years, but after a territorial commission cited inaccurate billing and poor maintenance this year, its contract wasn't renewed.

Companies scrambling for lucrative municipal water contracts have also been caught up in corruption scandals. In June, Katherine Maraldo, a New Orleans Sewer and Water Board member, and Michael Stump, the former president of Professional Services Group, which ran the city's wastewater system, were convicted on bribery charges. PSG is now part of Vivendi, which is bidding to take over New Orleans' drinking-water system. And in 2001, two associates of Bridgeport, Connecticut, Mayor Joseph Ganim pled guilty to racketeering, mail fraud, and falsifying tax returns in connection with a $806,000 payment from PSG, which was negotiating for the city's $183 million water contract.

Such incidents point to a fundamental problem with allowing private companies to take over public water systems, says the Pacific Institute's Gleick. In attempting to make attractive bids for long-term contracts, companies often underestimate the cost of maintaining a water system, and so are forced to either skimp on staffing or demand more money to keep turning a profit. "At least when you have public utilities, the money they take in stays in the community," Gleick says. "With the private companies, the profits are going to go out of your community, out of your state, and probably out of your country."

Nevertheless, Troy Henry, the southern regional manager of United Water, is convinced that private water providers can do a better job than public utilities. He readily admits that his company and Atlanta city managers have had problems "dealing with the complexities of the system" in Atlanta and says the company is spending "multiple millions of dollars [to] win back the citizens' and mayor's confidence." A biomedical and electrical engineer and former manager at IBM, Henry argues that private companies can do for water delivery what Big Blue did for computing—revolutionize technology and attract "the best and the brightest and most talented people."

Perhaps Henry can mend fences in Atlanta, which he insists is United Water's—and corporate parent Suez's—"No. 1 priority." But Clair Muller, chair of the City Council's utility committee, contends that even if United Water ends up saving its Atlanta contract, it will merely have proved that privatization can work only under tight city supervision. And if tight supervision is possible, why privatize? "If government is run correctly—and that's always a big if—there's no profit motive," she says. "So if this is about saving money, we should always be able to do it cheaper."

In the end, the debate is about more than money. Taking responsibility for a community's water, Muller argues, is simply not the same as running a sports stadium or a cable franchise. "Water is the worst thing to privatize," she says. "It's what we need to live. I think that's key to the whole debate—are we going to lose control over functions that are essential to life?"

The New Water Wars

BY BILL LAMBRECHT
THE WASHINGTON MONTHLY, MAY 2005

Bob Shadwell, the proprietor of the Point of View Lodge in Pollock, S.D., and a professional fisherman, is in the habit of sending emails to the White House on Monday mornings. He is not sure if they are ever read, and, if they are, they have certainly not yet turned up much in the way of response, but they are remarkable for their singularity of focus. Shadwell's obsession matches that of his customers, and indeed that of folks I met throughout the drought-prone Dakotas. He wants the Army Corps of Engineers to let the Missouri rise higher on his stretch of the river, Lake Oahe, and give the local river recreation industry something it desperately needs: water. He believes that the Corps is unfairly keeping the river low in the Dakotas to appease a few connected farmers and barge operators in Missouri.

> September 11, 2002
>
> Dear President Bush:
>
> I am writing this letter today on the anniversary of the World Trade Center attack. We feel like here in South Dakota we're under attack by bureaucracy and plain bad politics. We know of your promise to Missouri farmers during your campaign. Did you not know that South Dakota, North Dakota, and Montana are part of the Union?
>
> It's time to make changes in this system of GOOD OLD BOY POLITICS!!!! Start looking at the big picture. These states have as much right to Missouri River water as Missouri does. Remember what Mark Twain said: "Men will vote over whisky and go to war over water."

When I first visited Shadwell in the summer of 2002, he was emailing his Monday morning messages to the White House with an alluring offer: free lodging at Point of View Resort and a guided fishing trip for lunker walleyes. He hadn't heard back, and that's probably just as well. The president professes to be a sporting man, but sport is hard to find along Lake Oahe. Touring Shadwell's 60-acre property along Ritter Bay, I noted that the water was so low and had receded so far from land that the cove fronting his Point of View restaurant was situated roughly a half-mile from water. "It seems like the country really doesn't know our plight out here. It seems that, regardless of the situation, downstream barge traffic takes precedence," Shadwell told me over a beer at his empty bar.

There are plenty of Bob Shadwells in the Dakotas, people whose Missouri River recreation businesses need water in the worst way from federally managed dams. The drought that engulfed the region in the first years of the new century was the immediate cause for distress. In August of 1999, the elevation on Lake Oahe, calculated in feet above sea level, was 1,617. When I first visited there, it had dropped by 29 feet to 1,588. Water was also low at Fort Peck and Garrison. Together with Oahe, lakes at those dams hold 85 percent of the storage in the Missouri River system.

This was a punishing drought. But pain or not, the problem along the Missouri River is chronic. Routinely, there is not enough water in a system that gives priority to navigation. The Army Corps of Engineers interprets its Master Manual to say there must be sufficient water in the 732-mile stretch of lower river to maintain navigation, a criterion which in recent years has helped to keep the upper Missouri mighty dry. Congress and the courts have refused to stipulate otherwise, so somebody has to suffer. Right now, that somebody is Bob Shadwell.

I talked to Shadwell many times over the next two years, as the water continued to drop. He felt more desperate all the time, like a fish flopping in a boat and gasping for air. Abandonment can take over in a hurry in a remote land. The Point of View is situated near South Dakota's border with North Dakota where the earth is an exotic blend of camelbacks, swales, and hillocks, some perfectly round, that fellows hereabouts have named after parts of the female anatomy. Otherwise, you see nothing but a few cows on the five-mile gravel road back to Shadwell's lodge.

South Dakota and North Dakota have been trapped in a fight with Missouri over the river's level since the 1950s when the Army Corps of Engineers first began putting dams and locks on the river to control its flow. For a half-century, they have mostly lost. But their fight has recently taken on a greater urgency, given the $85-million-per-year recreation business on the Missouri—fly-fishing in Montana, trophy walleye hunting in the Dakotas, and weekend boating for tired suburbanites from Denver and Sioux Falls. That may not sound like much, but it dwarfs the shriveled, $9-million-per-year barge business the dams were originally built to protect, but which can no longer compete with cheaper trading and other modes of freight.

The fight over the Missouri is usually understood in Washington—when it's understood at all—as little more than a ruckus between the bearded, blue-jeaned biologists from the Fish and Wildlife Service (who want water levels in Missouri restored to some semblance of their natural flows to protect nesting birds and the pallid sturgeon) and military technocrats from the Corps, who are trying to keep their congressional paymasters and their allies along the river happy by keeping the river artificially controlled. But the dramatic decline in barge traffic between North Sioux City, S.D., and St. Louis, Mo., and the rise of the recreation industry further upstream, began to change that political calculus. By 2001, the legendarily intractable Corps suggested that it was ready to make some changes in river flows, handing a victory to the sturgeon and the Dakotas—a day that the odd coalition of fishers, Dakota pols, Fish and Wildlife biologists, and conservation groups thought would never arrive.

> Politics, like economics, eventually gives way to the law of supply and demand.

But the last four years have been far from a triumph for these groups. An aggressive congressional delegation, led by Sen. Christopher Bond (R-Mo.) and backed by a sympathetic White House eager to keep Missouri's electoral votes in the GOP column, has fought back, and the battle has drifted into a stalemate as knotty and dense as ever. Missouri River barges may be few, but they continue to get the water they need. And, as the drought persists, the Dakotas remain parched.

Now, similar political tensions are sparking battles over water in parts of the country that have never seen them before. In Florida, Arkansas, Georgia, and elsewhere, politically connected interests with declining economic rationales for the water are using the Corps to preserve their advantages usually over emerging populations and industries with a growing justification for that water. Water wars, a feature of Western politics for decades, have begun to move east.

This state of affairs won't last forever. Politics, like economics, eventually gives way to the law of supply and demand. The status quo of federal water management of American rivers is like the Soviet Union in the early 1980s, a grossly inefficient, economically senseless system kept alive by political and economic interests trying to protect their increasingly rickety power. One good blow and the whole thing could crumble.

Scripture of the Water Gods

Army engineers in suburban Omaha lord over the life of the Missouri River.

On a Monday in October 2000, my quest to understand how the Missouri runs and why has led me to the Reservoir Control Center in the Army Corps' Omaha District for the first of two weekly meetings that will decide how the waters of the river will flow.

Guiding this 21st-century command meeting on the river—and close at hand for easy reference—is the Corps' Master Manual. Like any scripture, the Master Manual inspires and incites. It is weighty—more than two pounds—and full of commandments as to where the water flows, when, and for whom. Written in stone long ago, these orders barely have changed over four decades. Recreation, fish, and wildlife come last in the litany "insofar as possible without serious interference" in the marching orders from Congress to the Corps.

Here in Omaha, the first order of business is taking stock of when it has rained along the river, and when it might, which takes some attention in a basin consisting of some 541,000 square miles. To calculate how much water might be entering the Missouri from the 220-plus rivers and streams that feed it, 14 Army engineers and civilian workers fix their eyes on an oversized computer terminal. As I watch, the Corps men and women study a series of National Weather Service reports.

A handful of reports forecast rain. This is news for rejoicing among the "god of navigable rivers" as the Army Corps of Engineers has been ordained by Congress. The Corps invokes satellites on high to consult readings from 800 rain gauges. The calculus of flow decisions also must factor in the volume of water in reservoirs behind the dams and the volume of water needed to generate the electricity that can be sold that day on the spot market.

Rain is forecast south of Sioux City, Iowa, so the team decides to release slightly less water into the lower stretch of river that flows from Sioux City into the Mississippi above St. Louis. The water gods command that the flow of river through Gavins Point be scaled back to 32,500 cubic feet per second from 33,000, as it had been. A flow of 33,000 cubic feet of water amounts to roughly 250,000 gallons, enough to inundate a football field to the depth of one foot.

They email their instructions to Gavins Point Dam, 160 miles north at the South Dakota-Nebraska border, where they arrive on Dennis O'Rourke's computer screen much faster than I can make the trip north to see them executed.

Releasing all this water from Gavins Point is a one-finger job, and I imagine Michelangelo's "Creation of Adam" as O'Rourke stretches out his finger to enter the command. Instantly, there's movement beneath us in the 54,000-horsepower turbines that generate electricity from the raging water. Inside the turbines, 10-feet high, four-ton wicket gates close ever so slightly, like Venetian blinds, diminishing the flow of water from Lewis and Clark Lake, a reservoir on the north side of the dam, through the dam and out into the Missouri River on the other side.

The Corps of Engineers' control of the water on the Missouri stems from the 1940s, when Congress, having just beaten the fascists and in search of grand projects at home, began to assign the Army to dam and manage rivers. Two audacious bureaucrats—an Army engineer named Col. Louis Pick who had headed the Corps' Omaha office, and an easygoing assistant chief in the Bureau of Reclamations Billings office named Glenn Sloan—had been pushing for a new regime of federal management of the Missouri. They were aided in their quest by municipal boosters from Montana to Missouri who were panicked by the river's regular floods and believed the river's barge industry would benefit if the vessels could more reliably traffic the river. Congress, its members smelling pork projects for their districts, agreed, allowing the Corps and the Bureau of Reclamation to combine their contradictory river development plans in the Pick-Sloan Act. Since then, the Missouri River has been managed under the precepts set down in the Corps' Master Manual, which makes the lower river's navigation for barge traffic a priority. But by the time the Corps completed its nine-foot-deep channel from St. Louis to Sioux City in 1981, the barge business it had been designed to accommodate was beginning to become economically obsolete.

Sunk!

"What we've got here is like an old-fashioned Western water fight," insists barge industry executive Don Huffman, a Missourian who retired recently after more than three decades in the barge business. "They want the water up there and we want it down here."

It takes perspective as long as Huffman's to defend the vitality of Missouri barging. We were headed toward success until the 1980 grain embargo, the barge industry says, one in a list of laments as long as it is arcane. Managed low flows have destroyed reliability and run off potential customers. We just need another chance. We're an industry under siege, facing off against conservationists, upstream recreationists, and shrinking revenues.

The Missouri River barge industry was bound for trouble. As suburbs have spread and trucking and rail have remained the dominant means of transporting goods up, down, and around the Midwest and Great Plains, it takes a mighty lean barging operation to steal shipping business. And barging on the Missouri—unlike on rivers like the Mississippi—has always been a dicey proposition. Even bank stabilization and the Corps' channel-digging haven't fully tamed this threatening, meandering river, as the Great Flood of 1993 showed. And the threat that some nesting terns will delay the shipping season another day, week, or month has taught clients that barging is not the most reliable way of getting your goods from Sioux Falls to St. Louis, or back.

And so the river's barging business has shrunk. An industry that was once essential for bringing all the produce of the Plains to market has dwindled to a $9 million annual business, according to calculations by a long-time ally of the barge industry—the Army Corps of Engineers.

Your Horse Is Pregnant

Not long after that nine-foot-deep channel was completed, advocacy groups objecting to the principles governing the Corps' management of the Missouri began to organize. They believed that the Master Manual (with its *Dr. Strangelove*-like name) gave unjust preference to barge interests and their chief allies, farmers along the river. Meanwhile, the Fish and Wildlife Service, which is charged with enforcing the 1973 Endangered Species Act, began to document how the Corps' finger-of-God raising and lowering of the Missouri's water line had rather remorselessly disturbed the natural rhythms of life for the river's animals. Particularly, they argued, the Corps was endangering two federally protected species of bird and the pallid sturgeon, a beast with a flat, shovel-like snout and a reptilian tail that looks like a genetic concoction of dinosaur, shark, and alligator.

Second, there were the upriver states—Montana, North Dakota, and South Dakota—in a region often plagued by drought, which argued that the manipulations of the river routinely starved their portion of the Missouri of needed water. North Dakotans are far and away the most zealous on this point: One of their distinguishing characteristics is a willingness to display bottles of their yellow, mineral-fouled water for any reporter or politician they meet. I have encountered these bottles everywhere from North Dakota to the halls of the Dirksen Senate Office Building in Washington, D.C. (One North Dakota rancher, Keith Farstveet, recalled, perhaps in jest, that he had once sent a yellowish sample of well water to a state lab for analysis. It came back with a note, which Farstveet recounted: "Your horse is pregnant.")

The upriver states, often in league with Indian tribes and recreation interests, typically lose Missouri River battles thanks to the critical, hand-in-hand relationship between the Corps and Congress that strengthened throughout those decades. The Corps, like the rest of the Army, serves the White House, but over the last century it has become effectively a branch of Congress. This tight relationship has long made sense: Both the Corps, which has wanted a grand role for itself, and Congress, which has wanted pork for favored districts, has had an interest in ginning up more and bigger Chamber-of-Commerce-pleasing projects such as dams, levees, and irrigation systems. By 1950, Harold Ickes, formerly FDR's long-serving Interior Secretary, was moved to write: "It is to be doubted whether a federal agency in the history of this country has so wantonly wasted money on worthless projects as has the Corps of Engineers. . . . No more lawless or irresponsible federal group than the Corps of Engineers has ever attempted to operate in the United States." It took another half-century for this mindset to trickle out beyond the world of liberal public-interest groups in Washington, but when it did, it meant trouble for the Corps.

"A Cockamamie, Godawful Project"

In the new century, it wasn't just liberals like Ickes or advocacy groups who were squawking. Budget hawks and Republicans with environmental sensibilities began pressuring the Corps. U.S. Rep. Wayne Gilchrist, a Maryland Republican and ex-marine, summed up the growing criticism: "The Corps of Engineers has been over-used by Congress," he told me in the summer of 2002. "They've dredged, they've levied, they've channelized, and they've degraded the environment of the United States more than they have needed to." For instance, independent experts at Virginia Tech concluded in 2000 that the Corps had overestimated by $144 million the benefits of a huge Mississippi project called Yazoo Pumps, which would drain 200,000 acres of Mississippi River wetlands to make new farmlands. Ex-Interior Secretary Bruce Babbitt called the Yazoo Pumps plan "a cockamamie, godawful project."

Similar sentiments echoed around the Department of the Interior after a Corps project to rescue the Chesapeake's native Virginia oyster, which relied upon "carpet-bombing" one million baby oysters into the Great Wicomico River, ended in laughable disaster when a herd of native stingrays descended and devoured the shellfish. "We didn't really know anything about the cow-nosed ray," Corps project manager Doug Martin told the Norfolk *Virginian-Pilot.* "It kind of surprised us."

The Corps' mismanagement of water and its often-bungled attempts to rework natural resources are being repeated around the country, its critics say. As municipalities in the South and East from Atlanta to Charlotte to Little Rock, have expanded out into fields, the strain they've put on existing water supplies has increased dramatically. "The level of conflict that we associate with the West is now occurring around the country," Robert Hirsch, associate director of the U.S. Geological Survey and the nation's chief water scientist, told me when I visited his office in suburban Washington, where the nation's water is watched and measured. "There are many concerns and even jealousy. Everyone worries that somebody's going to steal their water."

Rice growers in Arkansas, the backers and beneficiaries of a proposed $300 million Corps pumping project designed to keep their plantations irrigated, found themselves in conflict with a vast coalition of smaller farms, municipalities, and environmental groups, after the growers depleted a main aquifer with unsustainable farming. Residents along the Apalachicola River in Florida are furious at a decades-long Corps dredging project designed to build a canal for a barge industry that sends so few vessels downstream each month that locals can count them on a single hand. And the bursting-at-the-seams water needs of sprawling metropolitan Atlanta have meant a 10-year negotiation over how to distribute water among Georgia, Alabama, and Florida—a debate that shows no signs of reaching a conclusion.

In 2000, reporter Michael Grunwald wrote a series of stories in *The Washington Post* based on more than a thousand interviews and tens of thousands of pages of documents. The Corps was parlaying its congressional relationships into billions of dollars' worth of water projects, he concluded, and many of them charged heavy environmental costs for dubious economic value. At about the same time, the National Academy of Sciences took the Corps to task in two separate reports, saying the Army Engineers' methods and planning models for the Mississippi River were failing to balance economic and environmental benefits.

The tide seemed to be turning against the Corps. Besieged by Congress, environmental groups, and taxpayer advocates, by 2000, the Corps' then-new leader, Lt. Gen. Robert Flowers, had begun to realize that his agency's position was untenable. "The greatness of the Corps is being able to say no when no is the right thing to be said," he told me at Corps headquarters a block from the new MCI Center sports palace in Washington, D.C., and you could feel the wheels beginning to turn.

But in the 2000 presidential election, Gov. George W. Bush won Missouri, a state that had gone for Democrat Bill Clinton by wide margins in the two previous elections, and his advisors believed he had done so in part by siding with Missouri commercial interests—and the Corps—against the environmentalists and upriver states. (St. Louis, after the 1993 floods, had been particularly aggressive about building on the river's floodplains; millions of square feet of mall topped off by a Bentley dealership now sit on what had been the flooded neighborhood of Gumbo Flats. Its businessmen, consequently, had a lot to lose if the Corps dialed back its management of the river.) So, it was no surprise that the Bush administration fought the dramatic flow changes, including a summer draw-down of water, that would de-emphasize barge traffic and make the river more friendly to wildlife and recreation concerns. Gen. Flowers's professed reform impulse was nipped in the bud, and the status quo prevailed.

The Missouri Compromise

One of the current administration's least-favorite species, an aggressive, avowedly liberal federal judge, offered perhaps the biggest threat to that status quo. I first encountered Gladys Kessler in July 2003 in Washington, D.C., where she was charged with adjudicating a suit brought by environmental groups hoping to compel the Corps to protect endangered species by altering the Missouri's ebb and flow. On a hot summer day, Judge Kessler, a Clinton appointee and a founder of the activist Women's Legal Defense Fund, looked mad enough to climb down from the bench and throttle one of the half-dozen government lawyers frying on her griddle.

"The Army general counsel didn't think this was a significant enough matter to attend himself?" she asked one junior Army lawyer.

Nor had the Army's acting secretary, Les Brownlee, shown for a hearing. Brownlee had to be overseas, his staff had told her. Now, Kessler heard that he was busy at Fort Leavenworth. Which was it?

"I think that what was reported to my office was that he was in Europe, not Kansas. Kansas is a little closer than Europe," she snapped.

Environmentalists were downright giddy. Kessler ordered the Missouri to fall in order to protect nesting birds, the first such court ruling. Suddenly, the Corps' mission of river navigation—of keeping those barges running—had been trumped by the imperative of protecting species.

> An iron triangle of joined interests has kept the Missouri River battle stuck for so long.

It had the makings of a seismic ruling, yanking away decision-making from the Corps, which had run Big Muddy like a private stream. There was a second trembler underlying her ruling: If Kessler's logic held, the balance of control over the river might shift to upper basin states for the first time in decades. And her logic might well apply to other river wars across the country.

Among recorders of the shock waves was a *New York Times* editorial writer who observed: "On the eve of the 200th anniversary of Lewis and Clark's historic journey, Americans can begin to hope for a better future for the river that carried the expedition westward." Judge Kessler threatened to become draconian, declaring that the Corps would be fed a half-million dollars every day they failed to comply.

But Kessler never had the opportunity to drag the Corps officers into her courtroom again, or levy her fee, or get draconian. What happened next was the judicial equivalent of the Major League Baseball commissioner stepping in with a scheduling change during the World Series, a classic *deus ex machina*. On the afternoon before Kessler's deadline, the Judicial Panel on Multidistrict Litigation, of which I'd never heard but which had been set up in the 1960s to help federal courtrooms run more smoothly, transferred six Missouri River cases—among them the litigation in front of Kessler—to the Minnesota courtroom of a U.S. District Judge named Paul Magnuson, a senior, conservative jurist appointed by Ronald Reagan. The Bush Justice Department wasted no time in requesting a stay on the fee imposed by Kessler, and Magnuson granted it. Ultimately, his rulings would preserve the authority of the Army Corps of Engineers—and the status quo.

Till the Bank Shuts Me Down

An iron triangle of joined interests has kept the Missouri River battle stuck for so long: the Corps' political clout in Congress, the downstream barge industry, and Missouri's appeal as a presidential swing state. Arguably, the importance of each of those is diminishing, and the evolving economic realities suggest a coming political realignment on this most intractable of issues. Such a realignment might be triggered by a judge like Gladys Kessler; more likely, a future president will make the calculation that the political benefits of pleasing the senators in three states (N.D., S.D., and Mont.) outweigh the risks of crossing the barge industry in one state, Missouri. In any event, such a change is unlikely to occur under the present administration. The Bush White House has cast its lot with the downriver folks and has repeatedly cast a decisive veto to reject any efforts to alter the status quo.

So, for the moment, that status quo persists, and that's left some in an unpromising spot. When I spoke with Bob Shadwell in 2003, he told me he'd filed for bankruptcy protection. As the drought persisted, water levels along the Lake Oahe stretch of the Upper Missouri had continued to drop—by an amazing 11 feet. Cottonwoods submerged for a half-century protruded like a forest graveyard, he said, and getting on the river was spooky as well as dangerous.

A resort had closed nearby, a victim of drought and what Dakotans regarded as a water-allocation policy favoring downstream interests. But despite disastrous conditions, Shadwell insisted that he would not abandon his dream of running a fishing lodge with his family. "I can't give up on this," he said. "I'm going to hang on until the fat lady sings or the bank shuts me down."

Water War

CURRENT EVENTS (WEEKLY READER), NOVEMBER 12, 2007

Something is missing from Georgia's Lake Lanier. Its green islands, once at lake level, now sit 15 feet above the water on huge mounds of dirt. Billions of gallons of water that once filled the lake are gone.

The problem runs far deeper than it looks on the surface. People and animals in three states—Georgia, Alabama, and Florida—rely on that water for their survival.

Millions of people in the Atlanta area get their tap water from Lake Lanier. Coca-Cola and Pepsi plants need the water to make soft drinks and Gatorade. Downstream, other cities, power plants, and endangered creatures rely on the water as well.

Praying For Rain

Normally, water isn't a problem here, but the southeastern United States is in the midst of one of its worst droughts on record. The National Weather Service says the area needs at least a foot of rain to ease the drought, and it doesn't expect to see that much rainfall any time soon.

The hot, dry weather has been causing problems all across the Southeast. In Orme, Tenn., the town's spring is running so low that Mayor Tony Reames has to have water trucked in. Families in Orme get just three hours of water each night now to take showers and wash clothes. "I've heard some threaten to move out, but where are they going to go? The drought is everywhere," Reames says.

Farmers are suffering too. The drought wiped out hay crops and dried up pastures where cattle graze. People in Alabama have another worry: electricity. One power plant shut down because there wasn't enough water to run its cooling system. Another major power plant relies on water flowing out of Lake Lanier.

War Among the States

Lake Lanier has become a battlefield. The federal government created the lake when it built a dam on the Chattahoochee River in the 1950s. Today, the Army Corps of Engineers controls how much water stays in the lake and how much is let out so the river can continue flowing through Georgia and down the Alabama line.

TIME TRIP

THE DUST BOWL

The 1930s showed the nation how much damage a drought can do. When rain stopped falling in the Midwest, farm fields began to dry up. Corn wouldn't grow, and wheat struggled to sprout in a region long known as "the nation's breadbasket." After years of poor land management, fierce windstorms easily stripped the parched fields of their topsoil, blowing it into giant clouds of dust. Those storms led to the nickname the "Dust Bowl."

LeRoy Hankel started farming in the 1930s. "Boy, we had dust here. You couldn't keep a house clean or anything. . . . That's the way '34 [was]," he recalls in a taped interview, one of several about the era at www.uvinghistoryfarm.org. Other farmers went bankrupt and moved west, looking for work, but Hankel stayed. "Every year we was hoping this would be the good year," he says. He didn't get a good corn crop until 1941. That drought was the nation's worst, and it hit during the Great Depression. President Franklin D. Roosevelt created new programs to help farms survive. He also started conservation efforts to bring the "breadbasket" back to life.

After the water leaves Lake Lanier, several cities south of Atlanta tap it for drinking water and to run factories. Last—and some would argue least—are the mussels in Florida. Federal rules that protect endangered species say enough water must flow out of Lake Lanier to keep some endangered mussels, a type of shellfish, alive.

The Corps has been releasing Lake Lanier's water to comply with those rules. But because of the drought, more water has left the lake than has flowed into it. That has Georgia Gov. Sonny Perdue angry. If something doesn't change, he says, Atlanta could be without water in as little as three months.

If Atlanta goes dry, it will be a human and economic disaster, Perdue says. The governor sees it as a war of "man versus mussel," and he says the federal government is rooting for the shellfish. Perdue declared a state of emergency in October because of the drought. His state is now suing to keep water from leaving Lake Lanier.

The governors of Alabama and Florida say the water is just as crucial to their people—they need it to run factories and keep fisheries healthy.

"If the water is not released, then the industries will be forced to shut down, and thousands of . . . families will lose their source of income," Alabama Gov. Bob Riley wrote in the *Atlanta Journal-Constitution*.

Florida Gov. Charlie Crist says Georgia recklessly let Atlanta grow too big too fast without considering the consequences, such as water shortages.

The federal government is trying to find a solution. Meanwhile, people across the Southeast are cutting back on their water use. "You just don't know what's going to happen when you go messing with the ecosystem," Reames says. "You can count on one thing: It's going to tell on you."

Sharing the River Out of Eden

By Sandra Postel
Natural History, November 2007

When I first set eyes on the Jordan River, after a rainy winter in February 1992, I could scarcely believe that the thin ribbon of muddy liquid I saw winding its way southward could be the main prize in the contest for water in the Middle East. The Jordan is a small river. Its average annual flow is only 1.5 percent of what the Nile delivers to Egypt. By the time I encountered it, after several decades of its being dammed, diverted, and polluted, this legend of the biblical landscape, heralded in song as "deep and wide," appeared dirty and spent.

Rarely has such a modest river been asked to do so much for so many. The Jordan and its tributaries serve five distinct political entities: Israel, Jordan, Lebanon, the Palestinians, and Syria. And unsurprisingly—in this most contentious and water-scarce of places—there is still no agreement about how the blue golf should be shared among all the parties. The Palestinians in the West Bank and Gaza are chronically short of water, and use a quarter as much per capita as do the neighboring Israelis. Inequitable access fans the flames of tension. Meanwhile, downstream lies the fabled Dead Sea—the lowest-lying and saltiest lake on Earth, and the Jordan's final destination. But by the time the Jordan gets there, some 90 percent of its flow has already been diverted for domestic and agricultural uses upstream, so the river no longer sustains the sea. For the past quarter century, the lake level has been dropping about three feet a year; some warn that the Dead Sea could vanish by 2050.

As if those conditions weren't dire enough, climatologists warn that global warming and its attendant increases in drought and evaporation may intensify the water shortages in the Middle East. At the same time, the projected rise in sea level may expose the coastal aquifers of Israel and Gaza to ruinous invasions of saltwater, rendering ever more wells unfit to supply drinking water.

In many ways the water predicament in the Middle East seems as intractable as the decades-long feuds over territory, Jerusalem, and refugees. But is it really so unyielding? Are there untapped solutions waiting to be deployed? And could an equitable resolution of water disputes perhaps become the wedge that opens new pathways to the grail of peaceful coexistence?

As with so much in the Middle East, a little geography tells a lot of the story. The Jordan owes its flow to the confluence of three streams—the Hasbani River, which originates in Lebanon; the Dan River in northernmost Israel; and the Baniyas River, which emerges from Syria. The Jordan then flows south about twenty-five miles to the Sea of Galilee, Israel's sole natural freshwater lake, which holds about a third of the nation's renewable water supply. About six miles south of the Sea of Galilee, the Jordan is joined by its main tributary, the Yarmuk River, which originates in Syria and forms the Syrian-Jordanian border before merging with the Jordan River in Israel. The Jordan then continues its journey southward to the Dead Sea.

A source of water crossing so many political boundaries, especially given the overheated politics and thirsty terrain of the Middle East, is a recipe for tension. Political leaders have routinely threatened war over the control of water. Golda Meir warned in 1960, when she was the Israeli foreign minister, that any attempt by Arab nations to divert the northern tributaries of the Jordan would be "an outright attack on one of Israel's means of livelihood" and "a threat to peace." In 1990 Jordan's King Hussein declared that water was the only issue that could take him to war with Israel.

> In 1990 Jordan's King Hussein declared that water was the only issue that could take him to war with Israel.

Ever since the creation of Israel in historic Palestine in 1948, the quest for water security among the parties of the Jordan basin has veered between unilateral action and cooperation. Recognizing the importance of water-sharing to the region's stability, in 1953 the U.S. president, Dwight D. Eisenhower, appointed Eric Johnston, chair of the International Development Advisory Board, as special ambassador to the region to help negotiate a water-development plan. After two years, the so-called Johnston formula emerged. It allocated water according to the amount and location of irrigable land that could receive surface water by gravity—a sensible approach that placed water "needs" above water "rights." By overlaying political boundaries on the map of irrigation potential, the Johnston plan arrived at a fair and technically feasible way of divvying up the water. Amazingly, the Johnston plan was acceptable to all parties at the time (though the Palestinians were not yet viewed as a distinct political entity). In the end, however, politics won out over rationality, and the plan was never formally ratified.

A spate of unilateral moves to capture and claim water followed, dramatically changing the hydrological landscape. In 1964 Israel began conveying the upper Jordan into its National Water Carrier, a system of canals and tunnels that supplies water to Tel Aviv and other coastal cities, as well as to desert agriculturalists in the Negev. Attempts by the Arab nations to thwart Israel's diversion plans and capture the Jordan's headwaters for their own use led to skirmishes in the mid-1960s, including Israeli attacks on construction facilities at diversion sites in Syria.

It was Israel's military victories during the Six-Day War of June 1967, however, that sealed its strategic hydrologic advantage. None other than Ariel Sharon, an Israeli commander in that war, noted that "the Six-Day War really started on the day Israel decided to act against the diversion of the Jordan." Before the war, less than a tenth of the Jordan River watershed lay within Israel's borders; by the war's end, Israel had secured the vast majority of it. Israeli control extended to what had been Syria's Golan Heights (which drain into the Sea of Galilee) and Baniyas River, as well as to critical groundwa-

ter aquifers under the West Bank. The latter territory, previously the possession of Jordan, now provides Israel with about a third of its water.

The three underground aquifers of the West Bank figure centrally in any effort to delineate and constitute a Palestinian state. The Yarqon-Taninim aquifer, the largest, runs along the foothills of the West Bank and flows westward across the Green Line (the Israeli boundary before the 1967 war) toward the Mediterranean Sea. Israel can now tap this groundwater on either side of the Green Line, but the aquifer's main recharge zones lie under the West Bank.

During its occupation of the West Bank, Israel has prevented Palestinians from drilling wells for irrigation and has severely restricted Palestinian access to supplies. Journalist Fred Pearce reported in his 2006 book *When The Rivers Run Dry* that Palestinian families around Nablus spend between 20 and 40 percent of their income on water for drinking, cooking, and cleaning, while Israeli settlers nearby enjoy lawns and swimming pools.

This hydrologic inequity has worsened as a result of Israel's construction of the controversial separation barrier that it began building in 2002. Israeli military officials say the approximately 425-mile stretch of wall and fencing, which in many areas extends considerably east of the Green Line, is necessary to protect Israeli cities and towns from Palestinian suicide bombers, and that security concerns alone determine the barrier's route. The Palestinians dispute this, viewing the barrier instead as a land-and-water grab. According to the Applied Research Institute of Jerusalem (ARIJ), a nonprofit organization dedicated to protecting the Palestinians' natural resources, the barrier could ultimately isolate Palestinian villages from 134 wells and 62 springs, as well as from some 260,000 acres (about 405 square miles) of productive farmland.

Of course, the Palestinians themselves also bear some responsibility for their water predicament. Years of infighting between the two principal factions, Fatah and Hamas, have distracted officials from the basic needs of their people, a problem compounded by a severe lack of financial and technical resources.

The water infrastructure is decaying, pollution is rampant, and the coastal aquifer is nearly destroyed. The water for 1.4 million Gazans comes from shallow groundwater that has long been over-pumped—depleted faster than it can be replenished—and is already so contaminated by salt and pollutants that most of it does not meet the drinking-water standards of the World Health Organization.

As elusive as it may seem, water security for all—a *sine qua non* for lasting peace in the region—is within reach. Thanks to cooperation between scientists and citizen groups, advances in water-management technology, and agreements reached during peace talks in the early 1990s, there is a foundation on which to build lasting and more equitable water-sharing arrangements.

The Israeli-Jordanian peace treaty signed in October 1994, for instance, included water-sharing provisions that largely resolved the tensions between the two countries. Relying on the 1955 Johnston Plan to formulate his negotiating position, Jordan's lead water negotiator limited Israel's share of the Yarmuk River, critically important to his country's water security.

Nothing nearly as conclusive emerged from the Israeli-Palestinian talks culminating in the 1993 and 1995 Oslo Accords, though some progress was made. Because Jordan had disengaged from the Israeli-occupied West Bank in 1988, it was up to the Palestinians, then represented by the Palestine Liberation Organization, or PLO, to negotiate their own water deal with Israel. In the Taba Agreement, or Oslo II, signed by Israel and the PLO in September 1995, Israel formally recognized for the first time that the Palestinians have legitimate rights to West Bank groundwater—an important first step. How much water each side was entitled to, however, was left for the "final status" talks, which are yet to occur.

Coupled with further diplomatic initiatives to share water more equitably, a stronger push for straightforward measures to curb demand, expand supply, and use water more productively could generate enough water to satisfy the region's needs. And few countries have more technical know-how in water management than Israel does.

Half a century ago, Israeli engineers developed highly efficient drip irrigation methods, and they've been perfecting them ever since. Drip systems deliver water directly to the roots of plants at low volumes through perforated tubing installed on or below the soil surface. Drip systems nearly eliminate wasteful evaporation and runoff, and compared with more conventional irrigation, they can double or triple the crop yield per unit of water. Israel now applies drip and other micro-irrigation methods on two-thirds of its cropland. With the help of Israeli engineers, Jordan, too, has adopted those methods, and now applies them on 55 percent of its farmlands.

> Desalination—the removal of salt from seawater—could also yield sizable peace dividends.

Israel has also moved aggressively to treat, recycle, and reuse its urban wastewater. Seventy-three percent of treated sewage from Tel Aviv and other cities gets used a second time by farmers, in effect taking the "waste" out of wastewater. Recycled water makes up a fifth of Israel's total supply, and its share is projected to grow.

Despite such gains in efficiency, irrigated agriculture still accounts for about two-thirds of Israel's water use, yet it contributes only 2 percent to the nation's gross domestic product. Israel imports a good deal of its wheat and other staple foods, but it still irrigates substantial tracts planted with fruits, vegetables, and other high-return crops. By reducing agricultural water subsidies and paring back irrigated farming, Israel could free up a substantial quantity of water to share with its Palestinian neighbors—at little cost to its own economy.

Desalination—the removal of salt from seawater—could also yield sizable peace dividends. Although its costs are still high, they have fallen substantially in the past decade. In 2005, at Ashkelon, on the southern Mediterranean coast just north of Gaza, Israel opened the first of five planned desalination facilities. By a process called reverse osmosis, in which saltwater is filtered through a fine polymer membrane under high pressure to separate out the salts, the facility can produce 100 million cubic meters of desalinated water per year. That capacity makes the Ashkelon plant the largest reverse-osmosis seawater desalination plant in the world.

By 2010, Israel expects to be desalinating a total of 315 million cubic meters of seawater per year, nearly equal to its current use of freshwater from the West Bank aquifers. If Israel were to substitute desalinated seawater for West Bank groundwater, Palestinians there could double their current water use while easing up on the overpumping of the aquifers.

Unfortunately, no such deal is in the cards. Israeli officials have instead proposed that the United States help fund the construction of a desalination plant on the Mediterranean coast at Caesarea. From there, they suggest, the desalinated water could be transferred to the West Bank for use by the Palestinians. Under that proposal, Israel would retain its control of West Bank groundwater, and the Palestinians would get high-priced desalinated seawater from Israeli territory—hardly a recipe for Palestinian water security.

Why is Israel pushing for this approach? Driven by a deep mistrust of Palestinian motives, Israel feels a need to retain control over the region's water supplies. For their part, Palestinians publicly blame Israel's water greediness. Yet behind the scenes, even during the worst of the second *intifada*, ministers from both sides quietly met and agreed not to damage each other's water infrastructure.

Joined in destiny by the hydrological cycle, the people of the Jordan River basin know, whether consciously or subconsciously, that they must share the water of the basin and that cooperation can benefit them all. While traveling in the hills of Israel's western Galilee region in 1992, I visited an Arab village of 7,000 people called Kfar Manda. The sewage from the village was managed by a neighboring Jewish community, Yodfat. A series of small reservoirs stored Kfar Manda's wastewater and treated it biologically; it then became a source for drip irrigation in Yodfat's cotton fields. The Arab villagers got an inexpensive way of handling their sewage, which might otherwise have flowed untreated into their surroundings. And the Yodfat farmers got a reliable and less costly source of water for irrigation—water that carried enough nitrogen and phosphorus to markedly cut their fertilizer costs. By bridging the ethnic and religious divides, the two communities reaped benefits that neither would have achieved without the other.

With similar methods and goals in mind, EcoPeace/Friends of the Earth Middle East (FoEME), a private organization of Arab and Israeli environmentalists, initiated the "Good Water Neighbors" project in 2001. It aims to organize joint water-management projects between cross-border communities in Israel, Jordan, and the Palestinian territories. Seventeen communities are participating so far, each one working with its partner across their common border on the water problems they share. A mayors' network has been formed to give residents a voice on such larger issues as the health of the Jordan River, the demise of the Dead Sea, and the implications of the separation wall under construction in the West Bank.

Along with the drip irrigation lines and desalination units that increasingly dot the landscape of the Jordan River basin, technical and civilian cooperation has persisted throughout years of violence and political stalemate. That spirit of cooperation stands ready to be harnessed and augmented to build a secure water future for all in the region. If it is not, political leaders will have squandered far more than water.

III. POLLUTED WATERS

Editor's Introduction

Those who seek to conquer the world and shape it as they see fit never succeed. The world is a sacred vessel and cannot be improved. Whoever tries to alter it spoils it; whoever tries to direct it, misleads it.

—*Lao Tzu*

Throughout history humanity has settled near freshwater systems. Unfortunately, too often people have abused these systems—and not just in modern times. For example, in ancient Rome, sewers emptied into the Tiber River, causing the waters to became so polluted that the Romans were forced to construct their now-famous aqueduct systems to carry freshwater into the city.

Today, roughly 2.5 billion people suffer from diseases stemming from polluted water. Fertilizers, pesticides, industrial runoff, and sewage all contribute to this public health dilemma. However, the toll exacted from wildlife is even more severe; indeed entire ecosystems have been destroyed. According to Eleanor Sterling and Merry Camhi in "Sold Down the River," the first article in this chapter, numerous freshwater organisms, including dragonflies, damselflies, mussels, and birds, "now rank among the world's most threatened species."

The authors of "Troubled Waters" examine water pollution in China, India, and the West Bank. They report that China's rapid industrialization has gravely threatened the health of the Yangtze and Yellow Rivers. In India meanwhile, the strain of pollution and the demands of an expanding agricultural sector has left the majority of the country's citizens without access to clean water.

The Ganges River is sacred to India's vast Hindu population. Joshua Hammer, in his article, "A Prayer for the Ganges," explains the Ganges River's importance to the people of India and the ongoing efforts to restore its health. He reports that over the past three decades India's explosive population growth and its rapid industrialization and urbanization have placed unyielding pressure on the sacred stream. He also describes the work of the Indian environmentalist Rakesh Jaiswal, who has spent the last 15 years waging a lonely battle to clean up the river.

In "Breathless in Brooklyn," Frank Koughan reports on an oil spill in Newtown Creek, a waterway that divides the New York City boroughs of Brooklyn and Queens. Between 17 and 30 million gallons of oil are believed to have seeped below the creek, dwarfing the size of the notorious spill that issued from the *Exxon Valdez* oil tanker. Some attribute the Newtown Creek disaster to a massive gasoline explosion in 1950, while city officials blame gradual leakage from a nearby Mobil refinery. Little has been done to clean up the spill, and residents of the Brooklyn neighborhood of Greenpoint suffer from more than just the foul air, as rates of cancer and other conditions are alarmingly high.

The authors of "Dangerous Waters" explore how harmful chemicals and infectious pathogens contaminate freshwater supplies and examine what can be done to provide the world's population with clean water. They also report on the United Nations' Millennium Development Goals, one of which is to reduce the number of people who lack adequate water and sanitation.

In the final article, "Water," from the *New Internationalist*, the author lists six facts about water consumption over the last 40 years, presenting a dire portrait of water misuse, pollution, and climate change.

Sold Down the River

By Eleanor J. Sterling and Merry D. Camhi
Natural History, November 2007

The banks of the Mekong River in Vientiane, the capital of Laos, can be a lovely retreat at sunset. The river sweeps alongside the city in a wide elbow curve, offering a panoramic view of tranquil waters and tree-lined shores. Thailand rests on the opposite bank, seeming farther away than its half-mile distance. And as the setting sun lights the water ablaze, birds skim the surface, and fish make themselves known with the occasional splash, making an evening walk along the riverbank a pure delight.

At the start of a recent visit to Vientiane, however, one of us (Sterling) wound her way through the city to the river, anticipating a cool breeze and a quiet walk after a sweltering workday, only to stare into a scene from the desert. Clouds of dust rose from the riverbed, where a group of kids were playing soccer. Beyond that bone-dry sandbar, a vestige of the river was just visible as a thin stream along the far bank. By all appearances, one could easily have walked across to Thailand.

Such radical fluctuations are natural to the Mekong, and whole communities—human and wild—are adapted to its periodic floods and droughts. The river swells when rainfall rushes down its tributaries and shrinks again in drier weather. But the rise and fall of the Mekong is increasingly dictated by energy use in China and Thailand. Upriver hydroelectric dams dampen the fluctuations and change the timing of floods and dry spells, affecting water-dependent wildlife hundreds of miles away. The extent of those changes is likely to grow as more dams, scheduled for construction, make their mark on the river.

The dams are just one of the many troubles that confront the river and its denizens; water extractions, pollution, invasive species, and overfishing also threaten the ecosystem's health. And the Mekong's woes mirror those of freshwater systems worldwide, which are increasingly pressured by a growing human population that makes ever-greater water demands. The scale is enormous: people now appropriate more than half of the world's accessible surface freshwater, leaving precious little for natural systems and other species to thrive.

As a result, even as the human population of the globe has doubled, many species that depend on freshwater ecosystems have suffered steep declines. The list would bring tears to a conservationist's eyes: in the past three decades, a fifth of the world's water birds, a third of freshwater mammals, a third of amphibians, and more than half of freshwater turtles and crocodiles have become either threatened, endangered, or extinct. Freshwater fishes represent a quarter of the world's living vertebrate species, and yet more than a third are threatened or endangered. The ecology of freshwater systems may be irreversibly damaged if we humans don't improve the way we treat them.

The Mekong's name translates from Lao as "mother of the waters." It's no wonder: the river snakes some 3,000 miles from its headwaters on the Tibetan Plateau to its outlet through the Mekong River Delta into the South China Sea. It and the uncountable "feeder" rivers and streams in Cambodia, China, Laos, Myanmar, Thailand, and Vietnam make up the 300,000-square-mile Mekong River Basin.

That mesh of waterways is one of the most productive and diverse ecosystems on Earth, supporting more than 6,000 species of vertebrates alone. Its fish fauna, with some 2,000 species, of which sixty-two are endemic, exceeds all but those of the Amazon and Congo river basins. The wetlands harbor several threatened and endangered birds and mammals, including the eastern sarus crane, Grus antigone sharpii; the Bengal florican, *Houbaropsis bengalensis*; and the hairy-nosed otter, *Lutra sumatrana*, which was recently rediscovered after having been feared extinct. Sixty-five million people live there, too, 80 percent of them dependent on the river for their livelihood as farmers and fishers.

The Mekong River Basin is a microcosm of the Earth's freshwater resources—it includes almost all of the natural forms freshwater takes on Earth: groundwater, lakes, ponds, streams, and wetlands. (Wetlands are defined as shallow, often intermittently wet habitats, such as bogs, floodplains, marshes, and swamps.) Together, freshwater ecosystems cover less than 1 percent of the Earth's surface and hold a mere 0.008 percent of its water, but they support about 100,000 animal species—an inordinately large number for their size relative to marine and terrestrial habitats. That freshwater fauna includes a third of all known vertebrates and a whopping 40 percent of all known fish species.

Their rich biodiversity aside, freshwater systems bestow untold—and underappreciated—benefits on people. Indeed, they are the very foundation of our lives and economies. The value of all the services freshwater ecosystems provide worldwide, such as drinking water, irrigation for agriculture, and climate regulation, has been estimated at $70 billion per year—a figure that assumes, rather delusionally, that one could purchase the services elsewhere if they became unavailable in nature.

Dams are a dramatic example of a human activity that degrades freshwater ecosystems. Built to control flooding, store water, and generate electricity, dams have numerous ecologically disastrous side effects. They impede the movement and migration of aquatic species; some kill animals in turbines; and they change the timing and amount of flow downriver, which interferes with the reproductive cycles of fishes, frogs, and water birds that depend on seasonal flooding.

About a dozen hydroelectric dams in the Mekong River Basin provide the bulk of the region's energy—and another hundred or so are in the planning stages. To date, China has built two dams across the upper mainstream, but there are none across the lower mainstream—in fact, the Mekong is one of the world's few major rivers with so few mainstream dams. That may soon change: local governments view the free-flowing Mekong as an underutilized economic resource. Worldwide, an average of two large dams have gone up each day for the past fifty years, and today there are more than 45,000 dams taller than forty-five feet. Fortunately, increased awareness of the environmental problems they cause has contributed to a slowdown of large-dam construction in the United States and Europe. In the Mekong River Basin and elsewhere, however, big dams continue to rise.

> Dams are a dramatic example of a human activity that degrades freshwater ecosystems.

Species along the Mekong, as in other freshwater systems, depend on natural flood cycles for nutrients and for transportation to and from spawning grounds. More than 90 percent of the fish species in the Mekong watershed spawn not in rivers, but in seasonal lakes or periodically flooded forests and fields. Flow patterns altered by dams and other projects could prevent those species from reproducing. In addition to building dams, countries along the Mekong are destroying or modifying rapids and other natural features to improve navigation—changes that will disturb critical fish habitats and alter downstream water flow.

Another destructive practice is crop irrigation, the biggest consumer of freshwater both along the Mekong and worldwide. Most of the water withdrawn from the Mekong goes to irrigating crops, mainly rice. Demand for irrigation water has risen dramatically in the past decade, as new acreage has come under cultivation and new irrigation schemes have enabled farmers to produce a second or third rice crop each year. Removing so much water from freshwater systems can be devastating for wildlife, exacerbating flow problems caused by upstream dams.

Worldwide, irrigation guzzles about 70 percent of the freshwater people use. To grow food for expanding human populations, people divert rivers, drain inland seas, and extract fossil groundwater collected over thousands of years, often at unsustainable rates. Worse, current agricultural practices often waste as much water as they use: about half the water that flows through conventional irrigation systems never actually reaches a crop plant. A lesser—though still formidable—amount of water is siphoned off to slake the thirst of cities and industry, and when you add it all together, it's clear that people are using more than their fair share. The Mekong still manages to reach the sea. But at least ten other major rivers, including the Colorado, Ganges, Jordan, Nile, Rio Grande, and Yellow, now regularly run dry before they reach their outlets.

Agriculture, in addition to being the greatest consumer of freshwater, is also a major polluter—another bane for wildlife. In the Mekong River Basin, agriculture relies heavily on pesticides and fertilizers; it also drives deforestation, which causes erosion. Chemical, nutrient, and sediment runoff from farms winds up in the Mekong River Delta, where it degrades water quality, shifts natural nutrient cycles, and alters wildlife habitat. The six nations in the Mekong watershed have initiated a regional program to encourage agricultural development. If not done mindfully, the accelerated development could worsen water quality.

Other countries are already contending with the effects of major pollution. Fertilizer, pesticide, and livestock-waste runoff from farms in the American Midwest, for example, have created a dead zone at the mouth of the Mississippi River in the Gulf of Mexico. There, coastal algae populations thrive on the influx of nutrients and the misfortune of their natural predators, which are often curtailed by the pesticides. From spring until late summer, immense algal blooms rob the Gulf's water of oxygen. Such hypoxic conditions chase the swimming creatures away and kill clams and other sedentary species on the spot. The Gulf's seasonal dead zone now encompasses more than 8,000 square miles, an area the size of New Jersey, every spring and summer. Much smaller dead zones occur on the Mekong, too. Worldwide, there are 146, every one increasing in size, intensity, and often duration.

Besides agricultural runoff, pollution from industry and municipalities is also a big problem for freshwater systems. In addition to contributing extra nutrients that promote algal overgrowth, municipal wastewater also carries thousands of chemicals from products used in daily life: cosmetics, soaps, pharmaceuticals, cleaning supplies, and more. Most of it winds up in aquatic systems.

The long-term consequences of dumping so many chemicals in the water are just coming to light. More than 200 species are thought to have adverse reactions to endocrine disruptors—such as estrogen and its chemical mimics—that get into the environment via human and veterinary pharmaceuticals in wastewater and farm runoff. Sightings of frogs with deformities, such as extra legs, mushroomed in the Midwest about a decade ago. Ecologists think chemicals or an interaction between chemicals and parasites could be causing the deformities. Indeed, chemicals in freshwater may be a factor in the alarmingly sharp worldwide decline of amphibians.

Biological introductions to waterways, like chemical introductions, are extremely problematic. In their own communities, most species are held in check by natural predators or other environmental constraints. But organisms from afar can crowd, devour, or outcompete native species in their new neighborhoods, and can even change entire ecosystems. Most biological introductions by people are accidental, but some, such as fishes stocked for anglers or plants brought in to stabilize soils, are intentional.

Mimosa pigra, a spiny shrub native to the Americas and planted abroad as an ornamental or to control erosion, is now one of the world's worst aquatic invasive species. Once established, it quickly forms dense stands and outcompetes native plants. First spotted on the Mekong in 1979, it spreads in floodwaters and in truckloads of construction sand, and is now devastating parts of the watershed. The mimosa has taken over several irreplaceable wetlands, doubling its area almost every year in some places. Several endangered water birds that depend on native grasses for food and shelter are undergoing population declines as mimosa stands replace their habitat.

Controlling freshwater invaders and mitigating the damage they cause costs some 9 billion dollars each year in the U.S. alone. Yet the rate of invasions everywhere is on the rise as global commerce, trade, and travel increase.

So much for the organisms people add to freshwater systems. What about the ones—too many—that we take out? Overexploitation for food, medicine, and recreation poses a major threat to freshwater birds, crocodiles, fishes, frogs, and turtles, as well as some invertebrates. More than 40 million people rely on the waters of the Mekong River Basin for their protein and income, and they are overfishing numerous species—indeed entire fish assemblages in certain areas—as a result.

The Mekong giant catfish, *Pangasianodon gigas*, is just one of the region's struggling, overfished residents. Reaching nine feet in length and more than 600 pounds, it is the world's largest catfish. With such grand proportions, a jackpot of succulent flesh that once sold at a premium to urban restaurants, the giant catfish was a fisherman's prize catch. In the mid-twentieth century, hundreds of giant catfish—a naturally rare species—were caught each year, but recently the annual catch has declined to fewer than ten. Overfishing is the main cause of the decline, but habitat fragmentation and alteration of spawning grounds by dams and navigation projects also contribute. Today, the giant catfish is critically endangered, its range is greatly restricted, and the average size of individuals is declining. In recent years, Cambodia, Laos, and Thailand have outlawed catching the giant catfish. But the species is migratory, so a regional agreement may be necessary to prevent its demise.

Fish aren't the only victims of overexploitation. As many as 10,000 water snakes are fished from Tonle Sap Lake each day. The water snakes mainly go to feed hungry crocodiles raised for commercial export; they substitute for fish, whose populations have declined. People are fishing down the food chain in the Mekong River Basin, as in so many freshwater and marine systems. After depleting the top predators and the largest species, fishermen turn their nets on successively smaller organisms.

The upshot of all those assaults is that freshwater organisms rank among the world's most threatened species. Data on global trends are sparse, but what biologists do know paints a bleak picture of striking declines across taxa. Freshwater dragonflies, damselflies, mussels, fishes, amphibians, reptiles, birds, and mammals—all are suffering. To prevent a wave of irreversible extinctions and ecosystem collapses, people need to take better care of fragile freshwater habitats.

Fortunately, there is much people can do. We can remove obsolete dams and design new ones that take into account natural patterns of river flow. We can reduce the need for massive water extractions by changing the way we grow our food and our cities; more efficient irrigation techniques and increased capture of rainwater, even in wet areas, would help. Conservation may be the best "new" source of water, particularly as climate change begins to shift water supplies globally. We can start to reduce our polluting ways by avoiding harmful chemicals in the first place. In the end, keeping more water in freshwater habitats and maintaining its quality must be a top global priority.

The future of the Mekong lies in the balance. Today, it remains one of the world's least-degraded large rivers, but the primacy of economic growth threatens to tip the balance towards decline across the entire river system. Still, there are hopeful signs. Several transboundary initiatives are in the works among the six nations that share the Mekong, which should help balance the needs of people and wildlife. Then there's the Mekong River Commission. Formed in the 1950s, the commission has moved away from its original focus on dams and irrigation projects toward more holistic management that takes environmental health into consideration. But the MRC is only as strong as the resolve of the governments it represents; China and Myanmar are not members, which may undermine its effectiveness in protecting the basin.

Internationally, the Ramsar Convention on Wetlands, with 155 signatory nations, guides conservation of 1,675 globally important wetland ecosystems. As with the Mekong River Commission, however, Ramsar's strength rests on the decisions of its signatories: it has no enforcement mechanism. It should come as no surprise, then, that—as with conservation choices in general—most decision makers have consistently chosen short-term economic gain over the long-term health of aquatic systems.

Current societies value few things more than gold. But though one can survive, even live well, without gold, the same is not true for water. Ultimately, the true value of gold is reduced to this: it can buy you fresh, clean water—if there's any for sale.

Troubled Waters

By Mary Carmichael, Sarah Schafer, and Sudip Mazumdar
Newsweek, June 4, 2007

Daily life in the developed world has depended so much, for so long, on clean water that it is sometimes easy to forget how precious a commodity water is. The average American citizen doesn't have to work for his water; he has only to turn on the tap. But in much of the rest of the world, it isn't that simple. More than a billion people worldwide, lack clean water, most of them in developing countries. The least fortunate may devote whole days to finding some.

When they fail—and they fail more and more often now that rivers in Africa and Asia are slowly drying up after decades of mismanagement and climate change—they may turn to violence, fighting over the small amount that is left. Water has long been called the ultimate renewable resource. But as Fred Pearce writes in his book "When the Rivers Run Dry," if the world doesn't change, that saying may no longer apply.

Like the famines of the '80s, the global water crisis is far more than a straightforward issue of scarcity. Accidents of geography, forces of industry and the machinations of politics may all play a role in who gets water—just as warlords, as well as droughts, were responsible for starvation in Ethiopia. In many ways, the famines contributed to today's man-made droughts: the crops grown in the worldwide "green revolution" of the past three decades sated hunger but sapped water in the process. "As the globe gets more crowded," says Susan Cozzens, a policy professor at Georgia Tech who is working on water problems, the old arrangements just don't work anymore.

There is still time for nonprofits and governments to fix things. "Chlorination, gravity-fed distribution systems, taps at every household, all these could make a difference," says John Kayser of Water for People, a nonprofit working in the developing world. Ecoconscious start-ups in the United States and Europe are increasingly offering new ways of purifying water, from high-tech (but inexpensive) ultra-violet filters to simple tactics such as filling clear bottles and letting the hot sun kill the bacteria inside.

But thus far, there has been no worldwide "blue revolution." More likely, says Pearce, we'll "only really start to worry about the water when it isn't there." Here are some flashpoints, regions where the future of water is most worrisome.

China's Poisoned Water.

To look at the mighty Yangtze River, you might think China could not have a water crisis. The third longest river in the world, it funnels 8 million gallons into the East China Sea every second. The river drives the world's largest hydroelectric dam, the Three Gorges, and it is one of the backbones of the country's economy.

When you look more deeply into China's water supply, however, you'll see plenty to worry about. The government has long known that the Yangtze is polluted. In 2002, Beijing announced a $5 billion cleanup effort, but last year admitted that the river was still so burdened with agricultural and industrial waste that by 2011 it may be unable to sustain marine life, much less human life. An April report by the World Wildlife Fund and two Chinese agencies found that damage to the river's ecosystem is largely irreversible.

> Nowhere is China's pollution problem more visible than in the tiny cancer villages" that dot the country's interior.

Travel farther north, especially near the country's other major water system, the Yellow River, and the picture is even bleaker. Since the 1980s, drought and overuse have diminished the river to a relative trickle. Most of the year, little to none of its water reaches the sea, says Pearce. What does still flow in the Yellow is often unsuitable for drinking, fishing, swimming or any other form of human use. Every day, the river absorbs 1 million tons of untreated sewage from the city of Xian alone.

Nowhere is China's pollution problem more visible than in the tiny "cancer villages" that dot the country's interior. Shangba, a town of 3,000, captured national attention a few years ago after tests found that heavy metals in its local river far exceeded government levels. Officials from a nearby state-owned mine—suspected of dumping those chemicals into the water—persuaded the government to pay for a new reservoir and water system built by locals. But other, smaller cancer villages are still struggling. In the southern hamlet of Liangqiao, rice grown by villagers with water from a local river has taken on the reddish hue of contaminants from the same iron mine that blighted Shangba. Since the late 1990s, cancer has caused about two thirds of the 26 deaths in the village. "We have to use the polluted water to irrigate the fields, since we have no other choices. We don't have any money to start a water project," says Liangqiao resident He Chunxiang. "We know very well that we are being poisoned by eating the grain. What more can we do? We can't just wait to starve to death."

There is hope yet for Liangqiao. Environmental lawyer Zhang Jingjing is filing a lawsuit against the mine on behalf of the villagers, and she has a strategy that focuses on loss of crops instead of loss of life. (Chinese courts are often reluctant to link cancer to pollution.) But win or lose, Liangqiao is a tiny part of the problem. It has just 320 people. Meanwhile, almost 400 million Chinese, fully a third of the country's population, still have no access to water that is clean enough for regular use.

India's "Hydrological Suicide."

In this country of 1.1 billion, two thirds lack clean water. "Sanitation for drinking water is a low priority there, politically," says Susan Egan Keane of the Natural Resources Defense Council. The priority is agriculture. In the '70s and early '80s, the Indian government made this clear by pouring money into massive dams meant to pool water reserved for farms. "In many of these developing countries, the vast majority of their fresh water goes to irrigation for crops," says Egan Keane. "Agriculture may make up only 25 percent of the GDP, but it can get up to 90 percent of the water."

That's not to say, however, that India's farmers have enough. They are actually running low. The government built dams, but it failed to create the additional infrastructure for carrying water throughout the countryside. At the same time, factories have drawn too heavily on both the rivers and the groundwater. In Kerala, a Coca-Cola plant had to be shut down in 2004 because it had taken so much groundwater that villagers nearby were left with almost none.

Some farmers have reacted wisely to the dropping water levels by switching to hardier crops. Kantibhai Patel says he stopped growing wheat on his farm in Gujarat, the epicenter of India's water shortage, after eight years of watching his bounty and income shrivel in the sun. He farms pomegranates now, which require far less water than wheat. Experts hope more farmers will follow Patel's lead. So far, most farms still focus on water-guzzling crops like wheat, cotton and sugar cane. Indian dairy farmers also cultivate alfalfa, a particularly thirsty plant, to feed their cows, a practice Pearce calls "hydrological suicide." For every liter of milk the farmers produce in the desert, they consume 300 liters of water, says Saniv Phansalkar, a scholar at the International Water Management Institute. "But who is going to ask them not to earn their livelihood," he asks, if the dairy farms are keeping them afloat for now?

To nourish their plants and cows, most Indian farmers have resorted to drawing up groundwater from their backyards with inexpensive pumps. When the pumps don't bring up enough water, the farmers bring in professionals who bore deeper into the ground. There is constant pressure to compete. "If one [farmer] is digging 400 feet into the ground, his fellow farmer is digging at least 600 feet," says Kuppannan Palanisami, who studies the problem at Tamil Nadu Agricultural University. The water table, he says, drops six to 10 feet each year.

The West Bank's Water Wars.

Like the Chinese, the people of the West Bank wouldn't have a huge water problem if nature were the only force involved. Rain falls regularly on their hills and trickles down into the rocks, creating underground reservoirs. Unfortunately for denizens of the West Bank, that water then flows west toward Israel. Palestinians are largely banned from sinking new wells and boreholes to collect water, and they pay what they consider inflated prices to buy it. Meanwhile, the groundwater level is dropping, and Palestinians accuse Israelis of overusing. "[The Palestinians] sit in their villages, very short on water," says Pearce, "and they look up at their neighbors and see them sprinkling it on their lawns."

Battling over water in this region is nothing new—the Six Day War started with a dispute over water in the Jordan. Lately, on the West Bank, the water table is dropping and tensions are rising. Israeli soldiers have been accused of shooting up water tanks on the West Bank in retribution for terrorist acts, and Palestinians have been caught stealing from Israeli wells.

It is impossible to untangle the water problem in Israel and the Palestinian Authority from the overall animosity between the two groups. Conversely, says Pearce, "the wider problem between the Palestinians and the Israelis won't be solved until the water problem is solved." On the West Bank, it's a Catch-22, with water—and life—on the line.

A Prayer for the Ganges

By Joshua Hammer
Smithsonian, November 2007

A blue stream spews from beneath brick factory buildings in Kanpur, India. The dark, ribbon curls down a dirt embankment and flows into the Ganges River. "That's toxic runoff," says Rakesh Jaiswal, a 48-year-old environmental activist, as he leads me along the refuse-strewn riverbank in the vise-like heat of a spring afternoon. We're walking through the tannery district, established along the Ganges during British colonial rule and now Kanpur's economic mainstay as well as its major polluter.

I had expected to find a less-than-pristine stretch of river in this grimy metropolis of four million people, but I'm not prepared for the sights and smells that greet me. Jaiswal stares grimly at the runoff—it's laden with chromium sulfate, used as a leather preservative and associated with cancer of the respiratory tract, skin ulcers and renal failure. Arsenic, cadmium, mercury, sulfuric acid, chemical dyes and heavy metals can also be found in this witches' brew. Though Kanpur's tanneries have been required since 1994 to do preliminary cleanup before channeling wastewater into a government-run treatment plant, many ignore the costly regulation. And whenever the electricity fails or the government's waste conveyance system breaks own, even tanneries that abide by the law find that their untreated wastewater backs up and spills into the river.

A few yards upstream, we follow a foul odor to a violent flow of untreated domestic sewage gushing into the river from an old brick pipe. The bubbling torrent is full of fecal microorganisms responsible for typhoid, cholera and amoebic dysentery. Ten million to 12 million gallons of raw sewage have been pouring out of this drainpipe each day, Jaiswal tells me, since the main sewer line leading to the treatment plant in Kanpur became clogged—five years ago. "We've been protesting against this, and begging the [Uttar Pradesh state] government to take action, but they've done nothing," he says.

Half a dozen young fishermen standing by a rowboat offer to take us to a sandbar in the middle of the Ganges for "a better view." Jaiswal and I climb into the boat and cross the shallow river only to run aground 50 yards from the sandbar. "You have to get out and walk from here," a boatman tells us. We remove our shoes, roll up our trousers and nervously wade knee-deep in the toxic stream. As we reach the sandbar, just downstream from a Hindu cremation ground, we're hit by a putrid smell and a ghastly sight: lying on the sand are a human rib cage, a femur, and, nearby, a yellow-shrouded corpse. "It's been rotting there for a month," a fisherman tells us. The clothed body of a small child floats a few yards off the island. Although the state government banned the dumping of bodies a decade ago, many of Kanpur's destitute still discard their loved ones clandestinely at night. Pariah dogs prowl around the bones and bodies, snarling when we get too close. "They live on the sandbar, feeding on the remains," a fisherman tells us.

> Pariah dogs prowl around the bones and bodies, snarling when we get too close.

Sickened, I climb back into the rowboat. As we near the tanneries, a dozen boys frolic in the water, splashing in the river's foulest stretch. Jaiswal calls them over.

"Why do you swim in the river?" I ask one of the boys. "Aren't you worried?"

He shrugs. "We know it's poisonous," he says, "but after we swim we go wash off at home."

"Do you ever get ill?"

"We all get rashes," he replies, "but what can we do?"

Walking back toward the main road, Jaiswal seems despondent. "I would never have imagined the River Ganga could get like this, with stinking water, green and brown colored," he says. "It's pure toxic muck."

I shake my head at the irony. For more than two millennia, the River Ganges has been revered by millions as a symbol of spiritual purity. Originating in the frozen heights of the Himalayas, the river travels 1,600 miles across the teeming plains of the subcontinent before flowing east into Bangladesh and from there spilling into the Bay of Bengal. "Mother Ganga" is described by ancient Hindu scriptures as a gift from the gods—the earthly incarnation of the deity Ganga. "Man becomes pure by the touch of the water, or by consuming it, or by expressing its name," Lord Vishnu, the four-armed "All Pervading One," proclaims in the *Ramayana*, the Sanskrit epic poem composed four centuries before Christ. Modern admirers have written paeans to the river's beauty, historical resonance and holiness. "The Ganges is above all the river of India, which has held India's heart captive and drawn uncounted millions to her banks since the dawn of history," Jawaharlal Nehru, India's first prime minister, proclaimed.

For some time now, this romantic view of the Ganges has collided with India's grim realities. During the past three decades, the country's explosive growth (at nearly 1.2 billion people, India's population is second only to China's), industrialization and rapid urbanization have put unyielding pressure on the sacred stream. Irrigation canals siphon off ever more of its water and its many tributaries to grow food for the country's hungry millions. Industries in the country operate in a regulatory climate that has changed little since 1984, when a Union Carbide pesticide plant in the northern city of Bhopal leaked 27 tons of deadly methyl isocyanate gas and killed 20,000 people. And the amount of domestic sewage being dumped into the Ganges has doubled since the 1990s; it could double again in a generation.

The result has been the gradual killing of one of India's most treasured resources. One stretch of the Yamuna River, the Ganges' main tributary, has been devoid of all aquatic creatures for a decade. In Varanasi, India's most sacred city, the coliform bacterial count is at least 3,000 times higher than the standard established as safe by the United Nations World Health Organization, according to Veer Bhadra Mishra, an engineer and Hindu priest who's led a campaign there to clean the river for two decades. "Polluted river water is the biggest cause of skin problems, disabilities and high infant mortality rates," says Suresh Babu, deputy coordinator of the River Pollution Campaign at the Center for Science and the Environment, a watchdog group in New Delhi, India's capital. These health problems are compounded by the fact that many Hindus refuse to accept that Mother Ganga has become a source of illness. "People have so much faith in this water that when they bathe in it or sip it, they believe it is the nectar of God (and) they will go to heaven," says Ramesh Chandra Trivedi, a scientist at the Central Pollution Control Board, the monitoring arm of India's Ministry of the Environment and Forests.

Twenty years ago, then prime minister Rajiv Gandhi launched the Ganga Action Plan, or GAP, which shut down some of the most egregious industrial polluters and allocated about $100 million for constructing wastewater treatment plants in 25 cities and towns along the river. But these efforts have fallen woefully short. According to a 2001-2002 government survey the treatment plants could handle only about a third of the 600 million gallons of domestic sewage that poured into them every day. (The volume has increased significantly since then.) Many environmentalists say that the Ganges has become an embarrassing symbol of government indifference and neglect in a country that regards itself as an economic superpower. "We can send a shuttle into space, we can build the [new] Delhi Metro [subway] in record time. We can detonate nuclear weapons. So why can't we clean up our rivers?" Jaiswal laments. "We have money. We have competence. The only problem is that the issue is not a priority for the Indian government."

Early in 2007 the Ganges' worsening state made headlines around the world when Hindu holy men, known as *sadhus*, organized a mass protest against river filth during the Kumbh Mela festival. "The river had turned the color of Coca-Cola," says scientist Trivedi, who attended the festival and, against the advice of his colleagues at the Central Pollution Control Board, took a brief dip in the Ganges. ("I was not affected at all," he insists.) The sadhus called off the protests after the government opened dams upstream, diluting

the fetid water, and ordered another 150 upstream industrial polluters to close. "But it was a short-term solution," says Suresh Babu.
"It didn't achieve anything."

This past May, I followed Mother Ganga downstream for 800
miles, half its distance, to witness its deterioration firsthand and to
meet the handful of environmentalists who are trying to rouse public action. I began my journey high in the foothills of the Himalayas,
200 miles south of the river's glacial source. Here the cold, pristine
water courses through a steep gorge cloaked in gray-green forests of
Shorea rohusta, or sal trees. From a beach at the edge of a litchi
grove below the Glass House, an inn where I stayed, I watched rafts
of helmet-clad adventure-tourists sweep past on a torrent of white
water.

Fifteen miles downriver, at Rishikesh, the valley widens, and the
Ganges spills onto the northern Indian plain. Rishikesh achieved
worldwide attention in 1968, when the Beatles, at the height of
their fame, spent three months at the now-abandoned ashram, or
meditation center, run by the guru Maharishi Mahesh Yogi (who
today resides in the Netherlands). Built illegally on public land and
confiscated by the government in the 1970s, the ruined complex
rises on a thickly wooded hillside overlooking the Ganges. The place
has been unoccupied ever since it was seized—an intragovernmen-
tal dispute has prevented its being sold or developed as a tourist
resort—but I gave 50 rupees, about $1.25, to a guard, and he
unlocked the gate for me. I wandered among derelict, stupa-like
meditation chambers high above the river, which still conveyed a
sense of tranquillity. Baboons prowled the ghostly hallways of the
Maharishi's once-luxurious hotel and conference center, which was
topped by three domes tiled in white mosaic. The only sounds were
the chorusing of cuckoos and the cawing of ravens.

It's unlikely the surviving Beatles would recognize the busy, lit-
ter-strewn tourist town that Rishikesh has become. Down below the
ashram, I strolled through a riverside strip of pilgrims' inns, cheap
restaurants selling banana lassis and pancakes, and newly built
yoga schools. A boat packed with Indian pilgrims, wild-haired
sadhus and Western backpackers ferried me across the river, where
I walked past dozens of storefronts offering rafting trips and Hima-
layan treks. A budding boom over the past two decades has generated a flood of pollutants and nonbiodegradable trash. Each day
thousands of pilgrims drop flowers in polyethylene bags into the
river as offerings to Goddess Ganga. Six years ago, Jitendra Kumar,
a local ashram student, formed Clean Himalaya, a nonprofit environmental group that gathers and recycles tons of garbage from
hotels and ashrams every day. But public apathy and a shortage of
burning and dumping facilities have made the job difficult. "It's
really sad," Vipin Sharma, who runs a rafting and trekking company (Red Chdi Adventures), told me. "All of our Hindus come with
this feeling that they want to give something to the Ganga, and
they've turned it into a sea of plastic."

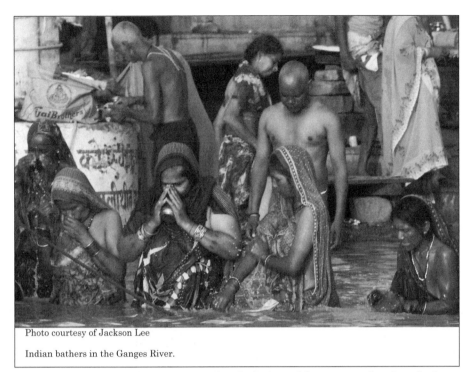

Photo courtesy of Jackson Lee

Indian bathers in the Ganges River.

From his base in Kanpur, Rakesh Jaiswal has waged a lonely battle to clean up the river for almost 15 years. He was born in Mirzapur, 200 miles downstream from Kanpur, and remembers his childhood as an idyllic time. "I used to go there to bathe with my mother and grandmother, and it was beautiful," he told me. "I didn't even know what the word 'pollution' meant." Then, one day in the early 1990s, while studying for his doctorate in environmental politics, "I opened the tap at home and found black, viscous, stinking water coming out. After one month it happened again, then it was happening once a week, then daily. My neighbors experienced the same thing." Jaiswal traced the drinking water to an intake channel on the Ganges. There he made a horrifying discovery: two drains carrying raw sewage, including contaminated discharge from a tuberculosis sanitarium, were emptying right beside the intake point. "Fifty million gallons a day were being lifted and sent to the water-treatment plant, which couldn't clean it. It was horrifying."

At the time, the Indian government was touting the first phase of its Ganga Action Plan as a success. Jaiswal knew otherwise. Kanpur's wastewater treatment plants broke down frequently and could process only a small percentage of the sewage the city was producing. Dead bodies were being dumped into the river by the hundreds every week, and most of the 400 tanneries continued to pour toxic runoff into the river. Jaiswal, who started a group called EcoFriends in 1993 and the next year received a small grant from the Indian government, used public outrage over contaminated drinking water to mobilize a protest campaign. He organized rallies and enlisted volunteers in a river cleanup that fished 180 bodies out of a mile-long stretch of the Ganges. "The idea was to sensitize the people, galvanize the government, find a long-term solution, but we failed to evoke much interest," he told me. Jaiswal kept up the pressure. In 1997, state and local government whistle-blowers slipped him a list of factories that had ignored a court order to install treatment plants; the state ordered the shutdown of 250 factories, including 127 tanneries in Kanpur. After that, he says, "I got midnight phone calls telling me, 'you will be shot dead if you don't stop these things.' But I had friends in the police and army who believed in my work, so I never felt my life was in real danger."

Jaiswal's battle to clean up the Ganges has achieved some successes. Largely because of his corpse-cleanup drive, a cemetery was established beside the Ganges—it now contains thousands of bodies—and a ban was enforced, obviously often violated, on "floaters." In 2000, the second phase of the Ganga Action Plan required 100 large- and medium-sized Kanpu tanneries to set up chrome-recovery facilities and 100 smaller ones to build a common chrome-recovery unit. Enforcement, however, has been lax. Ajay Kanaujia, a government chemist at Kanpur's wastewater treatment facility, says that "some tanneries are still putting chrome into the river without any treatment or dumping it into the domestic sewage system." This treated sewage is then channeled into canals that irrigate 6,000 acres of farmland near Kanpur before flowing back into the Ganges. India's National Botanical Research Institute, a government body has tested agricultural and dairy products in the Kanpur area and found that they contain high levels of chromium and arsenic. "The irrigation water is dangerous," Kanaujia says.

I'm in a motorboat at dawn, putt-putting down the Ganges in Varanasi, where the river takes a turn north before flowing into the Bay of Bengal. Called Benares by the British, this ancient pilgrimage center is the holiest city in India: millions of Hindus come each year to a three-mile-long curve of temples, shrines and bathing ghats (steps leading down to the river) along its banks. With a boatman and a young guide, I cruise past a Hindu Disneyland of Mogul-era sandstone fortresses and green, purple and candycane-striped temples. None of the pilgrims sudsing themselves in the Ganges, bobbing blissfully in inner tubes or beating their laundry on wooden planks, seem to pay the slightest attention to the bloated cow carcasses that float beside them—or to the untreated waste that gushes directly into the river. If toxic industrial runoff is Kanpur's special curse, the befouling of the Ganges as it flows past the Hindus' holiest city comes almost entirely from human excreta.

The boat deposits me at Tulsi Ghat, near the upriver entrance to Varanasi, and in the intensifying morning heat, I walk up a steep flight of steps to the Sankat Mochan Foundation, which, for the past two decades, has led Varanasi's clean-river campaign. The foundation occupies several crumbling buildings, including a 400-year-old Hindu temple high over the Ganges. I find the foundation's director,

Veer Bhadra Mishra, 68, sitting on a huge white cushion that takes up three-quarters of a reception room on the temple's ground floor. Draped in a simple white *dhoti*, he invites me to enter.

Mishra looks at the river from a unique perspective: he is a retired professor of hydraulic engineering at Banaras Hindu University and a *mohan*, a Hindu high priest at the Sankat Mochan Temple, a title that the Mishra family has passed from father to eldest son for seven generations. Mishra has repeatedly called the Ganga Action Plan a failure, saying that it has frittered away billions of rupees on ill-designed and badly maintained wastewater treatment plants. "The moment the electricity fails, the sewage flows into the river, and on top of that, when the floodwaters rise, they enter the sump well of the sewer system pumps and stop operations for months of the year," he tells me. (Varanasi currently receives only about 12 hours of power a day.) Moreover, he says, engineers designed the plants to remove solids, but not fecal microorganisms, from the water. The pathogens, channeled from treatment plants into irrigation canals, seep back into the groundwater, where they enter the drinking-water supply and breed such diseases as dysentery, as well as skin infections.

A decade ago, Mishra, with hydraulic engineers and scientists at the University of California at Berkeley, designed a water-treatment scheme that, he says, is far better suited to Varanasi's needs. Known as an "advanced integrated wastewater pond system," the process relies primarily on gravity to carry domestic sewage three miles downstream to four huge pools where oxygen-enriched bacteria break it down and pathogens are killed by sunlight and natural atmospheric action in a "maturation" pond. The projected cost of the system, which has been endorsed by the Varanasi municipal government, is $60 million.

Mishra was named one of *Time* magazine's Heroes of the Planet in 1999; in 2000, President Clinton praised him for his environmental work. But in spite of the honors that have come his way, Mishra has grown discouraged. The national government and the state government of Uttar Pradesh, which would have to fund the wastewater project, have openly opposed it on grounds ranging from doubts about the proposed technology to objections that treatment ponds would lie in a flood plain.

Meanwhile, the city's population keeps growing—it has doubled to three million in a generation—along with the bacteria count. Mishra says he's especially concerned for the future of India's most devout Hindus, whose lives are entirely focused on Mother Ganga. He calls them an endangered species. "They want to touch the water, rub their bodies in the water, sip the water," he says, "and someday they will die because of it," admitting that he himself takes a dip in the river every morning. "If you tell them 'the Ganga is polluted,' they say, 'we don't want to hear that.' But if you take them to the places where open sewers are giving the river the night soil of the whole city, they say 'this is disrespect done to our mother, and it must be stopped.'"

But how? Suresh Babu of the Center for Science and the Environment in New Delhi believes that if municipalities were obliged to draw their drinking water from downstream rather than upstream, "they would feel an obligation" to keep the river clean. But growing pressures on the Ganges seem destined to outstrip all efforts to rescue it. By 2030, according to Babu, India will draw eight times the amount of water from the Ganges it does today in the same time, the population along the river and its tributaries—up to 400 million, or one-third of India's total population—could double. Trivedi admits that the government "lacks a single coherent plan" to clean up the river.

Rakesh Jaiswal tells me that after all the years of small achievements and large setbacks, he finds it difficult to remain optimistic. "My friends tell me I've made a difference, but the river looks worse today than when I started," he says. In 2002, the Ford Foundation gave him enough money to hire 15 employees. But the next year, when the foundation cut its Environmental Equity and Justice Program, Jaiswal had to let his staff go and now works with one assistant out of a bedroom in his sister's house near the river. On his dresser stands a framed photograph of his wife, Gudrun Knoessel, who is German. In 2001, she contacted him after seeing a German TV documentary about his work; a long-distance courtship led to their marriage in 2003. They see each other two or three times a year. "She has a job in Baden-Baden," he explains. "And Kanpur needs me." So he often tells himself. But sometimes, in darker moments, he wonders if anybody really cares.

Breathless in Brooklyn

By Frank Koughan
Mother Jones, September/October 2007

Basil Seggos leans against the rail of the 36-foot harbor patrol boat as it chugs along Newtown Creek into an industrial wasteland of sewer pipes and flotsam, past a huge conveyor belt carrying skeletal cars to the scrap heap and a natural gas facility belching plumes of orange flame. A gentle headwind conveys the odors one at a time: salt, sewage, sulfur, and then the powerful stench of petroleum. "You can really smell it before you can see it," Seggos, the chief investigator for the environmental watchdog Riverkeeper, says, pointing to a black a metal bulkhead along the south bank. The boat draws closer, and a purple sheen appears on the surface. "That's all oil," he says. It's the bleeding edge of an environmental disaster, one of the largest oil spills in the world.

The discharge floating on this inland waterway, which divides the boroughs of Brooklyn and Queens, is just a hint at what lies beneath—anywhere between 17 million and 30 million gallons' worth, a spill more than 50 percent larger than the *Exxon Valdez*. But unlike the *Exxon Valdez*, this one has been allowed to grow and fester for half a century, directly below a residential area. Even in the neighborhood—an old-time blue-collar community pocked with hipster enclaves—many people don't know why the air smells like gasoline on rainy days.

"This is a working-class community with a dirty creek in a part of Brooklyn no one really cares about," Seggos says. "It would have perhaps been a better thing if these were river otters covered with oil. You'd have had immediate action."

No one's really sure how long the oil has been there, but most people point to a massive explosion that ripped through the city's sewer system in 1950, raining manhole covers down on the populace. City officials blamed gasoline leaking from what was then Mobil's Brooklyn refinery. Mobil denied it. That was pretty much the extent of the investigation, and for a couple of decades the oil quietly continued to drip into the soil and groundwater under the refinery, spreading beneath the neighborhood and oozing—a tenth of an inch every hour—toward the bank of Newtown Creek.

In 1978, a Coast Guard helicopter spotted an oil slick on the creek. Investigating further, the Guard discovered the 55-acre monster that had by then massed beneath the city. Chemical analysis fingered Mobil as the source, and again the company said it wasn't at fault. By now, Mobil had sold part of the refinery to Amoco and was using the rest for storage tanks. A few blocks away, a Texaco subsidiary also had a storage facility. The companies (now known as ExxonMobil, BP, and Chevron, respectively) pointed fingers at each other; government agencies, sensing that this was not a rumble they wanted to be involved in, did the same.

The Coast Guard, having spent half a million dollars investigating the spill, decided it had done enough; the case was turned over to the state of New York, which wanted no part of it either. Believing that the spill, while regrettable, posed no immediate hazard (no one drank the groundwater anymore, and the manhole-launching explosions had long ago subsided), officials decided not to apply their recently established oil spill fund to what was by far the state's largest oil spill, on the grounds that the spill predated the fund. So the buck was handed down to New York City—which, still reeling from its financial near-meltdown in the 1970s, chose not to do battle with a brace of oil company lawyers. For a decade, nothing happened. And the oil lake quietly grew.

"You become something of a stink connoisseur when you live in Greenpoint," says Teresa Toro, who lives two blocks from Newtown Creek. The neighborhood features rows of meticulously kept houses, manicured parks, and cafés catering to an influx of ex-Manhattanites, but it also remains the location of choice for projects that would never be placed along Fifth Avenue: sewage treatment, waste transfer, natural gas storage. For Toro, the oil fumes are the worst. "When the wind is just right, I can smell it blowing off the creek. Sometimes we can't open our windows.

Photo by Jim Henderson

The mouth of Newtown Creek in Brooklyn, New York.

"The [sewage treatment] plant people get very defensive when you call up and complain about the smell," Toro laughs. "They say, 'That's not us! It's the spill!'" But then she turns serious. "Every time I go to the creek, I just get so angry," she says. "I feel like I'm watching a crime in progress."

Local lore holds that it was the *Valdez* crash that finally shamed the state into action in 1990. "Not at all," says Joseph Lentol, the neighborhood's state assemblyman since 1972. The truth, he says, is worse: In 1988, Mobil had another leak—35,000 gallons—and felt the need to notify the city that, by the way, there happened to be 17 million gallons more underneath. The state's Department of Environmental Conservation began negotiating a consent order forcing Mobil to clean up its mess.

The deal, in the end, required no monetary damages, set no firm benchmarks for progress, and demanded removal of the oil floating on top of the groundwater but not of the contaminated soil. It also gave Mobil a powerful tool for staving off litigation—the company was, after all, complying with a government-mandated cleanup. "A consent decree is nothing more than another word for a plea bargain," says Lentol. "It was a slap on the wrist."

As time wore on, the people of Greenpoint would come to revile the environment department as much as, if not more than, the oil company itself. At least they weren't paying Mobil executives' salaries. A spokeswoman for the department, Maureen Wren, says the consent decree should be viewed in light of "the information available at that time" and that the state has always been committed to holding the company responsible. But by the time another decade had gone by, ExxonMobil and the other oil companies had removed less than 8 million gallons. There was no reason for them to pick up the pace. Until Riverkeeper showed up.

"We found out about it by stumbling across it, literally," Seggos says, recalling how he noticed the sheen on the water one day in 2002, while floating along Newtown Creek to educate immigrants about the dangers of fishing there. He assigned an intern to look into it and was soon presented with a fantastic-sounding story about a 17-million-gallon-plus underground lake of oil. "I said, 'You idiot! What the hell are you talking about? Go back and do more research!'" After almost another year of investigation, Seggos approached the state to see if Riverkeeper—a small, 41-year-old environmental group whose top attorney is Robert Kennedy Jr.—could help apply pressure on ExxonMobil. "They totally blew us off," he says.

In 2004, Riverkeeper notified the environment department that it planned to sue ExxonMobil, BP, and Chevron on behalf of a half-dozen local residents (including Teresa Toro). The suit sought no damages, only a proper cleanup. But behind the scenes, Seggos had begun laying the groundwork for a major toxic tort suit, facilitating a series of sometimes-awkward meetings between out-of-town trial lawyers and reticent locals. "It's a very difficult community to penetrate," he says.

That got a lot easier in the summer of 2005, when results of vapor tests Seggos had commissioned came back showing dangerous levels of explosive methane gas and benzene, a carcinogen. The neighborhood erupted as if the oil itself had been set ablaze. People who had long believed the spill to be merely a foul-smelling nuisance now began tallying the community's sick and its dead.

"It's up to 35 or 36 people that I know that have had cancer just on this block," says Tom Stagg, a retired detective who's lived near the spill his whole life. Sitting at his kitchen table, he rattles off the list: his mother, father, stepfather, his neighbor's wife, a friend of his daughter's, his pal Joey, a nine-year-old kid a couple streets over. "It's too many," he says. "Too many people."

Jane Pedota lives directly above the spill. A couple of her neighbors, she says, have exactly the same pancreatic problems; another neighbor has died of a brain tumor, and his wife died of myelofibrosis, a cancer linked to benzene. "I'm telling you, you're seeing odd things," Pedota says. "Too coincidental for me."

By the end of the year, the lawyers Seggos had brought in, Girardi & Keese—of *Erin Brockovich* fame—filed suit against the oil companies. Stagg and Pedota signed on. Brockovich herself showed up to rally the residents.

By the time the environment department convened a public meeting last year, the neighborhood had built up a full head of steam. Hundreds packed the Princess Manor banquet hall to hear presentations by ExxonMobil, BP, and Chevron, hectoring company representatives with catcalls of "liar!" and "shame on you people!" A health department spokesman tried to reassure the crowd, saying the state was unaware of any health threat but acknowledging that no studies had been done and none were planned. When state officials announced the cleanup would last another 20 years or more, the room fell silent.

That April, Riverkeeper obtained internal ExxonMobil documents showing that the company had known of high levels of benzene and other chemicals a decade earlier, when the substances were detected in a commercial property just 1,000 feet from the Pedota household. (ExxonMobil spokesman Brian Dunphy told *Mother Jones* that the tests, which were not conducted by the company, aren't proof of a health threat.)

The pressure continued to build until June 2006, when the talks between the environment department and ExxonMobil imploded (neither side will say why), whereupon the state finally referred the case to then-Attorney General Eliot Spitzer. Days later, Congress approved funding for a full EPA study of the spill, the federal government's first involvement in the case since the Coast Guard sailed away in 1979.

In February, Spitzer's successor, Andrew Cuomo, announced that his office intended to sue ExxonMobil (he filed the suit in July) to force a speedy cleanup. But the threat of litigation seemed to have the opposite effect. ExxonMobil shut down its groundwater pumps, which had been sucking up oil at a rate of 1,110 gallons per day, slowing the cleanup to a near halt. At the direction of the environment department, the company restarted the pumps this summer; the various lawsuits facing ExxonMobil remain ongoing. "I told my kids, 'This won't be settled until I'm dead and gone,'" says Pedota—who, like everyone else on her block, flies the Stars and Stripes in front of her house all year long. "But it would be nice to see that you could raise your children here." As she spoke, the oil beneath her home continued to creep, a tenth of an inch per hour, toward the creek.

Dangerous Waters

By Sharon P. Nappier, Robert S. Lawrence, and Kellogg J. Schwab
Natural History, November 2007

Drought in Australia. Water shortages in northern China. The desertification of western Africa. Almost daily, such headlines roll off the presses and issue from the airwaves.

Undoubtedly, diminished access to freshwater is a dire threat to people around the world. But consider the condition of the water when it finally trickles down people's throats. Infectious pathogens and harmful chemicals—from parasites to poisons—contaminate the world's freshwater and contribute to the deaths of millions of people worldwide every year. Understanding the effects of those contaminants holds the key to protecting our drinking water. And figuring out how we are exposed to harmful agents is the first order of business in choosing proper water-treatment techniques.

The burden of those agents weighs heavily on communities around the world. Nearly 2 million people—most of them children under five—die every year from diarrheal diseases. That statistic is not surprising when you realize just how much dirty water flows, or in many cases lies stagnant, across the continents. Nearly 20 percent of the 6.6 billion people in the world lack access to a supply of clean water, and 40 percent lack safe sanitation facilities. No new headlines there: as far back as 1981 the United Nations recognized the need for improved water supplies and sponsored a water-themed decade through 1990, in hopes of rallying international aid. Yet the percentage of people who have sufficient access to clean water supplies has remained fairly static.

Arguably, the battle is uphill. As quickly as innovative filters and water-transport systems enter the market, new contaminants and diseases arise, populations grow, and competing demands for water increase. Certain microorganisms can be elusive, causing severe illness, at doses as low as one infectious organism per drink of water. And those disease-causing organisms don't stand still while we figure out how to combat them: dirty water can lead to increased virulence, as in the case of antibiotic-resistant bacteria. Battling, let alone eliminating, those ever-changing organisms, along with the plethora of synthetic contaminants, seems only to be getting more difficult.

One thing will never change: people need water for survival. Circulating inside, outside, and across our cells, water constitutes as much as 70 percent of our body weight. Although we may survive four weeks without food, our bodies last, at best, only a few days without water. Furthermore, we use water for the most basic daily activities: drinking, cooking, bathing, washing, and sanitation.

For at least the past six thousand years, civilizations have understood the need to engineer water treatment techniques. Greek and Sanskrit texts discuss approaches to water sanitation that include boiling, straining, exposing to sunlight, and charcoal filtering. The ancient Egyptians employed coagulants—chemicals that are frequently used even today to remove suspended particles in drinking water—and other methods of purification. The earliest large-scale water treatment plants, such as the one built in 1804 to serve the city of Paisley, Scotland, used slow-sand filtration. By the 1850s London was sending all of its city water through sand filters and saw a dramatic reduction in cholera cases.

The discovery of chlorine as a microbicide in the early 1900s was a turning point in drinking-water engineering. That, in turn, led to a major advance in public health. Chlorination was initiated in the United States around 1910, and during the next several decades change was evident: the previously high mortality rate from typhoid fever—twenty-five deaths per 100,000—plummeted to almost zero. Although chlorine readily inactivates viruses and bacteria, its killing power flags when faced with hardy protozoan oocysts (developing cells), such as those of *Cryptosporidium parvum*—an agent of diarrheal disease. Another, and perhaps even nastier, drawback is that chlorine and organic matter may create carcinogenic by-products when they mix in the treatment plant. Nevertheless, chlorine is still one of the cheapest and most effective disinfectants in use today.

> For at least the past six thousand years, civilizations have understood the need to engineer water treatment techniques.

No panacea for water disinfection exists, however. To ensure that the water supply is clean enough to drink, most modern drinking-water plants amass an arsenal of treatment options. A multibarrier approach might include physical processes such as coagulation and flocculation (creating clumps of particles), sedimentation, and filtration, in conjunction with disinfectants such as chlorine, chlorine dioxide, chloramines, or ozone.

Such systems for cleansing community water are public investments that pay dividends. Clean water improves general health and reduces health-care costs, thereby enabling greater productivity among community members and redirection of public funds to other pressing needs. Unfortunately, rural and low-income localities cannot afford the infrastructure required for large, centralized drinking-water facilities.

On a global scale, of course, an ideal filter is natural vegetation. Protecting entire watersheds could vastly improve water quality worldwide; benefits could come from actions as simple as maintaining hillside growth to prevent soil erosion and flooding. But because many watersheds span several states or even countries, most management plans are politically complex. A comprehensive watershed-management plan must incorporate multiple stakeholders' needs and conflicting interests.

Water scarcity goes hand in hand with disease. As renewable freshwater becomes a dearer commodity worldwide, waterborne disease agents and other contaminants become harder to control. When dealing with diarrheal diseases, for instance, the quantity of available water often matters more than the quality, both to fend off the disease and to foil its spread. Then there's trachoma, a condition that can cause blindness; today it affects 6 million people and is associated with poor personal hygiene, often resulting from a dearth of water.

Every person, every day, needs at least thirteen gallons of water for drinking, cooking, bathing, and sanitation. In 1990 more than a billion of the world's people used less than that. By contrast, average per-capita water usage in the U.S. now exceeds 150 gallons a day. That discrepancy illustrates how the level of personal use correlates not only with the economic development of a region, but also with the degree of urbanization and with the overall public health in the region.

All that water filling swimming pools and soaking gardens might seem extraordinarily wasteful, but only 8 percent of the planet's freshwater supply goes toward personal, household, and municipal water use. Agriculture accounts for 70 percent, and industry for 22 percent, of current freshwater use. It takes more than fifty gallons of water to produce a single cup of milk. That's modest as virtual water content goes: consider a quarter-pound hamburger (470 gallons) or a cotton T-shirt (520 gallons). Then consider how many cotton T-shirts are tucked away in your closets. It's no surprise that demand is exceeding supply.

Daily water needs are exceedingly hard to meet in areas where rapid urbanization is taking place. Antiquated water-supply systems are simply not equipped to provide enough water and sanitation to people living in progressively crowded shantytowns or on the urban fringe. About half the world's people are now city dwellers. This new urban majority puts great stress on infrastructure, increasing the likelihood that illegal connections will be inserted into existing water systems and that, as a result, the piped drinking water will become contaminated.

Countries undergoing urban population booms often face acute microbial hazards. In countries where per-capita income is low, roughly 200 children under the age of five die every hour from a water-associated microbial infection. Many of the infections derive from the ingestion of water contaminated with human or animal feces that carry pathogenic bacteria, viruses, protozoa, or helminthes. That's the classic, but not the only, pathway for waterborne disease spread.

Exposure to contaminated water extends beyond the drinking fountain. Many diseases, once introduced into a population, can spread via person-to-person contact, in aerosol droplets, or through food preparation, rather than direct consumption of contaminated water. For example, malaria-carrying mosquitoes use stagnant water as a breeding ground; *Giardia* can be acquired during a swim in a local lake; clothing or bedding may carry scabies mites; noroviruses can be transmitted by eating oysters.

Emerging infectious diseases (the ones whose incidence in humans has increased in the past two decades or threatens to increase soon) have recently caused some public-health scares. Noroviruses—headlined for causing cruise ship infections—are already on the rise. *Cryptosporidium parvum* sickened some 400,000 residents of Milwaukee, Wisconsin in 1993, when the local water-treatment process was changed in what had seemed to be a minor way. *E. coli* O157:H7 is another of the more common emerging infectious pathogens in the U.S. joining the hefty ranks of dangerous bacteria, many of which are becoming resistant to multiple standard antibiotics.

But pathogenic microorganisms are not the sole cause of water-associated illnesses. Chemicals, too, pose serious risks. About a thousand new synthetic compounds are introduced every year, joining the ranks of tens of thousands more that are already in widespread use—dioxins, PCBs, and halogenated hydrocarbons included. Many inevitably seep into the water system and accumulate in the food chain. In the United States, for instance, some 700 chemicals have been detected in drinking water sources, and more than a hundred of those chemicals are considered highly toxic.

Advanced technologies enable investigators to detect harmful chemicals in the water supply, even in low concentrations—a critical step, since their effects on human health are often unknown. Several emerging chemicals of utmost concern are fuel additives, such as methyl tertiary-butyl ether, or MTBE; by-products of disinfection; antibiotics, hormones, and psychoactive drugs; the antibacterial soap ingredients triclocarban and triclosan; and persistent organic pollutants, such as perfluorinated chemicals and phthalates.

Most people have a sufficiently robust immune system to handle exposure to a certain amount of water pollutants. But some—infants, the elderly, people living with cancer or AIDS—are immunocompromised. Elderly adults often sicken on exposure to only a small fraction of the infectious dose that others require—an issue for the U.S. as its baby boomer population ages.

Just as an aging population poses a concern for public health, so too does an aging infrastructure pose a concern for water delivery. U.S. water infrastructure is outdated and deficient. In the next few decades, measures must be taken to reinforce or restore our water delivery pipes and systems, equipping them for both natural disasters and terrorist threats.

Once again the United Nations has declared a water decade: 2005 through 2015 will be the Water for Life Decade. Among the UN's Millennium Development Goals outlined for the decade are reducing the number of people worldwide who lack adequate water and sanitation by half. Additional efforts will concentrate on curbing the unsustainable exploitation of water. As with the UN's approach to increasing literacy, facilitating income generation, and curbing population growth, the focus will be on empowering women as a means of achieving its goals.

Certainly the goals are challenging. Achieving them will require cooperation among many stakeholders who are committed to expanding investments in water and wastewater infrastructure. New management strategies must embody conservation and efficiency for people everywhere, lest we find ourselves changing too slowly to quench the world's thirst.

WATER

NEW INTERNATIONALIST, MAY 2005

Water is a necessity for life. Yet, though life first evolved in the oceans, most terrestrial organisms cannot drink the salt water that makes up over 97 per cent of the world's total. Of the fresh water that makes up the rest, more than 90 per cent is locked away in glaciers and ice sheets, or hidden deep underground. Only 0.0001 per cent of fresh water is easily accessible; human settlements are clustered along the waterways and fertile floodplains.

This is all the fresh water available to us. It is not created anew but recycled, as the sun evaporates the oceans and water falls back to earth as rain and snow. What we drink is made up of ancient molecules of water that have fed rainforests, slaked the thirsts of dinosaurs and prophets, spent millennia frozen in glaciers. There is enough water in total for us all, but it is unevenly distributed. While the rich world uses more and more, many countries, particularly in Asia and Africa, suffer shortages. A third of the world's people live in dryland regions that have access to only eight per cent of the world's renewable water supply.

For centuries humans dumped waste in the nearest watercourse and drank from it too, but this works only when the waste is small and the people are few. The pollution of waterways by toxic industrial waste and sewage is one of the biggest environmental challenges of our time.

Modern improvements in human health are largely due to great public municipal works of sanitation that provide people with clean drinking water. Access to clean water is still one of the major distinctions between the world's 'haves' and 'have nots'. The wars of the future are likely to be over fresh water—and sooner than we think.

Meanwhile, as the Earth heats up and the polar ice caps melt, the rising, warming oceans are washing inland, salinizing freshwater tables and flooding human settlements. The oceans are the engines of global weather systems: as they warm, they are not only killing whales and coral reefs, they are triggering storm surges, droughts and new unpredictable weather patterns right across the planet.

WATER—THE FACTS

- Water withdrawals from rivers and lakes for irrigation, household and industrial use have doubled in the last 40 years.

- In some regions, such as the Middle East and North Africa, humans use 120% of renewable water supplies, due to the reliance on groundwater that is not recharged.

- Between 1960 and 2000 the storage of water in reservoirs quadrupled, so that the amount of water now stored behind large dams is estimated to be 3–6 times the amount held by natural river channels (excluding natural lakes).

- The construction of dams and other structures along rivers has affected flows in 60% of the large river systems of the world. Water removal for human uses has reduced the flow of several major rivers, including the Nile, Yellow and Colorado Rivers, to the extent that they do not always flow to the sea.

- As water flows have declined, so have sediment flows, which are the source of nutrients important for the maintenance of estuaries. Worldwide, sediment delivery to estuaries has declined by roughly 30%.

- Since about 1980, approximately 35% of mangroves have been lost, while 20% of the world's coral reefs have been destroyed and a further 20% badly degraded.

IV. CLIMATE CHANGE AND THE WATER SUPPLY

Editor's Introduction

Many see in the melting ice caps, increasingly powerful hurricanes, and rising temperatures of recent years the growing impact of global climate change. Most attribute the phenomenon to human fossil-fuel consumption—the burning of oil, coal and natural gas for energy—and believe that emissions must be reduced if catastrophic changes are to be forestalled. Widely considered the most pressing environmental challenge facing humanity, climate change is expected to pose a grave threat to water supplies throughout the world.

The articles in this chapter discuss the effects climate change has had on global water systems and how it will likely influence them in the future. From Seattle to Australia, changes in weather patterns are impacting water supplies and will require considerable adaptation if current trends continue.

In "A European Sahara," Eric Pape describes a report by the European Space Agency that estimates that 300,000 km^2 of Europe's Mediterranean coast is in danger of desertification due to climate change. As a harbinger of this new reality, Pape cites the August 2003 heat wave that struck Europe and killed tens of thousands of senior citizens. Protecting against such catastrophes, Pape contends, will be "a long-term battle," as Europe adjusts to these new and potentially deadly weather patterns.

Australia's Murray-Darling River is in deep trouble, a writer for *The Economist* reports in "The Big Dry." Years of drought have slowed the river's flow considerably, and though "few scientists are confident enough to ascribe any individual event, including the drought, to global warming," most believe that climate change is largely to blame. The shortage of water in the river has already hurt farmers and, unless adequately addressed, may threaten the sustainability of the cities that rely on the Murray-Darling.

In "Tapped Out?" Lisa Snider reports on what rising temperatures may mean for Boulder and other Colorado cities. These municipalities rely on the winter snowmelt to replenish their water supply every spring, the snowpack serving as a natural reservoir. Boulder has monitored recent climate changes to measure the potential impact. Scientists agree that greenhouses gases will warm up Colorado, but they are not certain whether the state will see less—or more—rain and snow as a result. Another concern is increased evaporation: Higher temperatures will cause more surface water to be lost in lakes and reservoirs. Snider also discusses Boulder's reservoir history, along with the challenges the city faces due to a growing population. Ultimately, she suggests that the state should consider employing water-efficient technologies and rebuilding older reservoirs.

Finally, in "Climate Change Could Mean More Massive Downpours," Lisa Stiffler and Tom Paulson report on the impact of climate change on water systems in the Pacific Northwest and what can be done to counteract it. In particular, they anticipate that floods will become more commonplace.

A European Sahara?

By Eric Pape
NEWSWEEK, OCTOBER 17, 2007

It looked and felt like hell. Swirling winds whipped flames along a 17-kilometer front of pine-forest scrub parched by the fiercest drought on the Iberian Peninsula in 60 years. A dozen firefighters, dwarfed by the massive blaze, fought the flames amid smoke, heat and the blackening countryside of Guadalajara, Spain. Before they could turn to flee, the fire swept over them. Eleven men and women died; the twelfth barely survived. The mid-July blaze was the most spectacular and deadly of the summer—so far. "The hurricane of fire was very big. I didn't think it was fire," Jesus Abad told Spanish television. To the shaken fireman, whose face and arms were bandaged like a mummy, the blaze had a diabolic will of its own: "I think it saw us and said, 'You, you're mine'."

With bursting thermometers, historic droughts and dozens of fires raging from Portugal to Greece, it isn't hard to imagine an apocalyptic future for southern Europe, almost as if the vast Sahara Desert were reaching out across the Mediterranean. Is this merely a long, hot summer, or are these the initial symptoms of enduring climate change, exacerbated by overpopulation and overdevelopment of a fragile ecological landscape? Evidence is mounting to support just such fears.

The Desert Watch project, led by the European Space Agency, reports that 300,000 square kilometers of Europe's Mediterranean coast—an area larger than Britain—with a population of 16.5 million, is threatened by "desertification." The Spanish minister of the Environment, Cristina Narbona, warned in June about a long-term decrease in rain and an increase in temperatures: "the beginning of a long cycle" of extreme drought. And while severe dry spells may be a normal component of Europe's climate, says Jose Luis Rubio, the head of the University of Valencia's Desertification Investigation Center, a weakening of the soil's resistance to drought among other things, along with human factors, are enhancing the risks of desertification. "We have observed a growing fragility," says Rubio. In places like Valencia, "the water levels are dropping and the soil is weaker."

This doesn't mean sand dunes will be drifting across the streets of Aix-en-Provence or Portofino any time soon. The word "desertification," in Europe, essentially means that the land itself dies and becomes agriculturally unproductive, even if people still build apartments on it or, indeed, greenhouses. And as with the broader debate on global warming, there is plenty of room for error when it comes to long-term forecasts. But optimism among scientists is increasingly hard to find, and the public has fresh memories—not to mention the broiling present—to fuel mounting concerns.

> Warmer weather and changing climates could bring malaria to Europe.

Remember the killer summer heat wave of 2003, when thousands of elderly French died while their children vacationed on beaches? That was the most intense in the 150 years of accurate weather history. This year's baking drought hasn't brought the same record heat—as yet. But eyeing southern Europe's cloudless skies, it's hard to escape the sense that this is no climatic aberration. Before the end of the century, summer temperatures in Italy are expected to increase by 7 to 8 degrees Celsius, according to the international panel on climate change, the IPCC (which was established by the world meteorological organization and the U.N. environment program). Meteo France projects that in the latter part of this century, 35-degree Celsius days will be "five to ten times more numerous" across the country. The city of Nîmes is expected to pass from four scorching days now to 40 by the latter part of this century (from the year 2070 onward), according to projections from Meteo France.

Such changes would transform everything from natural ecosystems—which can change dramatically with a tiny temperature variation—to basic water supplies, agriculture and tourism. Rainfall is expected to decline by 15 percent on average and 40 percent in the scalding summers before the end of the century, according to the IPCC. Experts warn that sea levels could rise as glaciers melt, even affecting the Mediterranean. Warmer weather and changing climates could bring malaria to Europe. And in North Africa the situation will surely be worse, as governments have far fewer resources with which to prepare for the future, says Dieter Schoene, an environmental specialist at the U.N.'s Food and Agriculture Organization. The result: even greater immigration pressure than exists today.

There's little doubt that Europe is getting warmer. During the last century, average temperatures increased by about 0.7 degrees Celsius. The 1990s marked the hottest decade since record-keeping began in the mid-1800s, registering two of the five hottest years ever recorded. This decade has already produced the other three hottest years, from 2001 to 2003. Last year was relatively cool, but the respite has been brief. This year, France has already endured the hottest late June in half a century, and Poland wilted under temperatures of 40 degrees Celsius last week.

With drier woods and fields, less water and hotter temperatures, the irresponsible people who attempted to prepare an illegal barbecue in Guadalajara, northeast of Madrid, merely precipitated a tragedy-in-waiting. Sixteen other fires burned around Spain at the same time. In some areas there's been no rain since October, and some Spanish water reservoirs are at just 20 percent of capacity. The whole of Portugal is enduring "serious" or "extreme" drought, according a report issued last week by the Portuguese Institute of Water—the worst ever recorded. Streams have dried up. Livestock are dying. Crops are withering. In generally lush France, more than 60 percent of the nation's departments face water restrictions. And the extremely dry weather of recent months has spawned swarms of locusts in France's Aveyron region, eating crops down to the stalks before sweeping through villages.

Farmers are not the only ones to suffer. As rivers fall, industries and hydroelectric plants are affected, says Stefano Ciafani, scientific coordinator of the Italian environmental association Legambiente: "The situation is alarming." Fierce competition for water is altering southern Europe's political relationships. France and Spain are in talks about sending huge amounts of French water to Barcelona, or even further down the Spanish coast. Portugal has asked Spain for 6 billion euros in compensation because water in the Douro River has fallen below levels set in a bilateral agreement. Provincial governments across Spain have begun accusing one another of illegal well-digging, overbuilding and water theft. (One province sent a spy plane to monitor the consumption habits of its neighbors and found ample evidence of misused resources.) "Historically, the Mediterranean has always fought over water," says Rubio. "We are now seeing a modern version of those historical water wars between regions in Spain."

The weather changes aren't just affecting the shores but the sea as well. Italy's Agency for Technology, Energy and the Environment concluded that its coastal ocean temperatures rose three degrees in the summer of 2003, a sharp spike highlighting a general trend. The Red Sea mullet, a warm-water native of the Suez Canal, has in recent years crossed into the Mediterranean and is now regularly sold in Italian fish markets. Other strange phenomena include the expanding reach of a 6,000-square-kilometer supercolony of Argentine ants that now stretches from Italy through France and Portugal to northwestern Spain. "Everything is linked to the changing climate," says Anne Rogers, senior economist at the U.N.'s Division for Sustainable Development.

The uncertainty gives an ominous undercurrent to this year's summer holidays. By mid-July, temperatures in much of southern France were already between 32 and 37 degrees Celsius. All major French cities have announced Level Three alerts—Four is an emergency—automatically bolstering, among other things, hospital staffing to flu-epidemic levels. Memories of the deadly heat wave of 2003 give every reason to worry. Italy's national statistics office recently revised its 2003 summer death toll, from 8,000 to an astounding 20,000. Overall, the number of European deaths from the heat two years ago is believed to have surpassed 40,000.

Protecting against similar catastrophes will be a long-term battle, not least because of short-term greed. Myopic land and water management figures large in the desertification phenomenon. In Spain, the greatest urban and agricultural expansion is taking place in the driest regions. Farmers can sometimes harvest three to four times annually in southern Spain, requiring plenty of water and depleting the soil. Three decades ago the Almeria region of Spain was verdant farmland. Today it is almost entirely devoid of greenery, thanks to 27,000 hectares of plastic-covered greenhouses. Development and the tourism boom are literally paving over the dying lands, and desiccating the countryside that's left. An estimated 350,000 new homes were built on Spain's Mediterranean coast in 2004, often with backyard swimming pools and nearby golf courses, each of which is estimated to consume as much water as a town of 13,000. Spanish television showed images last week of thousands of dying fish gasping in the depleted and mucky remnants of the Guardiaro River in Cadiz, their water allegedly diverted for urbanization and golf courses.

> Myopic land and water management figures large in the desertification phenomenon.

Against this background, raging wildfires may seem like some sort of Biblical retribution. Already, the average annual acreage burned off in Portugal, Spain, Italy and Greece has quadrupled since the 1960s. The fire that Jesus Abad was fighting in Guadalajara was ferocious almost beyond belief. As aircraft attacked the blaze, their 5,500-liter water-bombs evaporated before making contact. The 30,000-acre conflagration was brought under control only after three days and the bulldozing of a 10-kilometer long, 80-meter-wide fire break through the forest. The Alto Tajo nature reserve, home of numerous endangered species and plants, was left with little more than skeletal, blackened trees craning toward bright blue skies. At the same time, fires in neighboring Portugal were burning their way toward the 100,000-acre mark. Drought has cut Portuguese agriculture's financial projections by an estimated 35 percent this year—a loss of about 1.5 percent of the nation's GDP—and another firefighter was killed there last week. Amid the soaring temperatures, the fires and the locusts, you can almost feel the hot breath of the Sahara as it says to southern Europe, "You're mine."

The Big Dry

THE ECONOMIST, APRIL 26, 2007

The mouth of the Murray-Darling river sets an idyllic scene. Anglers in wide-brimmed sunhats wade waist-deep into the azure water. Pleasure boats cruise languidly around the sandbanks that dot the narrow channel leading to the Southern Ocean. Pensioners stroll along the beach. But over the cries of the seagulls and the rush of the waves, there is another sound: the mechanical drone from a dredging vessel. It never stops and must run around the clock to prevent the river mouth from silting up. Although the Murray-Darling is Australia's longest river system, draining a basin the size of France and Spain combined, it no longer carries enough water to carve its own path to the sea.

John Howard, Australia's prime minister, arrived here in February and urged the four states through which the Murray-Darling flows to hand their authority over the river to the federal government. After seven years of drought, and many more years of over-exploitation and pollution, he argued that the only hope of restoring the river to health lies in a complete overhaul of how it is managed. As the states weigh the merits of Mr Howard's scheme, the river is degenerating further. Every month hydrologists announce that its flow has fallen to a new record low. In April Mr Howard warned that farmers would not be allowed to irrigate their crops at all next year without unexpectedly heavy rain in the next few months. A region that accounts for 40% of Australia's agriculture, and 85% of its irrigation, is on the verge of ruin.

The drought knocked one percentage point off Australia's growth rate last year, by the government's reckoning. It is paying out A$2m ($1.7m) a day in drought-relief to farmers. If mature vines and fruit trees die in the coming months through the lack of water, the economic fallout will be more serious and lasting. Most alarming of all, the Murray-Darling's troubles are likely to worsen. As Australia's population continues to grow, so does demand for water in the cities and for the crops that grow in the river basin. Meanwhile, global warming appears to be heating the basin up and drying it out. Although few scientists are confident that they can ascribe any individual event—including today's drought—to global warming, most agree that droughts like the present one will become more common.

Many of the world's rivers, including the Colorado in America, China's Yellow river and the Tagus, which flows through Spain and Portugal, are suffering a similar plight. As the world warms up, hundreds of millions of people will face the same ecological crisis as the residents of the Murray-Darling basin. As water levels dwindle, rows about how supplies should be used are turning farmers against city-dwellers and pitching environmentalists against politicians. Australia has a strong economy, a well-funded bureaucracy and robust political institutions. If it is struggling to respond to this crisis, imagine how drought will tear apart other, less prepared parts of the world.

Droughts have long plagued the Murray-Darling. The region is afflicted by a periodic weather pattern known as El Niño. At irregular intervals of two to seven years, the waters of the central Pacific warm up, heralding inclement weather throughout the southern hemisphere. Torrential rains flood the coast of Peru, while south-eastern Australia wilts in drought. The duration of these episodes is as unpredictable as their arrival. They can range from a few months to several years. As a result, the flow of the Darling, the longest tributary of the Murray, varies wildly, from as little as 0.04% of the long-term average to as much as 911%. Although the most recent El Niño ended earlier this year, it has left the soils in the basin so dry and the groundwater so depleted that the Murray-Darling's flow continues to fall, despite normal levels of rainfall over the past few months.

Protracted droughts are a part of Australian folklore. Schoolchildren learn a hackneyed Victorian poem in praise of "a sunburnt country . . . of droughts and flooding rains". Dorothea Mackellar wrote those lines just after the "Federation drought" of the late 1890s and early 1900s. The recession that accompanied it was so severe that it helped nudge Australia's six states, at the time separate British colonies, into uniting as a federation, or commonwealth, as Australians tend to call it.

Water Politics

Negotiations over the federal constitution almost foundered on the subject of the Murray-Darling. South Australia, at the mouth of the river, wanted it kept open for navigation to the hinterland, allowing the state to become a trading hub. Its capital, Adelaide, also depended on water piped from the Murray to keep its taps running—as it still does. Further upstream, Victoria and New South Wales wanted to build dams to encourage agriculture. Queensland played little part in the row, since its stretch of the Darling was sparsely populated at the time. In the end, Victoria and New South Wales agreed to ensure a minimum flow to South Australia and to divide the remaining water equally between themselves. Like their counterparts elsewhere in the world, Australian engineers gaily pockmarked the basin with dams, weirs and locks, with little thought for what that would do downstream.

By the 1990s the drawbacks were evident. For one thing, states were allowing irrigators to use too much water. By 1994 human activity was consuming 77% of the river's average annual flow, even though the actual flow falls far below the average in dry years. The mouth of the river was beginning to silt up—a powerful symbol of over-exploitation. Thanks to a combination of reduced flow and increased run-off from saline soils churned up by agriculture, the water was becoming unhealthily salty, especially in its lower reaches. The tap water in Adelaide, which draws 40% of its municipal supplies from the river and up to 90% when other reserves dry up, was beginning to taste saline. The number of indigenous fish was falling, since the floods that induce them to spawn were becoming rarer. Toxic algae flourished in the warmer, more sluggish waters. In 1991 a hideous bloom choked a 1,000km (625 mile) stretch of the Darling.

Such horrors stirred indignation among urban Australians. The bad publicity put tourists off river cruises, fishing trips and visits to the basin's various lakes and wetlands. Many small businesses got hurt in the process. The citizens of Adelaide, which contains several marginal parliamentary seats, began to worry that the taps would run dry. Farmers were also starting to fear for the security and quality of their water supplies.

> Australia embarked on a series of reforms that in many ways serve as a model for the management of big, heavily exploited rivers.

So Australia embarked on a series of reforms that in many ways serve as a model for the management of big, heavily exploited rivers. New South Wales, Victoria and South Australia agreed to cap the amount of water they took from the river and to keep clear, public records of water-use rights. They also made plans to reduce salinity and increase "environmental flows". The commonwealth agreed to encourage this by allocating buckets of cash to compliant states. All these initiatives were to be managed by a body, called the Murray-Darling Basin Commission, in which the commonwealth and the various riparian states, including Queensland and the tiny Australian Capital Territory (ACT), had equal representation and where decisions were taken by consensus.

Moreover, Australia's politicians also agreed to a set of principles by which water should be managed throughout the country. There should be no more subsidies for irrigation. Farmers should pay for the maintenance of channels and dams. For each river and tributary, scientists would calculate the maximum sustainable allocations of water and states would make sure that extractions did not exceed that figure. To ensure that such a scarce resource was used as efficiently as possible, water should be tradable, both within and between states. And the minimum environmental flows necessary to keep the river in good health should be accorded just as high a status as water put to commercial uses.

Guided by these principles, the states and the commonwealth have made much progress. By 1999 the average salinity of the river in South Australia had fallen by over 20%. In the late 1990s salinity levels were falling within the prescribed limit over 90% of the time, compared with roughly 60% in the 1970s and 1980s. The construction of fish ladders around dams and weirs, and the release of extra water into important breeding grounds, has spawned a recovery in native species. The commission is spending A$650m to boost environmental flows, mainly by stemming losses from irrigation, and hence leaving more water in the river.

The trade in water has taken off. There are two basic sorts of transaction: sales of part of a farmer's water allocation for the year or a permanent transfer. Temporary exchanges between farmers in the same state topped 1,000 gigalitres (220 billion gallons) in 2003, or around a tenth of all water used for agriculture. That roughly matches the cumulative amount of water that has changed hands permanently within the same state.

Meanwhile, the commission has codified rules for trading water between users in different states. The volumes are much smaller, but the system is working as economists had hoped. In general, water is flowing from regions with salty soil to more fertile ones; from farms that are profligate with water to ones that are more efficient; and from low-value crops to more profitable ones. In particular, struggling dairy and rice farmers in New South Wales and Victoria have sold water to the booming orchards and vineyards of South Australia. A government assessment of a pilot scheme for interstate trade determined that such shifts prompted A$767m of extra investment in irrigation and food-processing between 1997 and 2001. Another study found that water trading helped to reduce the damage wrought by droughts.

But there are lots of problems. For one thing, the reforms concern only water that has already reached the river. Farmers in certain states can still drill wells to suck up groundwater, and tree plantations absorb a lot of rainwater that would otherwise find its way into the river. Little dams on farms, which block small streams or trap run-off from rain or flooding, are an even bigger worry. Little is known about how many there are or how fast their numbers are growing. In theory, most states are trying to regulate them, but the rules are full of loopholes and enforcement is difficult. Hydrologists fear that the severity of the drought has encouraged farmers to build more dams.

Some states are keener on the reforms than others. In 1995, when New South Wales, South Australia and Victoria agreed to cap the amount of water they took from the river, Queensland refused to join them on the grounds that it uses only a tiny share of the basin's water. The state government felt it had a right to promote irrigation along its stretch of the Darling to bring Queensland to the same level of agricultural development as the other states. It has since agreed to negotiate a cap. But earlier this year, despite the ongoing drought, it awarded new water-use rights to farmers on the War-rego, one of the tributaries of the Darling.

New South Wales, meanwhile, frequently exceeds its cap. Its farmers plant mainly annual crops, such as rice and wheat, instead of perennials like fruit trees or grape vines. If there is not enough water to go round, its farmers may suffer for a season, but their earnings are not permanently diminished. So the state tends to be less cautious in its allocation of water than Victoria or South Australia. However, the commission has no power to ensure that states stick to their caps. It can only denounce offenders publicly, in the forlorn hope that the shame will induce them to behave better.

Climate change is likely to exacerbate all these disputes. The Commonwealth Scientific and Industrial Research Organisation (CSIRO), a government agency, estimates that it could reduce the Murray's flow by as much as 5% in 20 years and 15% in 50 years. But other projections are much more cataclysmic. CSIRO cites a worst case of 20% less water in 20 years and 50% in 50 years. Peter Cullen, an academic and member of the government's National Water Commission, points out that inflows to the Murray have fallen to less than half of their long-term average over the past six years. He thinks it would be prudent to manage water on the assumption that low flows are here to stay.

Mr. Howard argues that the Murray-Darling Basin Commission moves too slowly to cope with all the upheaval. He wants the states to surrender their powers over the basin to the commonwealth. That will allow his government, he says, to work out exactly how much water is being siphoned off through wells and dams, and to use that information to set a new, sustainable cap on water use.

The government would also help farmers meet the new restrictions by investing in more efficient irrigation or by buying up their water rights—all without any of the typical bickering and foot-dragging that have held up collective action in the past. To entice the states to agree, he is offering to spend A$10 billion of the commonwealth's money on the various schemes. But the advantage of adopting policies by consensus, presumably, is that they may prove more durable than anything imposed from Canberra. National governments, even in Australia, are not immune to inefficiency and bias. They are often at loggerheads with the states.

Moreover, not all Australians want to move as quickly as Mr Howard does. He faces an election later this year in which his environmental record—and particularly his lack of action on global warming—will be a big issue. Nor does the federal government have any experience of managing rivers. In a recent book, "Water Politics in the Murray-Darling Basin", Daniel Connell argues that any institutional arrangement that fails to give enough weight to regional concerns will not last.

Running a River

Several state governments have their doubts about Mr Howard's plan. South Australia wants the administration of the river put in the hands of a panel of independent experts. Victoria, the only state to reject the prime minister's scheme outright, says that he could achieve the same goals without any extra powers by simply withholding money from recalcitrant states. Its government has also complained that the scheme would reward the most wasteful irrigators for their inefficiency, by helping to pay for improvements to their infrastructure and then allowing them to use much of the water saved. So the extravagant irrigators of New South Wales will end up with extra water, while their parsimonious counterparts in Victoria will benefit less.

Moreover, many Australians are uncomfortable with the idea of water trading, says Blair Nancarrow, the head of the Australian Research Centre for Water in Society, a division of CSIRO. People living in less fertile areas fear that local farmers will gradually sell all their water rights, eroding employment and commerce and killing off the area's towns. Concerned politicians have insisted on limits to the amount of water that can be traded out of regions and states each year and have refused to allow the commission to buy water directly from farmers for environmental flows. The National Party, the junior partner in Australia's coalition government, draws much of its support from the countryside and is particularly reluctant to give free rein to the water market.

In the eyes of Mr Cullen, however, many of the changes Australians fear are inevitable. As it is, he notes, the amount of money farms make for every million litres of water they use varies dramatically between states, from roughly A$300 in New South Wales to A$600 in Victoria and A$1,000 in South Australia. He believes that investment and water will continue to gravitate towards the bigger, more professionally managed farms. In the long run, the irrigation of pasture for livestock, which currently consumes about half of the basin's agricultural water, will not make sense. The number of small, family-owned farms will shrink.

Ian Zadow owns just such a farm, near Murray Bridge in South Australia, which has been in the family since 1905. He is also head of the local irrigators' association. His son used to work on the farm with him. But farming cannot support two families, so the younger man has taken a job tending graveyards instead. "If you can pay all your bills and get three meals on the table," says Mr Zadow, "that's about as good as it is going to get."

At the moment however, things are nowhere near that good. Last year, he saw his allocation of water slashed first by 20%, then by 30% and finally by 40%. Next season, unless much more rain falls, he stands to get no allocation at all. He feels that city-dwellers should do their bit to help farmers by conserving more water. When push comes to shove, he says, politicians will always give priority to the cities over the countryside, since they are home to more voters. He also thinks irrigators in New South Wales and Victoria should be trying harder to save water. Before too long Mr Zadow's complaints may be echoed by millions of farmers around the world.

If the Australian drought continues, the thousands who depend on irrigation water for a living will be in deep trouble. Many are already in debt and struggling to make ends meet. When asked what will happen if there is no water for them this year, Mr Zadow hesitates for a moment before replying, "Christ knows."

Tapped Out?

Melting Snow May Equal Less Water

By Laura Snider
Daily Camera (Boulder, Colorado), December 2, 2007

Now that the sting of winter's icy winds has finally settled on Colorado, snowflakes are beginning to coat the lumpy tundra around Silver Lake with deeper drifts, piling up under scraggly pines.

Island Lake and Goose Lake, which pour their frigid alpine waters into the larger Silver Lake, are coated with a fragile crust of ice, and snow dusts their winter armor.

All winter, snow will continue falling into Silver Lake's cirque, carved long ago by the then-mighty Arapaho Glacier and tucked high on the Continental Divide west of Boulder. In the spring, the deep snows will begin to melt, swelling North Boulder Creek and filling the city's reservoirs.

At least that's the plan. But now, Boulder—along with cities and towns across Colorado and the world that rely on snowmelt for their primary water supplies—has to consider how global warming may change its best-laid water strategies.

Boulder may well be the first city anywhere that has tried to model the potential effects of global warming on a scale small enough to predict how its water supply will be altered by warming temperatures and changing precipitation patterns. The results, according to a nearly completed study, show that Boulder probably has the flexibility to meet its future water demands under all but the most extreme scenarios.

"Boulder is really ahead of the game in looking at this seriously," said Lee Rozaklis, who has been helping the city model its water supply since the mid-1980s. "From my perspective, the city has been on top of it early and often, and we've got as good a picture as we can have."

A Slimmer Snowpack

Greenhouse gases will cause Colorado to heat up; that much most climate experts agree on. But scientists are still divided about whether the state will see less rain and snow—or more. Either way, the added heat will change the way municipalities on the Front Range manage their water.

"Warming, and changes in the form, timing and amount of precipitation, will very likely lead to earlier melting and significant reductions in snowpack in the western mountains by the middle of the 21st century," reads a report by the Intergovernmental Panel on Climate Change, worked on by hundreds of scientists and released earlier this year.

> In Colorado, it matters whether water falls from the sky as snow or rain.

In Colorado, it matters whether water falls from the sky as snow or rain. Snow will stick around until it's needed in the summer, melting in the sun's heat and feeding the added seasonal water demands for crops and lawns. But rain may run through the watershed immediately, soak into the spongy tundra or evaporate before it has a chance to flow down to Boulder.

"Snow in the winter in the West goes directly into runoff," Kenneth Strzepek, a civil engineering professor at the University of Colorado, told the city's Water Resources Advisory Board earlier this month. "Precipitation in the summer might evaporate right back into the sky. It's basically futile to have rain in the summer."

Even if summer rains added to the water in Boulder Creek, the city doesn't have enough manmade reservoirs to store the water until it's needed.

"The snowpack is our major reservoir, and we don't have artificial reservoirs sufficient in size to manage it in the way that nature manages it for us," said Kathleen Miller, a scientist at the National Center for Atmospheric Research in Boulder and author of the book *Climate Change and Water Resources: A Primer for Municipal Water Providers*.

Building more local reservoirs sufficient in size to offset an earlier-melting snowpack or late-season rains has its own problems, besides steep costs. Increased warming will mean more surface water will be lost through evaporation. Already, dry air steals a significant amount of water from major reservoirs across the West.

"We lose—the rough number—we lose almost 10 percent of the annual flow of the (Colorado) River in the main reservoirs on the river," said Martin Hoerling, a researcher at the National Oceanic and Atmospheric Administration in Boulder. "That's a lot of loss, and that evaporation is only going to increase."

A History of Forward Thinking

Today, Boulder's water-supply portfolio includes water from the Silver Lake watershed, water from Middle Boulder Creek that fills Barker Reservoir at the top of Boulder Canyon and even water drawn from the headwaters of the Colorado River, which eventually is stored in Boulder Reservoir after it makes a long, complicated trip across the Continental Divide.

The first reservoir built in Boulder was constructed in Sunshine Canyon in 1875, but it didn't take long before the water was tainted by mine tailings. At the turn of the century, Boulder made a move to start buying land in the Indian Peaks that could provide clean water to the growing town.

By the end of the 1920s, Boulder owned the entire Silver Lake watershed, which includes 13 reservoirs and natural lakes fed by the Arapaho Glacier.

But even with that wealth of water, severe droughts and an exploding population in the 1950s strained Boulder's supplies and pushed the city to acquire more water, this time from Barker Reservoir and new trans-basin projects, which would carry water to Boulder from the Colorado River.

A half-century later, Boulder water planners aren't as worried about population spikes—they estimate the city is 90 percent built out—and they've weathered the earth-cracking drought of 2002. The new threat to water is the increasingly accepted phenomenon of global warming.

Some signs of climate change in Boulder's watershed are mor -obvious than others—the seasoned Boulderite might not notice when there is a foot less snow in the Silver Lake basin than during the decade before. But nearly everyone who has taken the time to hike up in the Indian Peaks and peer down on the Arapaho Glacier will notice it's not as mighty as it once was.

Arapaho Glacier has shrunk so much that in 1998, the glacier officially became a "permanent snowfield," which means that the body of frozen water isn't crawling downhill anymore. All "real" glaciers move, even if they're melting up faster than they slide down.

For the next few decades—at the end of which some climate scientists predict all the glaciers in Colorado may be gone—the melting Arapaho Glacier may actually augment summer streamflows. But once it has disappeared, the city will be without one of its sources of backup water.

An Innovative New Study

For about 20 years, Boulder has been using a model of the Boulder Creek watershed that is now based on more than four centuries of historical streamflow data, most of which has been reconstructed from analyzing tree rings.

"There are droughts in the pre-history that are significantly worse than what we've seen in the last 100 years," said Rozaklis, an engineer for Hydrosphere Resource Consulting.

Because climate change is expected to magnify the swings in the natural cycles of precipitation and temperature, the study commissioned in 2005 to study the effects of global warming on the city's water supply began by overlaying a greater variability on the last 300 years of data.

Boulder's water system passed the test for reliability when planners modeled future supplies assuming that the next 300 years would resemble the last 300 years, only with 25 percent more variability—longer wet and dry spells. But Boulder failed when modelers decreased the long-term precipitation by 15 percent.

Rozaklis, along with Stratus Consulting's Joel Smith and CU's Strzepek, also modeled how Boulder's water supplies would perform in 2030 and 2070 based on three degrees of future warming and three scenarios for precipitation: drier, wetter and roughly the same.

The complicated matrix of results showed that, for the most part, Boulder could accommodate future water needs except if the warmest scenario overlapped with the driest scenario in the year 2070.

Next Moves

That's relatively good news for the city.

"I think that Boulder is in pretty decent shape," Rozaklis said. "It's great to think about this stuff, but it's probably premature to do anything about it."

That's partly because Boulder has fairly senior water rights and draws water from more than one source.

But Rozaklis and his colleagues cautioned that the real wild card is tied up in the Colorado River, where Boulder pulls 20 percent of its water annually. The Colorado River Compact of 1922—an agreement among the seven basin states and Mexico—already overappropriates the available flow in the river.

"There are major uncertainties in the law of the (Colorado) River," Rozaklis said. "If there are compact-call problems, it would be a statewide problem."

A restructuring of the Colorado River Compact may be decades away, but meanwhile, Boulder can consider water-efficient technologies and rebuilding older reservoirs that aren't now used but still carry senior storage rights, Rozaklis said.

No matter what the future climate holds, water planners may be the right people to deal with the massive uncertainties of global warming.

"The prospect of climate change is really just more of the same sort of thing we're used to," he said. "The only thing certain is that streamflows are highly erratic and hard to predict."

Climate Change Could Mean More Massive Downpours

By Lisa Stiffler and Tom Paulson
Seattle Post-Intelligencer, December 4, 2007

That sump pump you rented to suck out the standing water in your basement? You might want to ask Santa to leave you one under the tree this year.

Record-setting storms like the one Sunday and Monday that flooded the Northwest could become more of the norm as climate change skews our region's rainfall patterns and leads to more of these massive deluges as compared to the typical drizzle.

It's not guaranteed, but scientists said that multiple computer climate models predict an increased likelihood of more rain—and more episodes of heavier rainfall—in fall and winter, less in the summer.

Monday Seattle logged nearly 5 inches of rain and scored the second rainiest day on record. First place still goes to a rainy day in October 2003.

"There is a risk under climate change of having more storms of this nature," said Eric Salathe, a research scientist with the University of Washington's Climate Impacts Group.

"Given that this is also a La Niña year, I'd be very surprised if this is the last such storm you get up there this year," said Kelly Redmond, a climate scientist and interim director of the Western Regional Climate Center. The center, in Reno, Nev., is operated by the National Oceanic and Atmospheric Administration.

"The bigger question is whether the Northwest is seeing more of these kinds of events," Redmond said. "It isn't just a matter of increased rainfall. It's also about the form of that precipitation . . . whether you are getting more 'typhoon' moisture out of the tropical regions."

Some contend it's no longer much in question. A study released Tuesday by the non-profit Environment Washington reported that storms with heavy rainfall are 30 percent more frequent in Washington now compared with 60 years ago. The analysis was done using data from weather stations.

"The thing that's interesting about this report is that certainly no single weather event can be tied directly to global warming, but the fact that we're seeing a greater frequency of these events is evidence of global warming in Washington state," said Bill LaBorde, program director for the environmental group.

"We've tried to let people be aware that there is this risk that has to be managed in some way," Salathe said.

Redmond and another colleague at NOAA, climatologist Jim Ashby, said their data does show an uptick in Northwest rainfall amount over the past 15 years. But both said it would be premature to try to draw any definitive conclusions as to a trend.

"There isn't really a firm pattern or trend yet," Ashby said. Ashby said 1950 is still the wettest year on record for the Pacific Northwest and the rainfall pattern is notoriously chaotic when viewed over the longer term.

"It's a very important question and there is some evidence to support the claim that rainfall is increasing in the Northwest," Redmond said. "It's possible. But the jury is still out on whether you are getting more of these warm, tropical moisture events."

Assuming the climate models, if not necessarily Environment Washington's hard numbers, are accurate in predicting more massive deluges, an important environmental question is how to control the downpour that flooded roadways and basements and scoured streams where salmon have been laying eggs in recent weeks.

Some engineers, scientists and environmentalists think there are ways to control stormwater runoff that helps people as well as fish, bugs, birds and other wildlife.

In the past, trees and plants would catch rain in their leaves and needles, allowing it to drip to the ground more slowly or holding [it] so it evaporates. Once it reached the ground it was spongy with decaying leaves and needles. Streams weren't constrained and able to flood their banks.

When an area is developed, water runs from streets and houses into gutters and eventually into streams and Puget Sound, carrying with it oil, toxic metals and pesticides. A study by the Department of Ecology released Friday found that stormwater was the greatest pathway to carrying most pollutants to the Sound.

One option for dealing with the stormwater is building detention ponds that hold the water and release it slowly and allow it to soak into the ground.

But that alone won't solve the problem—particularly with rainfalls like Monday's that dumped some 5.8 billion gallons of water on Seattle.

Could you build a detention facility at today's property prices and construction costs that could hold that much water? asked Bob Spencer, watershed stewardship coordinator for Seattle Public Utilities. "You just couldn't."

Projects such as the restoration of Thornton Creek at Northgate help a little bit. The creek is being unearthed from buried pipes to flow like a normal stream, albeit in a heavily urbanized setting. The creek is being restored with broader banks to hold more water during storms. But it won't do much for typhoon-type rains.

"Individual people can do things to improve the amount of impervious surfaces on their property," Spencer said. That means gravel driveways and patios made of paving stones instead of concrete. While costly, people can install green roofs that are covered in plants. Another less expensive option is a rain garden—basically a deep depression lined with gravel and plants where water can collect and soak into the ground.

Seattle has received kudos for projects in select areas that increase natural drainage and reduce runoff by making streets more narrow and lined with water-absorbing ditches, using porous cement and rain barrels. Rich Horner, a research associate professor with the UW's Civil and Environmental Engineering Department has studied the projects.

"You can definitely cut down on surface runoff with these techniques," he said. "And you're going to cut down on flooding too."

V. WATER MANAGEMENT

Editor's Introduction

How water gets to our faucets, sinks, and toilets is not a question most of us in the industrialized world ask regularly. We take for granted that we have a continuous flow of water in our homes. However, not everyone in the world can so easily turn on a faucet.

Thanks in large measure to geography and climate, the industrialized world has developed an effective water distribution system, complete with dams, aqueducts, pipelines, and a host of other utilities. The articles in this chapter examine various water management strategies, from those employed in the comparatively water-rich West to those used in drought-ridden and water-deprived regions, taking into account the negative effects some of these methods may have on the environment and human health. Also covered is the potential threat posed by aging infrastructure.

In the first article, "How to Fix Our Dam Problems," James G. Workman explains a proposed cap-and-trade system to finance the destruction or rehabilitation of thousands of aging dams throughout the United States. The current funding mechanism, Workman contends, is fraught with inefficiency and ought to be discontinued. Moreover, of the more than 2.5 million dams in the United States, 85 percent will have "outlived their average 50-year lifespan" in the next 20 years. Unless they are repaired, these dams will pose a risk not only to the surrounding ecosystems, but to people and property as well.

The authors of "Scaling Up Drinking Water Services," the subsequent piece in this section, evaluate a variety of water management systems in Australia, India, and South Africa. On a case-by-case basis, they highlight the unique challenges faced by each nation and how each in turn responded. Ultimately, some common themes recurred in their individual solutions: "In all countries, valuing water as an economic good and introducing some level of user charges were essential to getting providers to become more accountable to consumers," the authors write. Increasingly, many believe that the solution to the global water crisis requires that we first start to view water as an economic good rather than a right.

Randal Archibold describes a plan to counteract water shortfalls using treated sewer water in "From California Sewage, Drinking Water." Designers envision that the water purifying plant of the Orange County Water District will process 70 million gallons of water per day. However, like desalinization, a process in which saltwater is converted into potable water, recycling sewer water is an energy intensive process and is thus not particularly efficient or environmentally friendly. Nevertheless, in certain water-deprived regions, there may be no alternative.

In "Clean and Green," the authors discuss stormwater management strategies in Santa Monica California; Kansas City, Missouri; and Mission Hills, Kansas; and the associated environmental benefits these initiatives have provided.

How to Fix Our Dam Problems

BY JAMES G. WORKMAN
ISSUES IN SCIENCE AND TECHNOLOGY, FALL 2007

California is the world's eighth largest economy and generates 13% of U.S. wealth. Yet Governor Arnold Schwarzenegger says high temperatures, low rainfall, and a growing population have created a water crisis there. A third of the state is in extreme drought and, if there's another dry season, faces catastrophe. The governor fears that his economy could collapse without a $5.9 billion program to build more dams.

His concerns are widely shared in the United States—not to mention in dry Australia, Spain, China, and India. Yet as California desperately seeks new dam construction, it simultaneously leads the world in old dam destruction. It razes old dams for the same reasons it raises new dams: economic security, public safety, water storage efficiency, flood management, job creation, recreation, and adaptation to climate change. Dam-removal supporters include water districts, golf courses, energy suppliers, thirsty cities, engineers, farmers, and property owners.

With 1,253 dams risky enough to be regulated and 50 times that many unregistered small dams, California is a microcosm of the world. There are more than 2.5 million dams in the United States, 79,000 so large they require government monitoring. There are an estimated 800,000 substantial dams worldwide. But within the next two decades, 85% of U.S. dams will have outlived their average 50-year lifespan, putting lives, property, the environment, and the climate at risk unless they are repaired and upgraded.

Neither dam repair nor dam removal is a recent phenomenon. What is new is their scale and complexity as well as the number of zeros on the price tag. Between 1920 and 1956, in the Klamath River drainage 22 dams were dismantled at a total cost of $3,000. Today, the removal of four dams on that same river—for jobs, security, efficiency, safety, legal compliance, and growth—will cost upwards of $200 million.

Which old uneconomical dams should be improved or removed? Who pays the bill? The answers have usually come through politics. Pro-dam and anti-dam interests raise millions of dollars and press their representatives to set aside hundreds of millions more tax dollars to selectively subsidize pet dam projects. Other bills bail out private owners: A current House bill earmarks $40 million for repairs; another one sets aside $12 million for removals. The outcome is gridlock, lawsuits, debt spending, bloated infrastructure, rising risks, dying fisheries, and sick streams.

Dam decisions don't have to work that way. Rather than trust well-intentioned legislators, understaffed state agencies, harried bureaucrats, or nonscientific federal judges to decide the fate of millions of unique river structures, there's another approach. State and federal governments should firmly set in place safety and conservation standards, allow owners to make links between the costs and benefits of existing dams, and then let market transactions bring health, equity, and efficiency to U.S. watersheds. Social welfare, economic diversity, and ecological capital would all improve through a cap-and-trade system for water infrastructure. This system would allow mitigation and offsets from the vast stockpile of existing dams while improving the quality of, or doing away with the need for, new dam construction.

Big Benefits, Then Bigger Costs

A new dam rises when its public bondholder/taxpayer or private investor believes that its eventual benefits will outweigh immediate costs. When first built, dams usually fulfill those hopes, even if the types of benefits change over time. In early U.S. history, hundreds of dams turned water mills or allowed barge transport. Soon, thousands absorbed flood surges, diverted water for irrigation, or slaked the thirst of livestock. Later still, tens of thousands generated electrical power, stored drinking water for cities, and provided recreation. North America built 13% of its largest dams for flood control, 11% for irrigation, 10% for water supply, 11% for hydropower, 24% for some other single purpose such as recreation or navigation, and 30% for a mix of these purposes. Today, the primary reason is drinking water storage and, to a far lesser extent, hydropower and irrigation.

Unfortunately, we usually fail to heed all the indirect, delayed, and unexpected downstream costs of dams. With planners focused primarily on near-term benefits, during the past century three large dams, on average, were built in the world every day. Few independent analyses tallied exactly why those dams came about, how they performed, and whether people have been getting a fair return on their $2 trillion investment. Now that the lifecycle cost is becoming manifest, we are beginning to see previously hidden costs.

First, it turns out that a river is far more than a natural aqueduct. It is a dynamic continuum, a vibrant lifeline, a force of energy. Dams, by definition, abruptly stop it. But all dams fill with much more than water. They trap river silt or sediment at rates of between 0.5% and 1% of the dam's storage capacity every year. Layer by layer, that sediment settles in permanently. By restraining sediment upstream, dams accelerate erosion below; hydrologists explain that dams starve a hungry current that then must scour and devour more soil from the river bed and banks downstream. Silt may be a relatively minor problem at high altitudes, but it plagues U.S. landscapes east of the Rockies, where precious topsoil is crumbling into rivers, backing up behind dams, and flowing out to sea. Removing trapped sediment can cost $3 per cubic meter or more, when it can be done at all.

> What we didn't appreciate until recently is that dams also pollute the air.

The second enemy is the sun. Whereas sediment devours reservoir storage from below, radiant heat hammers shallows from above. In dry seasons and depending on size, dam reservoirs and diversions can evaporate more water than they store. Rates vary from dam to dam and year to year, but on average evaporation annually consumes between 5% and 15% of Earth's stored freshwater supplies. That's faster than many cities can consume. It's one of the reasons why the Rio Grande and Colorado Rivers no longer reach the sea and why precious alluvial groundwater is shrinking, too. Nine freshwater raindrops out of 10 fall into the ocean, so the trick is to see the entire watershed— from headwater forest to alluvial aquifers through downstream floodplain—as potentially efficient storage and tap into water locked beneath the surface. Today, irrigators pump more groundwater than surface water. In arid landscapes, water is more efficiently and securely stored in cool, clean alluvial aquifers than in hot, shallow, polluted reservoirs.

The third threat to dam performance, as both a cause and a consequence, is climate change. Dams are point-source polluters. Scientists have long warned that dams alter the chemistry and biology of rivers. They warm the water and lower its oxygen content, boosting invasive species and algae blooms while blocking and killing native aquatic life upstream and down. Rivers host more endangered species than any other ecosystem in the United States, and many of the nation's native plants and animals, from charismatic Pacific salmon to lowly Southern freshwater mussels, face extinction almost entirely because of dams.

What we didn't appreciate until recently is that dams also pollute the air. The public may commonly see dams as producers of clean energy in a time of dirty coal and escalating oil prices. Yet fewer than 2% of U.S. dams generate any power whatsoever. Some could be retrofitted with turbines, and perhaps various existing dams should be. But peer-reviewed scientific research has demonstrated that dams in fact may worsen climate change because of reservoir and gate releases of methane. Brazil's National Institute for Space Research calculated that the world's 52,000 large dams (typically 50 feet or higher) contribute more than 4% of the total warming impact of human activities. These dam reservoirs contribute 25% of human-caused methane emissions, the world's largest single source. Earth's millions of smaller dams compound that effect.

Worse, as climate change accelerates, U.S. dams will struggle to brace for predicted drought and deluge cycles on a scale undreamed of when the structures were built. This brings us to the fourth danger. Dams initially designed for flood control may actually make floods more destructive. First, they lure people to live with a false sense of security, yet closer to danger, in downstream floodplains. Then they reduce the capacity of upstream watersheds to absorb and control the sudden impact of extreme storms. Looking only at mild rainstorms in October 2005 and May 2006, three states reported 408 overtoppings, breaches, and damaged dams. Only half of the nation's high-hazard dams even have emergency action plans.

The scariest aspect of dams' liabilities is the seemingly willful ignorance in the United States of their long-term public safety risks. Engineers put a premium on safety, from design to construction through eventual commission. Yet after politicians cut the ceremonial ribbon, neglect creeps in. As dams age they exhibit cracks, rot, leaks, and in the worst cases, failure. In 2006, the Kaloko Dam on the Hawaiian island of Kauai collapsed, unleashing a 70-foot-high, 1.6-million-ton freshwater tsunami that carried trees, cars, houses, and people out to sea, drowning seven. This is not an isolated exception, but a harbinger.

These preventable tragedies happen because both public and private dams lack funds for upkeep and repair. In 2005, the American Society of Civil Engineers gave U.S. dams and water infrastructure a grade of D and estimated that nationwide, repairing nonfederal dams that threaten human life would cost $10.1 billion. The U.S. Association of State Dam Safety Officials (ASDSO) placed the cost of repairing all nonfederal dams at $36.2 billion. Yet Congress has failed to pass legislation authorizing even $25 million a year for five years to address these problems.

Cash-strapped states generally don't even permit dam safety officials to perform their jobs adequately. Dozens of states have just one full-time employee per 500 to 1,200 dams. Hence state inspectors, like their dams, are set up to fail. Between 1872 and 2006, the ASDSO reports, dam failures killed 5,128 people.

As environmental, health, and safety regulations drive up the cost of compliance, owners of old dams tend to litigate or lobby against the rules. Others simply walk away. The number of abandoned or obsolete dams keeps rising: 11% of inventoried dams in the United States are classified under indeterminate ownership.

To date, warnings have been tepid, fitful, disregarded, or politicized. In 1997, the American Society of Civil Engineers produced good guidelines for the refurbishment or retirement of dams. They have been ignored. In 2000, the landmark World Commission on Dams established criteria and guidelines to address building, managing, and removing dams, but its report so challenged water bureaucrats that the World Bank, the commission's benefactor, has tried to walk away from its own creation. Environmental organizations have published tool kits for improving or removing old dams, but activists often target only the most egregious or high-profile dozen or so problems that best advance their profile or fundraising needs.

Dams have always been politically charged and often the epitome of pork-barrel projects. For the same reasons, dam removal can get bipartisan support from leading Democrats and Republicans alike. The switch from the Clinton to Bush administrations led to attempted alterations of many natural resource policies, but one thing did not change: the accelerating rate of dam removals. In 1998, a dozen dams were terminated; in 2005, some 56 dams came down in 11 states. Yet despite bipartisan support, there has never been any specific dam policy in either administration. A dam's demise just happened, willy-nilly, here and there. Dams died with less legal, regulatory, or policy rationale than accompanied their birth.

Thoreau Had It Right

No laws, no regulations, no policy? Federal restraint remains an alluring ideal in a nation that feels cluttered with restrictions. It's a deeply ingrained American sentiment, embodied in Henry David Thoreau's famous remark in Civil Disobedience: "That government is best which governs least." Yet the founder of principled civil disobedience was also the first critic of seemingly benign dams because of their unintended effects.

While paddling with his brother on the Concord and Merrimack Rivers in 1839, Thoreau lamented the disappearance of formerly abundant salmon, shad, and alewives. Vanished. Why? Because "the dam, and afterward the canal at Billerica . . . put an end to their migrations hitherward." His elegy reads like an Earth First! manifesto: "Poor shad! where is thy redress? . . . armed only with innocence and a just cause . . . I for one am with thee, and who knows what may avail a crow-bar against that Billerica dam?"

Thoreau restrained himself from vigilante dam-busting, but 168 years later the effects of the country's dams have only multiplied in number and size. Happily, the end of Thoreau's tale might nudge us in the right direction. He did not complain to Washington or Boston for results, funds, or a regulatory crackdown. He looked upstream and down throughout the watershed and sought to build local consensus. Because the dam had not only killed the fishery but buried precious agricultural farmland and pasture, Thoreau advocated an emphatically civic-minded, consensus-based, collective, economically sensible proposal, in which "at length it would seem that the interests, not of the fishes only, but of the men of Wayland, of Sudbury, of Concord, demand the leveling of that dam."

In other words, if those watershed interests were combined, they could sort out fixed liabilities from liquid assets. The economic beneficiaries of a flowing river, including the legally liable dam owner, should pay the costs of old dam removal, just as the beneficiaries of any new dam pay the costs of its economic, environmental, and security effects. In a few words, Thoreau sketched the outlines of what could emerge as a policy framework for existing dams that could be adapted to a river basin, a state, or a nation.

The most successful and least intrusive policies can be grouped under the strategic approach known as cap and trade. That is, the government sets a mandatory ceiling on effects, pollution, or emissions by a finite group of public and private property stakeholders. This ceiling is typically lower than present conditions. But rather than forcing individual stakeholders to comply with that target by regulatory fiat, each one can trade offsets, what amount to pollution credits, with each other. Those who cut waste, emissions, and effects better may sell their extra credits to laggards or newcomers. This approach leverages incentives to reform, innovate, and improve into a competitive advantage in which everyone benefits, and so does nature.

Although it did not involve dams, a cap-and-trade policy was tested nationally under the 1990 Clean Air Act revisions aimed at cutting acid rain–causing sulfur dioxide emissions of U.S. factories in half. When it was announced, the utility industry gloomily predicted a clean–air recession, whereas environmentalists cried sell-out over the lack of top-down regulatory controls. But cap and trade turned out to reduce emissions faster than the most optimistic projection. The industry grew strong and efficient, and the result was the largest human health gains of any federal policy in the 1990s. Annual benefits exceeded costs by 40:1.

Since then, cap-and-trade policies have proliferated from India to China to Europe. Though far from flawless, a cap-and-trade carbon policy is one success story to emerge from the troubled Kyoto Protocol to reduce emissions that accelerate climate change. Nations and multinational corporations such as General Electric and British Petroleum used it to reduce polluting emissions of carbon dioxide and methane while saving voters and shareholders money in the process. More recently, atmospheric cap and trade has been brought down to earth; the valuation and exchange in environmental offsets have been applied to land and water ecosystems. Certain states use cap and trade in policies to curb nitrogen oxides and nonpoint water pollution, others to reduce sediment loads and water temperature, and still others to trade in water rights when diversions are capped. California's Habitat Conservation Plans work within the Endangered Species Act's "cap" of preservation, yet allow "trade" of improving, restoring, and connecting habitat so that although individuals may die, the overall population recovers. Under the Clean Water Act, a cap-and-trade policy encourages mitigation banking and trading, which leads to a net gain in wetlands.

In each case the policy works because it lets democratic governments do what they do best—set and enforce a strict uniform rule—while letting property owners, managers, investors, and entrepreneurs do what they do best: find the most cost-effective ways to meet that standard. Given the documented risks of the vast stockpile of aging dam infrastructure in the United States, a cap-and-trade policy for dams could be tested to see if it can restore efficiency, health, and safety to the nation's waters.

Making the Policy Work

The first step would be to inventory and define all the stakeholders. In air-quality cap-and-trade cases, these include factory owners, public utilities, manufacturers, refineries, and perhaps even registered car owners. In the case of dams, one could begin with the 79,000 registered owners in the National Inventory of Dams. Tracking down ownership of the estimated 2.5 million smaller unregistered dams may prove a bit challenging, until their owners realize that dismantling the dams can yield profit if removal credits can be bought and sold.

The second step would be to recognize the legitimate potential for trades. Dams yield (or once yielded) economic benefits, but every dam also has negative effects on air emissions and water quality, quantity, and temperature, therefore on human health and safety, economic growth, and stability. Even the most ardent dam supporter acknowledges that there is room for potentially significant gains in performance from dams as well as from the rivers in which they squat. Whereas the top-down goal in the past had been to subsidize or regulate new dams for their economic benefits, the aim in this case is horizontal: to encourage an exchange to reduce old dams' economic and ecological costs.

> Every dam also has negative effects . . . on human health and safety.

Third, quantify the kind, extent, and nature of those negative effects. Our scientific tools have advanced considerably and are now ready to measure most if not all of those qualitative damages observed by amateurs since Thoreau. By breaking them down into formal "conservation units," degrees Celsius, water quality, cubic meters of sediment, and so forth, we can quantify potential offsets in ecological and economic terms. The United States could set out rigorous scientific standards modeled on the Clean Air Act cap-and-trade policy or wetlands mitigation banking.

Fourth, start small, then replicate and scale up with what works best. The pilot exchanges could be structured by geography or by type of effect. But both kinds of pilot programs have already begun. One creative company in North Carolina, Restoration Systems, has begun to remove obsolete dams to gain wetlands mitigation credits that it can sell and trade, in most cases, to offset the destruction of nearby wetlands by highway building. In Maine, several dams in the Penobscot River watershed have been linked through mitigation as part of a relicensing settlement. On the Kennebec River, also in Maine, the destruction cost of the Edwards Dam was financed in large part by upstream industrial interests and more viable dams as part of a package for environmental compliance. On the west coast, the Bonneville Power Administration is using hydropower funds to pay for dam removals on tributaries within the Columbia River basin.

These early efforts are fine, but restricted geographically; each approach could be allowed to expand. The larger the pool of stakeholders, the greater are the economies of scale and the more efficient the result. But a national consensus and standards do not emerge overnight, nor should they, given that there are so many different dams. Each dam is unique in its history and specific in its effects, even though the cumulative extent and degree of those effects are statewide, national, and sometimes even global. A cap-and-trade policy will emerge nationally only as it builds on examples like these.

Finally, work within existing caps while using a standard that lets the amoral collective marketplace sort out good from bad. The beauty of this framework is that many of the national standards are already in place. Legal obligations to comply with the National Environmental Policy Act, Endangered Species Act, Clean Water Act, and Clean Air Act all have strong bearing on decisions to remove or improve dams. Some tweaking may be required, but perhaps not much. Recently, Congress revised the Magnuson-Stevens Act to pilot cap-and-trade policies in fishery management, in which fishermen trade shares of a total allowable or capped offshore catch of, say, halibut or red snapper.

Those overworked state and federal agencies responsible for enforcing laws—the ASDSO, the Army Corps of Engineers, the Fish and Wildlife Service, the National Marine Fisheries Services, and the Environmental Protection Agency—need not get bogged down in the thankless task of ensuring that each and every dam complies with each and every one of the laws. Dam owners may have better things to do than argue losing battles on several fronts with various government branches. All parties can better invest their time according to their mandate, strengths, and know-how: officials in setting the various standard legal caps and ensuring that they are strictly applied to the entire tributary, watershed, state, or nation; and dam owners in trading their way to the best overall result.

A Cap-and-Trade Scenario

Suppose, for example, that a worried governor determines to cap at one-third below current levels all state dam effects: methane emissions, sedimentation rates, evaporative losses, aquatic species declines, habitat fragmentations, artificial warming, reduced oxygen content, and number of downstream safety hazards. He wants these reductions to happen within seven years and is rigorous in enforcing the ceiling. That's the stick, but here's the carrot: He would allow dam owners to decide how to get under that ceiling on their own.

Taking note of seemingly contradictory trends around dam construction and destruction worldwide, one might ask, "How far will the current trends go? How many old dams are we talking about repairing or removing? Hundreds? Thousands? A few big ones? A million little ones? Do we need more dams or fewer?"

Such questions largely miss the point of the policy envisioned here. We don't need a specific number of dams, but rather we need healthier rivers, safer societies, and a more efficient and disciplined water-development infrastructure. How we get there is beyond the capacity of a single person to decide; only through a flexible horizontal market can we answer, together. A government policy can be the catalyst for and guide the direction of this market because it removes personal, political, ideological, and geographic biases from the equation. Nothing environmental and safety activists say or do can prevent new dam construction, and nothing dam supporters say or do can prevent old dams from coming down. But if the nation's anti-dam and pro-dam interests were gathered collectively under the same fixed national ceiling and left to their own devices, Adam Smith's "human propensity to truck, barter and exchange" could unite with the spirit of Thoreau's civil "wildness:" A cap-and-trade dam policy's embedded incentives would encourage the market's invisible hand while ensuring its green thumb.

The United States once led the world in the construction of dams, but over time, many have deteriorated. Now, under a cap-and-trade policy, it can bring horizontal discipline to that vertical stockpile of fixed liabilities, reducing risks while improving the health and safety of living communities. The United States can once again show the way forward on river development. Through such a cap-and-trade policy it can help dams smoothly and efficiently evolve with the river economies to which they belong.

Let us close where we began, with Governor Schwarzenegger. If states are indeed the laboratories of U.S. democracy, he stands in a unique position to mount a market-based experiment for the United States as part of his agenda to build bigger, higher, and more new dams for water storage. He has already expanded in-state cap-and-trade schemes in water transfers, endangered species habitats, ocean fishery rights, and carbon emissions. He is open to the idea of removing the O'Shaughnessy Dam that has submerged Hetch Hetchy Valley in Yosemite National Park, even while he seeks more water storage elsewhere. Now, as the governor makes his pitch for big new multibillion dollar dams to save California from parched oblivion, he and other governors, not to mention heads of state from Beijing to Madrid to New Delhi to Washington, DC, could institute effective new policies to protect Earth's liquid assets.

Scaling Up Drinking Water Services

By Junaid K. Ahmad, David Savage, and Vivek Srivastava
Development Outreach (World Bank), March 2004

Worldwide there have been many successes in the delivery of drinking water services. The reform of Phnom Penh's public utility in Cambodia and Cartaghena's water privatization in Colombia are outstanding examples. But, there are also cases of dramatic failures—Cochabamba, Bolivia, or Bangladesh's arsenic crisis. These successes and failures offer a host of lessons for reformers, but one stands out in particular: the success of service delivery depends on whether institutions of service provision are accountable to citizens. The challenge is thus "not to fix the pipes, but to fix the institutions that fix the pipes."

Institutional changes, which ensure that service providers are accountable to all citizens, are a highly political endeavor. Undertaking such changes on a pilot basis is difficult enough; scaling it up across jurisdictions and sustaining it over time, is a daunting challenge. Yet, it is precisely the scaling up of institutional change that is needed to ensure that the goal of universal access to basic services can be realized. How can governments ensure that all citizens have access—and quickly—to a basic level of water and sanitation services, that these services are provided on a sustainable basis, that service providers respond to a variety of consumer preferences across income levels, and can adapt endogenously to changing circumstances?

The historical experience of three countries—Australia, India, and South Africa—offers important insights into the process of institutional change in service delivery and the challenges of scaling up of service provision. The country settings—demographics, political systems, geographical size, economics, and income levels—are different; but it is precisely this diversity that enables us to draw common lessons and principles from their experiences.

The Case of Australia

Restructuring in the Australian water sector was initiated in the context of broader economy-wide reforms. Between 1960 and 1992, Australia slipped from being the third richest nation in the world to the fifteenth. This decline drove successive governments in the 1980s and 1990s to initiate wide-ranging economic reforms, including reform of public utilities in the infrastructure sector.

In this context, a compact was signed in the Council of Australian Governments between different tiers of government—the federal tier, the Commonwealth, and the states—to create an economically viable and ecologically sustainable water industry. The states decided to restructure their public agencies in the sector on the basis of agreed upon principles. These included introducing commercially viable and justifiable water pricing; costing and transparency of (cross) subsidies; institutional reforms of public monopolies to achieve separation of key institutional roles—policy, service delivery and regulation; performance monitoring; intensive public consultations and education; and measures related to natural resource sustainability, including allocation and trading in water entitlements.

In view of Australia's federal structure, the actual reform path—the implementation of the principles—was left to the discretion of the states. Different states and territories are introducing the reforms at different rates and in different ways. For examples, some states have viable state-wide utilities, others use local government utilities, some have state-wide regulators, others rely significantly on performance monitoring, and so on. These differences in implementation approaches reflect the differences in the initial legislative, economic, and political conditions of the separate jurisdictions. But in all cases, the institutional choice adopted by the states is defined by the agreed upon principles.

> Australia's water sector has become an important model for infrastructure reform.

As an incentive, the Commonwealth makes fiscal payments to the states and territories for achieving the milestones of reform. Although not large—less than one percent of the overall budget of the Commonwealth and states—the fiscal transfers provide sufficient incentive at the margin for the states to stay committed to the reform program. The initial reform timetable was optimistic and underestimated the complexity of the reform program requiring extensive research and analysis for effective implementation, the need for extensive consultative and educative processes and the demand that these reforms placed on governments, institutions, and stakeholders. But, after more than a decade of sustained institutional reform, Australia's water sector has become an important model for infrastructure reform.

The Case of Rural India

Rural India, with 700 million people, is currently undergoing a major reform in its drinking water and sanitation sector. A state subject under India's Constitution, rural water services have traditionally been provided through state water boards and departments. Water has been treated as a social good by the state agencies, supplied without any user charges or local stakeholder involvement in the delivery process. Top down in their approach, the boards were proficient at delivering hardware, but less inclined to undertake the operations and maintenance and manage service delivery. This was not surprising, as the boards were underwritten by Central and State budgetary outlays regardless of performance. The bias was for greater spending and often spending captured by political interests.

Drawing on the lessons learned from smaller projects—often financed in partnership with donors—central government in 1999 piloted the Sector Reform Program across all the states covering 70 million people. In the SRP, communities were mobilized through user group committees to determine their choice of service standard and process for managing service provision. Capital costs were shared between central government and communities, but communities were expected to pay fully for operations and maintenance. Water was treated as an economic good—valued for its use—thus increasing accountability to communities and enhancing their sense of ownership.

The SRP experience showed greater sustainability of services and more responsiveness to consumer preferences. But, scaling up of community delivery systems has proven to be a challenge—the problems of managing collective action, capacity constraints, and addressing the political context of existing state agencies are important policy issues that need to be addressed. Increasingly, local governments—panchayats—are being seen as the key link to managing a process of scaling up the SRP.

State governments are now being asked to develop a plan for shifting drinking water services in rural areas to a completely demand-driven, participatory approach where communities and local governments are partners in the provision of drinking water. In the process, states are being asked to re-define the role of the water agencies. The principles are fixed, but the state governments have the full flexibility to develop their individual approaches to implementation. Once endorsed by the political leadership of the states, the plans will form the basis of a Memorandum of Understanding between the state and central government, where the center will support the funding of the MoU against pre-agreed milestones of change proposed by the states. In addition, the center will provide funding for capacity support and clear monitoring and evaluation of the process with the possibility of benchmarking performance of the states.

The transition from state agencies, to community systems, and now to the proposed local government and community management of water and sanitation, reflects changes in the politics of India. While federal in structure—with a central government and several states—India adopted a centralized economic and a political model after independence. Over time, broader economic liberalization and strengthening of the federal system, including the introduction of local governments into the Constitution about a decade ago have changed the overall view of how services should be managed. Water and sanitation will not be an exception to these fundamental changes and success in scaling up service delivery will depend on the political, fiscal, and administrative relationship between the different tiers of governments.

The Case of South Africa

South Africa's water services sector has undergone far-reaching transformation since the advent of democracy in 1994. This transformation process has been underpinned by a strong commitment to eliminate the inequities of South Africa's apartheid past, but driven by a broader program to decentralize functions and finance to local government.

Although water services are defined as a local government function in the Constitution, the national government initially took the lead in expanding access to services. The Community Water Supply and Sanitation program was developed as a national investment program, implemented directly by the Department of Water Affairs and Forestry (DWAF) or through nationally owned water boards or NGO's. Initially, in the context of weak local government authorities, community management structures were established—although considerable emphasis was placed on large regional scheme investments.

> South Africa's water services sector has undergone far-reaching trans-formation since the advent of democracy in 1994.

The restructuring of the local government system through re-demarcation of municipal boundaries and a redefinition of local government functions created a structural conflict between community management structures and elected local government authorities. This occurred at a time of growing concern over the cost and sustainability of the national investment program. A program of fiscal decentralization, which involved the consolidation and decentralization of operating and capital transfers to local government, sought to address these problems through placing accountability for investment decisions with the operating authority and ensuring greater coordination between investment programs of all spheres of government.

Although DWAF has begun to transfer schemes it has built and operated to local government, concerns about their capacity to manage water distribution remain. Recognizing the positive relationship between functional assignments and actual capacity, DWAF has responded to the new environment through re-positioning itself as a "developmental regulator" of water services, rather than an investment agent or service provider. This focus on capacity building efforts at the local government level includes a policy framework that distinguishes between "authority" and "provider" functions and thus allows local authorities to engage other agencies, whether public or private sectors, to undertake actual provision of services under contract to the local authority. DWAF has also placed considerable emphasis on building local planning and infrastructure investment capacity and on developing effective monitoring and evaluation systems.

Some Lessons

Accountability to clients is at the heart of successful service provision. How to expand this relationship of accountability across the sector is central to the challenge of scaling up drinking water services. How can this be brought about? Australia, India and South Africa offer many lessons.

To begin with, scaling up of services is a political process. In Australia the broader forces of liberalization started it; in India it is the gradual opening up of the economy and the democratic forces of federalism; and in South Africa it was the end of apartheid and the emergence of a completely new democratic setting. These changes are complex and take time. None were big bang approaches to service reform and none saw the politics of reform in the water and sanitation sector come from within the sector.

Where the politics are not conducive to scaling up reforms, innovative pilots may have a demonstration role to play. But as the case of SRP in India suggests, scaling up pilots is not simply a replication of the pilots themselves. While pilots suggest important principles, the wider implementation of the principles may require a very different approach, as exemplified by the shift from SRP to a MoU between different tiers of government—similar to Australia's federal-state compact.

In all countries, valuing water as an economic good and introducing some level of user charges were essential to getting providers to become more accountable to consumers—rich and poor alike. This may well be a sine qua non of achieving universal services. Once the value of water is reflected in the transaction, allowing choices about standards and service delivery organization to be dictated by local preferences of communities becomes essential.

Separation of roles is also an essential element of the reform process. Within the sector, the policy making, regulatory, and service provision functions need to be kept in separate organizations and processes. Equally important, separating the powers and roles of different tiers of government is essential to enable the center to play a role of providing incentives for change. But this requires that the fiscal rules of the game between different tiers of government are clear and binding. In Australia, and increasingly South Africa, this is the case. In India, the reforms of rural drinking water may well be delayed because the rules of India's fiscal federalism are still in a state of flux. Importantly, the evolution of multi-tiered governments may well facilitate the separation of policymaking from regulation and service provision, which is essential to the sector—the two processes are interlinked.

With the separation of roles emerges the potential for independent benchmarking of providers and tiers of government responsible for service delivery. In effect, information becomes an important tool for catalyzing and sustaining reforms, and one which is being widely used in Australia and increasingly in the other countries.

Finally, reforms require mobilization of citizens and capacity support to governments and communities to understand and undertake the changes. Central governments can play a proactive role in designing such systems of capacity support. But the lesson is clear: such support is best delivered in the context of on-going reforms.

From California Sewage, Drinking Water

By Randal C. Archibold
The International Herald Tribune, November 28, 2007

It used to be so final: flush the toilet and waste be gone.

But this week, for millions of people here in Orange County, pulling the lever will be the start of a long, intense process to purify the sewage into drinking water—after a hard scrubbing with filters, screens, chemicals and ultraviolet light and the passage of time underground.

On Friday, the Orange County Water District will turn on what industry experts say is the world's largest plant devoted to purifying sewer water to increase drinking water supplies. They and others hope it serves as a model for authorities worldwide facing persistent drought, predicted water shortages and projected growth.

The process, called by proponents "indirect potable water reuse" and "toilet to tap" by the wary, is getting a close look in several cities.

The San Diego City Council approved a pilot plan in October to bolster a drinking water reservoir with recycled sewer water. The mayor vetoed the proposal as costly and unlikely to win public acceptance, but the council will consider overriding it in early December.

San Jose-area water officials announced a study of the issue in September, water managers in southern Florida approved a plan last week calling for abundant use of recycled wastewater in the coming years in part to help restock drinking water supplies, and planners in Texas are giving it serious consideration.

"These types of projects you will see springing up all over the place where there are severe water shortages," said Michael Markus, the general manager of the Orange County district, whose plant, which will process 70 million gallons, or nearly 3 billion liters, a day, has already been visited by water managers from across the globe.

The finished product, which district managers say exceeds drinking water standards, will not flow directly into kitchen and bathroom taps; state regulations forbid that.

Instead it will be injected underground, with half of it helping to form a barrier against seawater intruding on groundwater sources and the other half gradually filtering into aquifers that supply 2.3

million people, about three-quarters of the county. The recycling project will produce much more potable water and at a higher quality than did the mid-1970s-era plant it replaces.

The Groundwater Replenishment System, as the $481 million plant here is known, is a labyrinth of tubing and tanks that sucks in treated sewer water the color of dark beer from a sanitation plant next door and runs it through microfilters to remove solids. The water then undergoes reverse osmosis, forcing it through thin, porous membranes at high pressure, before it is further cleansed with peroxide and ultraviolet light to break down any remaining pharmaceuticals and carcinogens.

The result, Markus said, "is as pure as distilled water" and about the same cost as buying water from wholesalers.

Recycled water, also called reclaimed or gray water, has been used for decades in agriculture, landscaping and by industrial plants.

And for years, treated sewage, known as effluent, has been discharged into oceans and rivers, including the Mississippi and the Colorado, which supply drinking water for millions.

But only about a dozen water agencies in the United States, and several more in other countries, recycle treated sewage to replenish drinking water supplies, though none here steer the water directly into household taps. They typically spray or inject the water into the ground and allow it to percolate down to aquifers.

Namibia's capital, Windhoek, among the most arid places in Africa, is believed to be the only place in the world that practices "direct potable reuse" on a large scale, with recycled water going directly into the tap water distribution system, said James Crook, a water industry consultant who has studied the issue.

The projects are costly and often face health concerns from opponents.

Such was the case on Nov. 6 in Tucson, Arizona, where a wide-ranging ballot measure that would have barred the city from using purified water in drinking water supplies failed overwhelmingly. The water department there said it had no such plans, but the idea has been discussed.

John Kromko, a former Arizona state legislator who advocated the prohibition, said he was skeptical about claims that the recycling process cleanses all contaminants from the water and he suggested that Tucson limit growth rather than find new ways to feed it.

"We really don't know how safe it is," he said. "And if we controlled growth, we would never have to worry about drinking it."

Mayor Jerry Sanders of San Diego, in vetoing the City Council plan there, said it "is not a silver bullet for the region's water needs" and the public has never taken to the idea in the 15 years it has been discussed off and on.

Although originally estimated at $10 million for the pilot study in San Diego, water department officials said the figure would be refined and the total cost of the project might be hundreds of millions of dollars. While the council wants to offset the cost with government grants and other sources, Sanders predicted it would add to already escalating water bills.

"It is one of the most expensive kinds of water you can create," said Fred Sainz, a spokesman for the mayor. "It is a large investment for a very small return."

San Diego, which imports about 85 percent of its water because of a lack of aquifers, asked residents this year to curtail water use.

Here in Orange County, the project, a collaboration between the water and sanitation districts, has not faced serious opposition, in part because of a public awareness and marketing campaign.

Early on, officials secured the backing of environmental groups, elected leaders and civic groups, helped in part by the fact the project eliminated the need for the sanitation district to build a new pipe to spew effluent into the ocean.

Orange County began purifying sewer water in 1976 with its Water Factory 21, which dispensed the cleansed water into the ground to protect groundwater from encroaching seawater.

That plant has been replaced by the new one, with more advanced technology, and is aimed at coping with not only current water needs but also expectations that the population in the county will grow by 500,000 by 2020.

Still, said Stephen Coonan, a water industry consultant in Texas, such projects proceed slowly.

"Nobody is jumping out to do it," he said. "They want to make sure the science is where it should be. I think the public is accepting we are investigating it."

Clean and Green

By Donald Baker, Les Lampe, and Laura Adams
American City and County, March 1, 2007

Public desire for open space that includes clean streams and lakes, along with more stringent federal environmental regulations, have prompted many communities to adopt environmentally friendly stormwater management methods. Rather than using the traditional practices of enclosing channels in pipes and draining wetlands, which often permanently alter the ecosystem and destroy habitats, alternative methods mimic natural landscape features to improve water quality and waterside environments.

Traditional stormwater practices typically decrease water quality because they do not include a natural ecosystem to assimilate pollutants. In addition, they tend to shorten flow paths, creating higher peak flows. Many communities face flooding issues as a result.

Environmentally friendly approaches to stormwater management are designed to resemble the natural functions that support habitats and protect water quality. In addition, they slow water flow and often detain it, which results in lower peak flows and less flooding.

Stream Cleaning

Santa Monica, Calif., has adopted new stormwater management methods to improve its water quality. Situated on the Pacific Coast north of Los Angeles, the city is surrounded on all sides by other cities or by Santa Monica Bay, which collects all of the city's stormwater runoff. To protect the water quality of the bay, as well as the beauty of area beaches, the city has begun building additional stormwater treatment facilities to remove pollutants—such as organic compounds, metals and trash—from runoff before it reaches the beach. Because space is limited, the city is building the facilities underground.

One recently completed facility was built under a parking lot in a park owned and operated by Los Angeles. The Westside Water Quality Improvement Project, which treats stormwater runoff from a large portion of Santa Monica, was designed with no moving parts, chemical additives or electrical power requirements. "Urban runoff pollution is a major problem for our coastal waters, and this project is one big step in a long and continual process to ensure cleaner water and a healthier coastline, and to safeguard life," says Santa Monica Senior Environmental Analyst Neal Shapiro.

The system is designed to remove chemicals, such as pesticides, as well as organic compounds from automobile emissions and other sources from stormwater runoff. While not its primary purpose, the facility may collect chemicals from accidental spills, preventing them from reaching the bay. Santa Monica currently is identifying other sites for similar treatment systems.

While Lenexa, Kan., is not as confined as Santa Monica and other cities, it has plenty of stormwater and must plan for its proper management now and in the future. In the late 1990s, Lenexa officials began adopting more stringent stormwater design criteria, a stream buffer ordinance, and erosion and sediment control ordinances. To raise money to pay for better stormwater management, the city created a stormwater utility and instituted a capital development charge, and residents approved a sales tax to fund construction of new treatment facilities that also could be used as recreational areas.

The city's stormwater quality efforts are primarily designed to manage nutrients and sediment—the main pollutants from residential areas that comprise the majority of the city's landscape. Nutrients attach to the sediment, and the sediment clogs streams and chokes out aquatic vegetation.

Lenexa is creating multi-use facilities that manage stormwater, prevent floods, improve water quality and provide recreational outlets for residents. The city displays information about watershed protection on signs throughout the park-like areas and uses environmentally friendly construction materials where possible.

Taking a Holistic View

In Kansas City, Mo., as in many large cities, outdated stormwater infrastructure has inadequate capacity to carry runoff from large storms and to adequately treat it to meet current standards. A large portion of the city's stormwater infrastructure is in a combined sewer system that transports both stormwater and sewage. During heavy storms, increased runoff can cause overflows that discharge untreated sewage into area waterways.

To update the system and ensure it can handle future growth, local officials are reviewing the city's entire stormwater management program, including physical components as well as administrative and financial management procedures, to identify areas for improvement. In the months ahead, they will update existing flood control plans to reflect a holistic approach to stormwater management that involves flood control, combined sewer overflow reduction, water quality management and natural resource protection.

As part of the effort, Mayor Kay Barnes kicked off a program in November 2005 to encourage residents to plant rain gardens, which are shallow basins or depressions foliated with native plants that have deep roots that help water infiltrate the soil. The mayor's goal is for 10,000 rain gardens to be planted to demonstrate that if residents and businesses manage their own stormwater, peak flows to the city's infrastructure will reduce—as will costs for infrastructure improvements—and water quality in local streams will improve. The program also is raising residents' awareness of how their daily activities can affect stormwater runoff.

Nearby Mission Hills and Mission, Kan., also are addressing flooding issues, which have been caused by lack of regulations and upstream development that has generated more runoff. Mission Hills is an affluent community in the Kansas City metropolitan area in which residents frequently use public areas for walking, biking, jogging and relaxation. However, recent developments threaten to change the streamside corridors that residents have come to enjoy.

Development upstream of the city over the years has increased the amount of runoff channeled to area streams. Combined with aging stream channel walls and other infrastructure, the runoff is causing stream banks to fail, jeopardizing adjacent roads, water and gas mains, sanitary sewers, driveways and other property.

Rather than addressing each issue individually, city officials have begun studying the stream network in its entirety and searching for stormwater management practices that can improve large parts of the network at once. Numerous city staff as well as the planning commission, parks board and city council members are involved in the study. "This process has changed people's opinions on how city government manages its streams," says Mission Hills City Administrator Courtney Christensen. "Instead of more limited city government involvement, people feel it is imperative that the city protect our important natural resources."

As a result of the study, city officials will develop stream protection guidelines for buffers, landscaping and channel walls. They also will address land disturbance issues, lawn chemical applications, impervious lot coverage, and develop educational materials for residents. The measures will stabilize runoff from impervious areas and will protect—and eventually improve—the stream corridors by setting back human intervention and activities from streams. The buffers also will filter pollutants from the runoff before it enters the waterways.

Mission, Kan., began changing its stormwater management practices approximately three years ago, when costly floods prompted the city to complete large-scale flood control improvements and to redevelop its downtown area. As the city continues making improvements, it is incorporating environmentally friendly practices and stream restoration projects where they are feasible. City leaders now are looking for methods to decrease runoff and improve water quality citywide.

The city is conducting a study funded by the U.S. Army Corps of Engineers to identify locations for new treatment facilities and stream restoration projects. The project will provide a plan for constructing facilities and stream restoration projects that will improve the environment and the water quality of area streams. In addition, the study includes the development of a geographic information system tool that will identify suitable locations for the projects based on land use, topography and stream connections. The tool will select appropriate projects based on those parameters and on the stream quality. From there, cost estimates for project construction will be developed, and improvements will be prioritized for construction.

The city is working with Kansas State University to monitor the effects of the improvements. It also is constructing demonstration projects that will be monitored for their effects on water quality and will be used to help educate residents about the importance of managing stormwater in an environmentally friendly way.

Like Santa Monica, Kansas City and Mission Hills, many communities throughout the country are embracing environmentally friendly stormwater management methods because of the ecosystem improvements and social benefits they provide. Such holistic and "green" approaches aim to ensure that the natural beauty that residents enjoy does not disappear in the future.

BIBLIOGRAPHY

Books

Allan, J. A. *The Middle East Water Question: Hydropolitics and the Global Economy*. London: I.B. Tauris, 2001.

Altman, Nathaniel. *Sacred Water: The Spiritual Source of Life*. New York: HiddenSpring, 2002.

Barlow, Maude and Tony Clarke. *Blue Gold: The Fight to Stop the Corporate Theft of the World's Water*. New York: The New Press, 2005.

Barlow, Maude. *Blue Covenant: The Global Crisis and the Coming Battle for the Right to Water*. New York: The New Press, 2007.

Barnett, Cynthia. *Mirage: Florida and the Vanishing Water of the Eastern U.S*. Ann Arbor, Mich.: University of Michigan Press, 2007.

Bastasch, Rick. *Oregon Water Handbook: A Guide to Water and Water Management*. Corvallis, Ore.: Oregon State University Press, 2006.

Clarke, Robin and Jannet King. *The Water Atlas*. New York: The New Press, 2004.

Colby, Bonnie G. *Arizona Water Policy: Management Innovations in an Urbanizing, Arid Region*. Washington, D.C.: Resources for the Future, 2006.

Doods, Walter K. *Freshwater Ecology*. Oxford, U.K.: Elsevier, Inc., 2002.

Erie, Steven P. *Beyond Chinatown: The Metropolitan Water District, Growth, and the Environment in Southern California*. Palo Alto, Calif.: Stanford University Press, 2006.

Garcetti, Gil and Peter H. Gleick. *Water Is Key: A Better Future for Africa*. Glendale, Calif.: Balcony Press, 2007.

Glennon, Robert Jerome. *Water Follies: Groundwater Pumping and the Fate of America's Fresh Water*. Washington, D.C.: Island Press, 2002.

Ho'ala , Lono Kahuna Kupua. *Don't Drink The Water: The Essential Guide to Our Contaminated Drinking Water and What You Can Do About It*. Twin Lakes, Wisc.: Lotus Press, 2003.

Holland, Marjorie, et al. *Achieving Sustainable Freshwater Systems: A Web of Connections*. Washington, D.C.: Island Press, 2003.

Jehl, Douglas. *Whose Water Is It?: The Unquenchable Thirst of a Water-Hungry World*. New York: Random House, 2004.

Kandel, Robert. *Water From Heaven*. New York: Columbia University Press, 2003.

Kerley, Barbara. *A Cool Drink of Water*. Washington, D.C.: National Geographic Society, 2002.

Koeppel, Gerald T. *Water for Gotham: A History*. Princeton, N.J.: Princeton University Press, 2001.

Leslie, Jacques. *Deep Water: The Epic Struggle Over Dams, Displaced People, and the Environment*. New York: Farrar, Straus and Giroux, 2005.

Leuven, R. S. E. W., et al, eds. *Living Rivers: Trends and Challenges in Science and Management.* New York: Springer Verlag, 2006.

Lewis, William. *Water and Climate in the Western United States.* Boulder, Colo.: University Press of Colorado, 2003.

Livingston, James V. *Focus on Water Pollution Research.* Happauge, N.Y.: Nova Science Publishers, 2006.

Marq de Villiers. *Water: The Fate of Our Most Precious Resource.* Boston: Houghton Mifflin, 2000.

Masood, Ehsan and Daniel Schaffer. *Dry: Life Without Water.* Cambridge, Mass.: Harvard University Press, 2006.

Morris, Robert D. *The Blue Death: Disease, Disaster, and the Water We Drink.* New York: HarperCollins Publishers, 2007.

Murphy, Dallas. *To Follow the Water: Exploring the Ocean to Discover Climate.* New York: Basic Books, 2007.

Olivera, Oscar and Tom Lewis. *Cochabamba! Water War in Bolivia.* Cambridge, Mass.: South End Press, 2004.

Peter Annin. *The Great Lakes Water Wars.* Washington, D.C.: Island Press, 2003.

Pollert, J. and Bozidar Dedus. *Security of Water Supply Systems: Systems from Source to Tap.* Dordrecht, The Netherlands: Springer, 2006.

Postel, Sandra and Brian Richter. *Rivers for Life: Managing Water for People and Nature.* Washington, D.C.: Island Press, 2003.

Rouyer, Alwyn R. *Turning Water Into Politics: The Water Issue in the Palestinian-Israeli Conflict.* New York: Palgrave Macmillan, 2000.

Shiva, V. *Water Wars: Privatization, Pollution, and Profit.* South End Press, 2002.

Sullivan, Patrick, et al. *The Environmental Science of Drinking Water.* Oxford, U.K.: Elsevier, Inc., 2005.

Swain, Ashok. *Managing Water Conflict: Asia, Africa, and the Middle East.* New York: Routledge, 2004.

Trawick, Paul B. *The Struggle for Water in Peru: Comedy and Tragedy in the Andean Commons.* Palo Alto, Calif.: Stanford University Press, 2003.

Viessman, Warren Jr., and Mark J. Hammer. *Water Supply and Pollution Control*, 7th ed. Upper Saddle River, N.J.: Prentice Hall, 2004.

Web Sites

Readers seeking additional information about the global water supply may wish to refer to the following Web sites, all of which were operational as of this writing.

Global Health and Education Foundation: Safe Drinking Water Is Essential

http://www.drinking-water.org/flash/splash.html

The Global Health and Education Foundation, a division of the National Academy of Sciences, provides information on the state of the world's water supply. Their highly interactive Web site, which includes videos and maps as well as feature articles and news reports, is divided into sections on water sources, treatment, and distribution.

U.S. Department of the Interior: Bureau of Reclamation

http://www.usbr.gov

The Bureau of Reclamation, a branch of the U.S. Department of the Interior, manages water in the western United States. Its Web site contains information about water management in the region, including a database and maps.

U.S. Environmental Protection Agency (EPA): Ground Water and Drinking Water

http://www.epa.gov/safewater/

This Web site, which is maintained by the Office of Ground Water and Drinking Water (OGWDW), the branch of the EPA responsible for overseeing implementation of the Safe Drinking Water Act, provides videos, an A to Z topic list, and other resources focusing on delivering safe, potable water to the nation's citizens.

U.S. Geological Survey (USGS): Water Resources in the United States

http://water.usgs.gov/

The USGS is charged with providing water information to the U.S. citizens. The organization's Web site features state-by-state analyses, as well as downloadable software applications, maps, and other data.

U.S. Geological Survey (USGS): Water Science for School

http://ga.water.usgs.gov/edu/

This portion of the USGS Web site, which is aimed at educating students, provides information about water and water management.

UNESCO: Water

http://www.unesco.org/water/index.shtml

Contains news, events, publications, and information on global freshwater resources from UNESCO, the science and educational arm of the United Nations. Among the material provided, are case studies, news reports, and other publications as well as links to government and non-government Web sites.

University of Arizona Water Resource Research Center
http://ag.arizona.edu/AZWATER/

Established in 1964, the WRRC is a research unit of the University of Arizona and is designated as the state's water resource center. It conducts water policy research and analysis, and publishes its findings on this Web site. Also provided are resources for freshwater research, including news reports and lecture transcripts.

WaterPartners International
http://water.org/index.aspx

The mission of WaterPartners International, a non-profit organization (NPO) based in the United States, is to ensure that the developing world has access to safe drinking water and adequate sanitation. Its Web site features a variety of resources on the global water crisis, including articles, links to other Web sites, and lesson plans for teachers.

World Health Organization (WHO): Water Sanitation and Health (WSH)
http://www.who.int/water_sanitation_health/en/

A division of the United Nations (UN), the WHO "works on aspects of water, sanitation and hygiene where the health burden is high, where interventions could make a major difference and where the present state of knowledge is poor," according to its Web site, which features information on water crisis centers throughout the world and what can be done to help.

World Wildlife Foundation (WWF): Freshwater—Conserving the Source of Life
http://www.panda.org/about_wwf/what_we_do/freshwater/index.cfm

The WWF is a global non-profit organization dedicated to preserving the world's resources by fostering activism and disseminating information to the public. This division of their Web site relating to freshwater, includes data on water usage, pollution, and depletion and offers strategies to better conserve water resources.

Additional Periodical Articles with Abstracts

More information about the global water supply and related subjects can be found in the following articles. Readers who require a more comprehensive selection are advised to consult the *Readers' Guide Abstracts* and other H.W. Wilson publications.

Tainted Water on Tap. Stephanie Chalupka. *American Journal of Nursing* v. 105 pp40–53 November 2005.

The author describes some of the possible health effects from contaminated water. An estimated 900,000 cases of waterborne illness occur each year in the U.S., and, although the EPA regulates the levels of 87 natural and synthetic contaminants in drinking water, thousands more are unregulated. In 2001–02, 31 outbreaks of disease associated with drinking water were reported in 19 states. The main types of contaminants are described, and some steps that nurses can take to help reduce the risk of waterborne illness in vulnerable populations and improve the status of local drinking water supplies are also discussed.

Hard Truth. Dry Times. Rod Davis. *D* v. 33 pp68–75+ September 2006.

Northeast Texas must be flooded in order to meet Dallas's water needs, Davis reports. Lake Lavon is already ten feet below normal and losing volume daily under the rainless skies of Collin County. The problems at the 21,400-acre reservoir could spell the end for the suburbs that have developed on the tenuous, semi-arid soil north and east of Dallas. These areas rely on the lake as their primary source of water. Moreover, the economies of north Texas are so interdependent that the collapse of even one of the three major municipal water suppliers would prompt emergency water-borrowing and desperation. The nearest water resources are in northeast Texas, and obtaining them means constructing several new reservoirs over the next 50 years. The most controversial of the new sites, Marvin Nichols, would flood 72,000 acres when finished in 2040.

For the Good of Our Water Supply, Kick the Bottle. *ENR* v. 259 p104 July 2–9, 2007.

The author applauds the decision by Gavin Newsom, the mayor of San Francisco, California, that the city will not pay for bottled water if tap water is available. Newsom's stance counters the pernicious marketing of bottled water companies and promotes the environmental benefits of tap water. His executive order maintains that over 47 million barrels of oil a year are used to produce plastic bottles, over a billion of which end up in California landfills every year. If people drink tap water, they will care about its quality and politicians will spend the money needed to ensure that America's drinking water remains the best in the world.

Providing Basic Utilities in Sub-Saharan Africa: Why Has Privatization Failed? Kate Bayliss and Terry McKinley. *Environment* v. 49 pp24–32 April 2007.

The widespread failure of the privatization of water and electric utilities in sub-Saharan Africa highlights the need for public investment, Bayliss and McKinley contend. Contrary to expectations, private investors have shied away from investing in water and electricity utilities in sub-Saharan Africa, making it costly for governments to motivate them to invest. Moreover, the focus of investors on cost means that societal objectives, such as reducing poverty and promoting equity, have not been met. The current situation highlights the necessity of building up the capacity of the public sector and financing more extensive public investment in water and electric utilities. A dramatic scaling up of external and domestic resources will be required to finance this expansion. This approach is consistent with the adoption of more ambitious Millennium Development Goals in the region.

Drugged Drinking Water. Carol Potera. *Environmental Health Perspectives* v. 108 pA446 October 2000.

Scientists are beginning to monitor the extent of pharmaceutical and personal health-care products (PPCPs) in the aquatic environment and their consequences, Potera observes. PPCPs that are excreted from or washed off the body naturally end up in the sewage that flows into sewer systems and septic tanks. However, researchers are now finding that, through leaching from septic tanks and escaping intact through sewage treatment processes, a selection of these substances is ending up back in the drinking water. The big unknown is whether or not PPCPs present a health concern now or in the future.

The Ecology of Hollywood. Rory Spowers. *Geographical* v. 72 pp52–8 August 2000.

In this article, Spowers examines the impact that Los Angeles, California, has had on the natural environment and the rise of environmentalism in the city. With today's intensive farming methods, it takes 20,000 liters of water to produce what an average Californian eats in a day, so the issue of water supply is never far away. The city, which must import over a trillion gallons of water per year via the 720 km Californian aqueduct, loses much of its considerable winter rainfall due to concrete drainage systems, and 40 percent of wells in southern California are contaminated above federal limits. In the past, Los Angeles has destroyed wetland areas and its very own L.A. River. However, plans are under way to restore this river for the sake of ecological sustainability, the linking of disparate communities, and symbolism. There is a feeling of optimism about the future of nature in a city that has always been viewed as being in fundamental opposition to it.

Foreign Faucet. Tom Arrandale. *Governing* v. 16 pp38–40 June 2003.

U.S. cities that use private firms to run water systems are increasingly hiring foreign companies, Arrandale reports. The water services industry in America has been consolidating into larger firms that operate in many states. In the past few years, European-based utility corporations have been acquiring those companies and bidding aggressively for new contracts to operate U.S. water systems. Some previously unspoken worries about the global reach of foreign corporations have started seeping into water-privatization debates, but local officials may have few alternatives to dealing with the foreign-controlled water conglomerates.

Water as a Human Right: The Understanding of Water in the Arab Countries of the Middle East. Simone Klawitter and Hadeel Qazzaz. *International Journal of Water Resources Development* v. 21 pp253–71 June 2005.

The international community has affirmed the human right to water in a number of international treaties, declarations and other documents, Klawitter and Qazzaz report. Most notably, the United Nations (UN) Committee on Economic, Social and Cultural Rights adopted in November 2002 a General Comment on the Right to Water setting out international standards and obligations relating to the right to water. Based on the UN concept of water as a human right for selected Arab countries in the Middle East (Egypt, Palestine, Jordan, Lebanon), the paper analyzes if and to what extent these concepts are acknowledged. It aims to identify the scale of knowledge of and commitment to the UN concept in the region, and the main areas of concern in each country regarding water as a human right. The paper summarizes the main challenges facing strategic and coordinated action towards the UN concept of water as a human right, identifies what types of processes and institutions need to be developed to meet the challenges of the concept, and provides best practice examples from countries that have shown innovation. Objectives and priority ideas for activities of non-governmental organizations are recommended.

Scientists Tackle Water Contamination in Bangladesh. Samuel Loewenberg. *Lancet* v. 370 pp 471–2 August 11–17, 2007.

An innovative, multidisciplinary research effort is under way to tackle arsenic contamination in Bangladesh, Loewenberg notes. More than 70 million people in Bangladesh are estimated to be exposed to toxic levels of arsenic from their drinking water. The arsenic is thought to occur naturally in wells where the people obtain their water. The response of international aid agencies to the problem has been scant, especially since researchers estimate that substantial mitigation could be achieved for less than $100 million. Experts and scientists from among the world's elite research institutions are devising a variety of ways to address the problem, and they have already developed innovative and inexpensive solutions. All of those involved in the initiative agree that the arsenic contamination is solvable but say that lack of political will and funding continue to impede progress.

Tijuana's Toxic Waters. Lori Saldana. *NACLA Report on the Americas* v. 33 pp31–47 November/December 1999.

In this article, part of a special section on the U.S.-Mexico borderlands, Saldana discusses the toxic waters that are present in the Mexican city of Tijuana. Within the city, many are employed in facilities that are termed *maquiladoras*. The large number of these factories has had numerous social, economic, and environmental implications. The maquiladoras' demand for water has put pressure on the city's water supply and its ability to ensure clean water for a rapidly growing population. It has also led to a shortage of clean water. Although these industries are causing many problems, support for them remains very strong. The majority of those that own these industries would choose to endure continuously high rates of labor turnover rather than change their hiring practices and the conditions under which their employees must work.

Dangerous Waters. Sharon P. Nappier, Robert S. Lawrence, and Kellogg J. Schwab. *Natural History* v. 116 pp 46–49 November 2007.

Contamination of drinking water is an ongoing problem in some regions of the world, the authors contend. Current estimates suggest that almost 20 percent of the global population does not have access to a supply of clean water. Water supplies are contaminated by infectious pathogens and harmful chemicals; such contamination contributes to the deaths of millions of people worldwide every year. As soon as innovative water filters and water-transport systems are developed, new contaminants and diseases become an issue. The problem is exacerbated by rising populations and increased water consumption, with agriculture and industry accounting for 70 percent and 22 percent, respectively, of current freshwater use. As part of its Millennium Development Goals, the UN aims to reduce the number of people worldwide who lack adequate water and sanitation by half and curb the unsustainable exploitation of water.

Thirsty Dragon at the Olympics. Dai Qing and Geremie R. Barme, trans. *The New York Review of Books* pp8+ December 6, 2007.

The writer discusses how China's dam projects have damaged the local environment and criticizes the waste of natural resources epitomized by preparations for the 2008 Olympic Games in Beijing. Water for farmers living on the outskirts of greater Beijing is strictly rationed, yet those in charge of preparations for the Olympics in Beijing are celebrating the creation of the ultimate "water follies," which will include the enormous lake surrounding the National Grand Theater and the biggest fountain in the world. The environment of Beijing might have been able to withstand such a spectacle if it had been held 300 years ago, or even 100 years ago, given that the city is bordered by mountains on three sides, has five significant water sources, and once had many lakes and marshes with underground springs. Beijing is totally different today, however. Its reservoirs are 90 percent empty, and all of its rivers contain unprecedentedly low levels of water.

Under China's Booming North, the Future Is Drying Up. Jim Yardley. *The New York Times* ppA1+ September 28, 2007.

In this article, part of a series entitled "Choking on Growth" that examines China's epic pollution crisis, Yardley contends that water has been a vital part of China's rapid economic growth over the past three decades, but the country's often wasteful use of its resources is pushing it toward a water crisis. Pollution is widespread, and water scarcity is already severe in north China. The Communist Party has long insisted on grain self-sufficiency, a policy that consumes enormous quantities of groundwater in the North China Plain.

No Longer Waiting for Rain, an Arid West Takes Action. Randal C. Archibold and Kirk Johnson. *The New York Times* ppA1+ April 4, 2007.

In the grip of a severe drought since 1999 and realizing that the Colorado River can no longer sustain its burgeoning population, Western states are now springing into action, the authors observe. Arizona has resurrected an idled desalinization plant, while neighboring Nevada has laid plans for a 280-mile pipeline which would divert water from the northern part of the state to Las Vegas. However, fierce competition for the limited water supply has re-ignited old rivalries and prompted some states, as in the case of Wyoming and Montana, to wage legal battles over what they believe are rightful claims.

The Future Is Drying Up. Jon Gertner. *The New York Times Magazine* pp68–77+ October 21, 2007.

The West, as well as being the most rapidly growing part of America, is the driest, and climate change could be greatly exacerbating matters, Gertner observes. Last June, environmental engineer Bradley Udall, head of the Western Water Assessment, testified before a Senate subcommittee that was hoping to understand how severe the nation's fresh-water problems could become in an age of global warming. Udall talked about the importance of the water near Lee's Ferry, where the annual flow of the Colorado River is measured in order to divide up its water among the seven states that rely on it. A report by the National Academies on the Colorado River Basin has recently found that the combination of limited Colorado River water supplies, rising demands, warmer temperatures, and the prospect of repeated droughts indicate a future in which the potential for conflict among those who use the river will be constant. The writer describes a trip to the Rockies in the company of Udall and his meetings with water manager Peter Binney.

Cool, Clear Water. Christian Caryl. *Newsweek* v. 150 p71 October 1, 2007.

According to Caryl, humans are facing an urgent water crisis, with global warming, population growth, and spreading deserts worsening the problem. Over 1 billion people live without safe drinking water, and modern solutions such as giant dams often cause more problems than they solve, and so development specialists are rediscovering water technologies so old that they are virtually forgotten. New programs worldwide are proving the usefulness of "primitive" water systems: Farmers and anthropologists in Peru have worked together to re-create an irrigation network that evolved there 1,000 years ago; in southern Africa, the relief organization Pump Aid is supplying farmers with foot-powered devices based on a 2,000-year-old Chinese design; and an innovative aid group backed by the United Nations and the Italian government, the Jal Bhagirathi Foundation, has been reviving centuries-old techniques to collect and store the monsoon rains of Rajasthan, India.

Where China's Rivers Run Dry. Orville Schell. *Newsweek* v. 149 pp84+ April 16, 2007.

In this article, part of a special section on leadership and the environment, Schell reports that the most dramatic national transformation in human history is taking place in China, but it is under threat from lack of water. For 150 years, China's inability to defend itself against the industrialized world imbued it with a profoundly felt desire to regain *fuqiang*, or wealth and power. The nation's hell-bent development has, however, had serious consequences for the environment. A person can drive 100 miles in any direction from Beijing and never cross a healthy river. In addition, in 80 percent of rivers that are still flowing in Shanxi province, water quality has been rated Grade V by Chinese officials, unfit for human contact or for agricultural or industrial use.

Safe Water: A Quality Conundrum. Peter Borkey and Brendan Gillespie. *The OECD Observer* pp16–18 March 2006.

Under the UN's Millennium Development Goals, a commitment was made to "halve, by 2015, the proportion of the people without sustainable access to safe drinking water and basic sanitation," Borkey and Gillespie observe. Unfortunately, achieving that goal is turning out to be rather complicated. In particular, the indicators used to assess progress do not take into account whether the water that people use is really safe to drink and whether access is sustainable.

Water For Everyone—The Time Has Come. Kirby A. Chaney. *Phi Kappa Phi Forum* v. 87 pp14–19 Summer 2007.

Chaney reports that the average American uses 160 gallons of water and emits an average of one-fifth of a pound of pollution back to the environment each day, while in that same 24 hours almost 5,000 people worldwide die from causes traceable to a lack of access to safe drinking water or basic sanitation. According to the WHO, 1.1 billion people do not have access to improved water-supply sources, and 2.4 billion lack access to any kind of improved sanitation facilities. Every time those in the Western, developed world draw safe water from the tap or flush waste down a drain, they take for granted the vital, life-giving nature of water and sanitation and their cheap and plentiful access to them, but they frequently forget that numerous people struggle through their day and even perish for the lack of them.

Rethinking Desalinated Water Quality and Agriculture. U. Yermiyahu, A. Tal, and A. Ben-Gal. *Science* v. 318 pp920–21 November 9, 2007.

An evaluation of the effects of water from a new desalination plant in southern Israel has revealed some surprising negative results that suggest that future water management orientation will need to be modified and desalination standards reviewed, the authors report. Desalination separates undesirable salts from water, but also removes ions that are essential for plant growth, and on farms using water from the new plant, crops began showing symptoms of $Mg2+$ deficiency that had to be remedied by fertilization. If the minerals required for agriculture are not added at desalination plants, farmers will require sophisticated and costly control systems to deal with the variable quality of the delivered water. On the basis of the Israeli experience, the water-quality parameters in desalination plants should be expanded in a way that does not contradict or compromise the quality of water for human consumption.

Prolonged Drought Threatens Australia's People, Wildlife, and Economy. Emily Sohn. *Science News* v. 172 pp266–68 October 27, 2007.

The people, wildlife, and economy of Australia are under threat from a prolonged drought, Sohn reports. Although the Australian continent has experienced dry spells since ancient times, the length and severity of the current crisis have surprised even veteran climate experts, and the rapid population growth in recent decades means that water is in heavy demand. Rivers have dropped to record low levels, temperatures have risen to new highs, there are wildfires, and ecosystems are degrading, and climate models are predicting that the situation will remain the same or grow worse for many years to come. Researchers are striving to develop innovative means of ensuring that Australia's thirst for water is met, a struggle that may provide important lessons for the rest of a warming globe.

Second Thoughts about Fluoride. Dan Fagin. *Scientific American* v. 298 pp74–81 January 2008.

New research has reopened the debate about water fluoridation, Fagin reports. Since the 1950s, many municipal water supplies in the U.S. have been fluoridated, with almost 60 percent of the U.S. population consuming fluoridated water today. A report released by the National Research Council in

2006, however, concluded that the U.S. EPA should lower its current limit of 4 mg/l fluoride in drinking water because of health risks to both children and adults. Although the report has neither caused public outrage against fluoridation nor prompted the EPA to lower its fluoride limits, it has caused researchers to question whether even 1 mg/l of fluoride is too much in drinking water, given the increasing recognition of the concentrations of fluoride that are found in many foods, beverages, and dental products.

Fresh from the Sea. Mark Fischetti. *Scientific American* v. 297 pp118–19 September 2007.

Fischetti provides information on how seawater is converted into drinkable freshwater. The production of drinking water by desalination is long established in the Middle East and the Caribbean, and use of the method may grow in the United States as people move to coastal communities, which often have insufficient groundwater. The most popular desalination processes are multistage flash distillation and reverse osmosis, although hybrid plants combining the 2 processes are now being promoted.

Climate Change Refugees. Jeffrey D. Sachs. *Scientific American* v. 296 p43 June 2007.

According to Sachs, the potential negative effects of global warming could spark a wave of forced migrations, with water being the most important determinant of these population movements. Alterations in the relationship between water and society will be widespread as locations are subjected to rising sea levels, stronger tropical cyclones, decreasing soil moisture, more intense precipitation and flooding, more frequent droughts, melting glaciers, and changes in the seasonal snowmelt. Areas of particular interest will be low-lying coastal settlements, farm regions dependent on rivers fed by snowmelt, subhumid and arid regions, and humid areas in Southeast Asia that are vulnerable to changes in monsoon patterns. Although some places will be able to adjust, in areas where adaptation cannot occur, suffering populations will most likely move. Attention will turn away from understanding and mitigating against climate change to adapting to the changes and aiding those most affected.

Sin City's Continuous Flow. Alex Markels. *U.S. News & World Report* v. 142 pp48–50 June 4, 2007.

In this article, part of a special section on water as a diminishing resource, Markels examines Las Vegas's water usage and what the city is doing to ensure its future supply. An annual influx of 65,000-plus new residents has had an impact on the city's water and on its fragile desert ecosystem, which is currently in the depths of a seven-year drought. In late April, Pat Mulroy, the tenacious water czar of southern Nevada, secured the state water regulator's approval for a plan to pump almost 20 billion gallons of water from a vast underground aquifer near the state's east central ranchlands. This decision was followed days later by an even more significant development: a historic agreement to alter the way Colorado River water is shared among Nevada and the six other Western states.

Water Fights. Alex Markels. *U.S. News & World Report* v. 134 pp58–61 May 19, 2003.

Although spring storms have produced flooding in parts of the Midwest and refilled some eastern reservoirs, much of the West is still struggling with drought, Markels notes. Reservoirs in some cities remain less than one-third full, and even average precipitation will not replenish them for at least three years. Unfortunately, the National Weather Service is predicting more dry weather in much of the region, all but guaranteeing a return to the water shortages that have already cost people from Colorado to California billions of dollars in water bills and withering vegetation. Some climatologists blame global warming for the drought's severity, but such episodes are not a new phenomenon, although this time around it is not just farmers and ranchers who are suffering. Now, the agrarian sector must compete with the region's burgeoning suburbs and even with endangered species that need ample stream flows to survive.

Index

40—